BUILDING TRADITIONAL KITCHEN CABINETS

BUILDING TRADITIONAL KITCHEN CABINETS

Jim Tolpin

The Taunton Press

COVER PHOTO: Charles Miller

The Taunton Press
Inspiration for hands-on living™

© 1994 by The Taunton Press, Inc.
All rights reserved.

10 9

Printed in the United States of America

A FINE WOODWORKING Book
FINE WOODWORKING® is a trademark of The Taunton Press, Inc.,
registered in the U.S. Patent and Trademark Office.

The Taunton Press, 63 South Main Street, Box 5506,
Newtown, CT 06470-5506
e-mail: tp@taunton.com

Distributed by Publishers Group West

Library of Congress Cataloging-in-Publication Data

Tolpin, Jim, 1947-
    Building traditional kitchen cabinets / Jim Tolpin.
        p.   cm.
    "A Fine Woodworking book"—T.p. verso.
    Includes index.
    ISBN 1-56158-058-9
    1. Kitchen cabinets. 2. Cabinetwork. I. Title.
TT197.5.K57T65   1994   94-14110
684.1'6—dc20   CIP

I dedicate this book to the memory of David "Bud" McIntosh,
designer and boatbuilder of the old New England school
and author of a classic text on wooden boatbuilding.
In word and deed, Bud taught me to love all that I do but to
write only about what I know.

CONTENTS

ACKNOWLEDGMENTS

I wish to thank the following people who helped me put this book together:

Brian Vanden Brink for his contributions to the color gallery; Jacob Middleton, Audrey Dewey and Craig Wester for their help during the photo shoot; and, of course, Pat Cudahy (once again!) for his prodigious efforts in getting well over 100 clear images onto film.

Scott Swantner and Libby Keefer of the Wooden Boat Foundation for their support and patience.

And at The Taunton Press: John Lively for initiating the book in the first place; Helen Albert for shepherding the work through the publishing process; and Peter Chapman for his insightful editing skills.

I also thank these companies for supplying materials or photographs:

American Design and Engineering, Inc.
CMT Tools
Excalibur Machine and Tool Co.
Feeny Manufacturing Co.
Häfele America Co.
Julius Blum, Inc.
Knape and Vogt Manufacturing Co.
Kreg Tool Co.
The Old Fashioned Milk Paint Co.
Pat Warner Router Accessories
Rev-A-Shelf, Inc.
Robert Bosch Power Tool Corp.
Smith Woodworks and Design
Timbercraft Homes (Charles and Judith Landau)
Veritas Tools, Inc.

INTRODUCTION

I won't deceive you, building a fine set of traditionally styled cabinets for a complete kitchen is not a job for the faint of heart. It's a big undertaking that will keep you in your workshop for a couple of months' worth of weekends. But what better way to spend your recreational time than in creating such an attractive and useful addition to your home? While a quality kitchen undeniably adds significant investment value to your property, it also brings much pleasure to those who will spend many years using it.

At first thought, the idea of designing and building your own cabinets might seem like a complex and daunting process — huge in scale and full of mysteries. But although the scale is admittedly large, the process is surprisingly straightforward. If you follow the step-by-step procedures described in this book and learn a few relatively simple layout and cutting skills, the building of your kitchen cabinetry should go smoothly and relatively quickly.

While specialized cabinetmaker's tools such as a panel-cutting saw, a line-boring machine and perhaps a wide belt sander would admittedly make the job go faster, they are by no means necessary. Be assured that the average basement/garage shop outfitted with standard woodworking machinery and a modest selection of hand and power tools are all that you'll need.

The cabinets that I show you how to build in this book, as you can no doubt tell by leafing through these pages, are decidedly traditional in design. The door and drawer-face styles and the trim-molding profiles (along with some of the finishes) pay homage to some of the primary roots of our design heritage — for example, the Colonial, Shaker and Mission eras.

I find building cabinets in these styles to be exciting, challenging and hugely rewarding — the fruits of these labors never cease to enrich my home and my life. If you share my visions of what makes for a good kitchen and an aesthetically pleasing set of cabinets, I hope that this book inspires you to get to work building your own.

1
DESIGNING YOUR CUSTOM KITCHEN

A kitchen is probably the most complex room in your home to design. Within the confines of a relatively small floor space you must plan to store packaged foods and produce, locate kitchenwares, prepare and cook meals, do cleanup and provide room for waste disposal. In addition, you may want to create areas for buffet-style serving, eating and perhaps even a small desk for planning meals and talking on the telephone. It's no piece of cake — at least not until you're done.

DESIGNING FOR YOUR LIFESTYLE

When it comes to designing a kitchen to fit your lifestyle, give the old "you are what you eat" adage a little twist and consider "you are how you eat." How you eat strongly influences the way you should think about laying out your kitchen.

If, for example, your family is big on fresh produce and bulk staples, your kitchen must feature a greater volume of storage and food-preparation areas than that of a family that subsists mainly on microwaved packaged freezer foods (see the drawing on the facing page). The "on-the-go" family wants a big freezer, but can do without your voluminous pantry storage and expansive cutting board.

If your family regularly consumes fresh-baked breads and pastries, you may want to devote a separate area of the kitchen to a baking center. Conversely, if baked goods are foreign to your diet, you have little need to create space to store bulk

flour and sugar or to provide an area to roll out dough. Certainly you have little need to burden the layout with a double oven.

But considerations about how you eat do not give you the whole picture. Look at how life in your kitchen relates with the activities throughout the rest of the home. Unless the family cook is a complete recluse (and wants to stay that way), you'll design the kitchen cabinetry to allow access (visually if not directly) with many other rooms in the house. The dining area must, of course, be directly adjacent and accessible to the kitchen, whether or not the cook is reclusive. If your family includes infants or other bystanders who demand the cook's attention, you may want to design a run of base cabinets to form a peninsula between the kitchen and family playroom area. Extending the peninsula's counter provides an eating area within the kitchen itself, which is appreciated by the gregarious cook. To be strictly practical, you may have to break up the cabinetry to allow a utility entrance to open into the kitchen (for arriving groceries) or to give easy access to a bathroom (within earshot of an over-boiling pot).

In a family with two cooks or with tag-along children, you'll need to design your kitchen to be as large as possible. All passageways between the cabinets, for example, must be at least 4 ft. wide to allow two people to pass freely. Providing for a second cook (or junior cook) may mean designing in an additional sink or food-preparation area to keep the two cooks out of each other's angel hair.

DESIGNING FOR SAFETY

A poorly designed kitchen can be hazardous to you and your family's health: over 40% of all household accidents happen here. Some design elements are clearly accidents waiting to happen — for example, sharp corners on counters or on pull hardware. Others are more subtle, such as drawer slides and door hinges that do not self-close. It's not much fun walking into the nearly invisible edge of an upper cabinet door or having your hip (or your child's head) find a partially closed drawer. It's also very important to have adequate lighting, especially in the area where people are working with sharp knives.

Surveys reveal that most kitchen accidents happen around the cooking area. Check to be sure that the layout of your cooktop and wall oven follow these basic guidelines:

LIFESTYLE FLOOR PLANS

'Country-life' kitchen

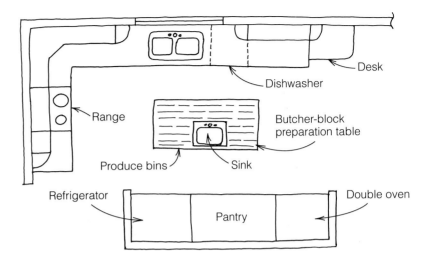

Desk
Dishwasher
Range
Butcher-block preparation table
Produce bins
Sink
Refrigerator
Double oven
Pantry

'On-the-go' kitchen

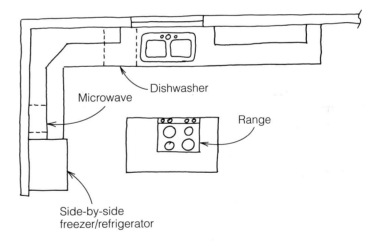

Dishwasher
Microwave
Range
Side-by-side freezer/refrigerator

Locate the cooktop away from open windows, where a draft could extinguish a gas flame or blow combustible objects into the burners. The edge of the cooktop should be at least 12 in. away from a wall — in the event of a pan fire, you want to be able to step away to either side.

Place counters at least 12 in. long to either side of the cooktop. (You should never locate a cooktop at the end of a counter.) At least one of the counters should have a heat-resistant surface. These areas offer landing pads for hot pans and keep pot and pan handles out of reach of curious young hands. If you plan to include a small work area for children within the kitchen, keep it away from the cooktop — to the side of the sink away from the stove is one good location.

Install a wall oven so its open door comes to about 6 in. below the cook's elbow. This makes it easy on the back when removing the Christmas goose (and other heavy meals). Locate a grease-fire extinguisher near to, but not directly under or over, the cooking unit. Finally, prepare for the inevitable burn or cut by installing a first-aid kit.

DESIGNING FOR THE MOBILITY IMPAIRED

In recent years, kitchen-design researchers at Cornell University have conducted studies of how kitchens might better meet the needs of people with restricted mobility. If you know that your kitchen will be used by an elderly person or someone suffering from a mobility impairment (though not in need of a wheelchair), consider the layout and cabinet-design suggestions given here. If the kitchen must accommodate a wheel-chair user, you should consider more extensive modifications. Refer to the Sources of Supply on pp. 194-196 for sources of information; or consult with a Certified Kitchen Designer who specializes in this field.

Bring the cooktop close to the sink, leaving only 12 in. of counter in between. This design eases the transfer of pots to the sink for draining foods and cleanup, and it allows the cook to fill the pots with water from the sink's spray hose. Consider making the counter in the food-preparation area at table height (30 in. to 32 in.) so the cook can sit at this task. Either modify the base cabinets or provide room for a 30-in. deep by 40-in. long table. Place the microwave oven at counter height.

Design most of the base-unit storage cabinets as banks of drawers with full-extension slide hardware. Install easy-to-grasp pulls (avoid knobs) on all doors and drawers. The lowest drawer pull should be at least 18 in. from the floor. Install upper cabinets lower than the standard 17 in. to 18 in. above the counter — dropping down to 15 in. above the counter makes these units easier to access. Explore all the fixture options that bring kitchenwares out of the cabinets for you. These include slide-out bins and shelf units, door-mounted pot-lid and spice racks, and swing-up appliance shelves.

Plan to use more lighting in the kitchen (an 80-year-old needs three times the light of a 20-year-old to perform a task safely). If you opt for under-cabinet lighting, be sure to install a valance to reduce glare.

DESIGNING FOR STYLE

When choosing the style of the cabinetry for your kitchen, you should consider making this room reflect the architectural period of the rest of your house. As an example, a home trimmed out with Colonial-style moldings and doors, and furnished with early American pine furniture, cries out for kitchen cabinets built of honey-stained pine with raised-panel doors hung on wrought-iron hinges. Upper cabinets should be joined to a soffit with a cornice molding matching the profile found throughout the rest of the house. Other traditional American design themes include Shaker, Arts and Crafts (Mission), Victorian, Taos and Art Deco. In the chart on pp. 6-7, note how the particular elements that tend to identify different periods might help to define the style of the cabinetry.

Even if you choose not to relate the kitchen directly to the style of your home's finish trim and furnishings, consider reflecting other prevalent design elements (see the photo at right). For example, arched passageways in sight of the kitchen area might influence you to use cabinet doors with arched top rails (and arched apron boards across open shelving). As another example, a prevalent use of certain materials in the home, such as stained oak trim or perhaps a tiled floor, could inspire you to incorporate these materials into the cabinets.

The purpose of attempting to relate the style of your kitchen to the rest of the house is to make this room feel an integral part of your home, and of your life within it. And as any realtor will tell you, a beautifully integrated kitchen makes a house "show well" — and is thus much easier to sell when the time comes.

This kitchen, designed and built by Rodger Whipple, exhibits a number of distinguishing Victorian-era features: tall over-counter cabinets topped with crown molding, tongue-and-groove siding on the cabinet ends and doors, porcelain knobs and surface-mounted brass hinges. (Photo by Charles Miller)

Designed and built by cabinet-maker Alex Kayner, this kitchen reflects the strong interior design elements of the house: the circular window and circular dining bay. Note, for example, how the tongue-and-groove paneling follows the curves of the rounded ends of the soffits and cabinets. (Photo by Brian Vanden Brink)

TYPICAL DESIGN ELEMENTS OF THREE MAJOR AMERICAN STYLE PERIODS

	Door Type	Hardware
COLONIAL	Raised panel or battened plank	Butterfly, "H" and "L" hinges Surface-mounted wrought-iron pulls
SHAKER	Flat recessed frame and panel	Butt hinges Wood pulls Wood turn latches
ARTS AND CRAFTS	Leaded glazed windows in wall cabinets (flat recessed panels in base units)	Hammered copper pulls and knobs Butt hinges on doors

Moldings	Wood/Finish	Special Features
Cyma recta cornice Beaded edges Scalloped valances and aprons	Amber-stained knotty pine or whitewashed/milk-painted pine or maple	Freehanging or under-cabinet plate rack
Single-board cornice with rounded face Curved side supports Aprons and valances with curved lower edge	Natural finish cherry or clear pine Milk paint (muted colors)	Pegboard trim Horizontal bank of drawers
Unmolded board cornice… …or molded with single curve Cavetto	Light-walnut-stained white oak (to mimic traditional "fumed" ammonia finish)	Decorative pins at mortise-and-tenon door joints Through tenons visible at case sides

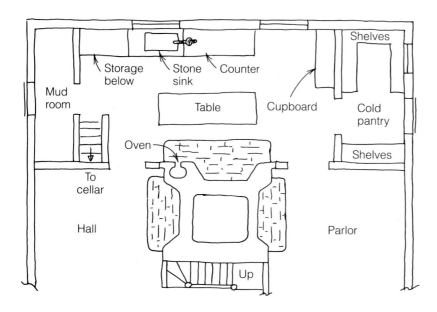

DEVELOPING THE LAYOUT

In the earliest American homes, most kitchens were laid out by placing the work areas and larder along the north wall of the house directly opposite the central fireplace. (The floor plan shown above is of an 18th-century Cape-style house I once lived in in Barrington, New Hampshire.) These days, modern appliances have eliminated the need for a north-facing wall to keep larder goods cool, or for a cooking area to be located next to the chimney. Now you can face the kitchen and its appliances in any direction you wish — to the east for a family of early birds, to the west for sunset diners or to the interior of the house for relentless entertainers.

While paying heed to certain basic efficiency principles (see below), you can choose from a wide variety of layout schemes. A good way to discover what seems to work best for you is to spend time in other people's kitchens. Ask what they like and dislike about the layout of their kitchen, and see if you feel the same way. Visit showrooms and building fairs to expand your view of layout options. Look through magazines, clipping out photos of kitchens you find not only attractive but also particularly appalling. It won't be long before you have a pretty good idea of what type of layout holds the most appeal.

Before sitting down to develop a scale view of your ideal kitchen, first consider some basic principles of kitchen ergonomics. As you will see below, there are distinct reasons why certain appliances and their attendant work areas should be grouped close to one another.

The classic work triangle

Back in the early 1950s, researchers at Cornell University conducted extensive studies to determine how kitchens were used and how to make them work as efficiently as possible. One result of their tests was the creation of the "work triangle" concept. The idea was based on the simple observation that nearly all cooking processes revolved around three points: the stove, the sink and the refrigerator. Connecting these points created a triangle that defined the kitchen's predominant traffic pattern.

The Cornell studies indicated that to keep a kitchen as efficient as possible this unobstructed triangle should not exceed 22 ft. in perimeter or be under 12 ft., and no leg of the triangle should exceed 7 ft. As the most heavily trafficked leg fell between the cooktop and sink, it followed that the most efficient layout would make this the shortest leg of the triangle. The longest (and least traveled) leg would stretch between the refrigerator and the cooktop.

You can further increase the effectiveness of the work-triangle concept by designing storage for the kitchenwares and foodstuffs used for many common tasks along the legs of the triangle. For example, when making coffee, you should be able to find coffee beans, grinder, brewer, filters and cups all within the triangle (and preferably close to the sink for easy cleanup).

You need not, however, feel constrained to a rigid triangular traffic pattern between the major appliances. If, for example, you intend to install a second small refrigerator or sink, you can fudge the pattern considerably without losing efficiency (see the bottom drawing at right).

Locating major appliances and work areas

A layout scheme begins by deciding where to locate the main sink area. While most builders and architects assume that everybody wants the sink in front of a wide window, this layout may not be best for you. Because the cook spends the most time at this "appliance," what she or he sees from this vantage point becomes very important. Of course a nice view is wonderful, but if your family includes elderly people or children who require the cook's constant attention, you might consider facing the sink toward the family area within the house (see, for example, the kitchen shown in the bottom photo on p. 19). And besides, the view outside your kitchen might be lousy.

The next major appliances to locate are the cooktop and refrigerator. Adhering to Cornell's work-triangle principle, an unobstructed path should be maintained between these points, with a total walking distance between these two appliances and the sink falling under 22 ft. Locate the cooktop, rather than the refriger-

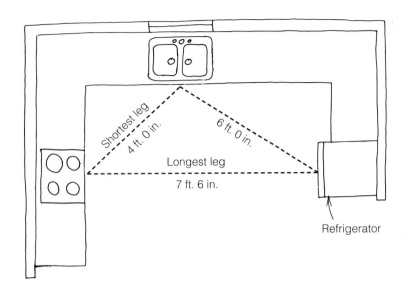

TRADITIONAL WORK TRIANGLE

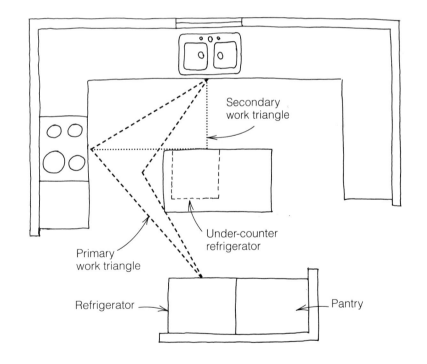

MODIFIED WORK TRIANGLE

ator, closer to the sink. In fact, the closer the better, as long as you leave at least 12 in. in between — a good place for a cutting board. But keep the refrigerator within 7 ft. of the sink, and be sure its door swings from the opposing side.

You've probably noticed my leaning toward a cooktop rather than a full-function stove unit. I have my reasons: Ovens are much more rarely used in most kitchens than are cooktops, and can thus be located outside the work triangle. This layout increases efficiency two ways: It allows a second person to perform oven chores out of the primary cook's way; and it creates space for a useful storage area under the cooktop — perhaps a bank of pot and pan drawers. Leaving space under the cooktop also suits my preference for vented range hoods over downdraft cooktop units. Because the motor and ductwork of a downdraft severely limit the cooktop cabinet's storage space, they defeat one of the advantages of a separate oven unit. I also like the way that range hoods can add visual interest to a run of upper cabinets, and how well they provide task lighting to an area that clearly needs it.

Locating secondary appliances

The location of the dishwasher is almost always next to the sink. Besides the obvious need to keep plumbing confined to one area, an efficient work pattern also demands that common processes be grouped in the same area — in this case, cleanup. This area, then, is also the place to install a trash compactor, garbage compost and recycling bins. The microwave, however, is used for at least two different primary purposes. If it is to be used often for cooking, locate it close to the food-preparation

area. If used primarily as a defroster, locate it near the refrigerator.

Small appliances such as toasters, blenders and coffee makers are handiest when left on the counter. For the sake of appearance, design an appliance garage to hide them in. Keep them plugged into a switched outlet strip (for safety, turn the strip off when closing the door). Larger appliances such as mixers, juicers and food processors can be mounted on swing-up shelf fixtures, but be aware that this does eat up considerable storage space.

Locating cabinets

To make a kitchen a pleasure to work in, design the cabinets to be interactive with the needs of specific work areas — not merely a random grouping of empty boxes. Your cabinets should help you organize kitchenwares where they are most needed, and bring them close to hand without requiring the skills and temperament of a spelunker. As a general rule, locate the most frequently used items between the height of the cook's knees and shoulders, and be generous with full-extension drawers and slide-out shelves throughout the base units.

The following are some examples of ways that cabinets can become interactive with specific work areas. The numbers refer to locations indicated in the drawing on the facing page.

1. A bank of drawers stores cooking utensils and hot pads near the cooktop.
2. A knife drawer slides out below the cutting board.
3. Pots and pans reside in deep drawers under the cooktop. A shallow top drawer holds spices.
4. Cookie sheets and oven trays store in vertical racks in a cabinet under the oven.

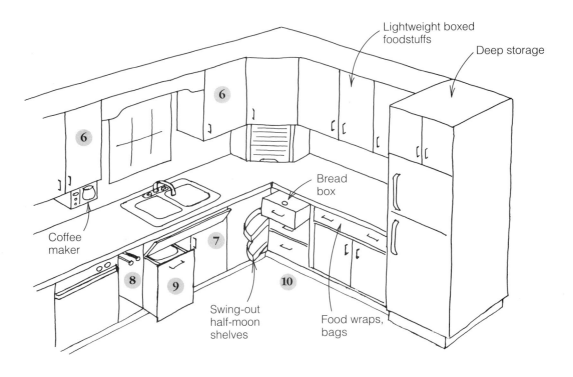

Lightweight boxed foodstuffs

Deep storage

Bread box

Coffee maker

Swing-out half-moon shelves

Food wraps, bags

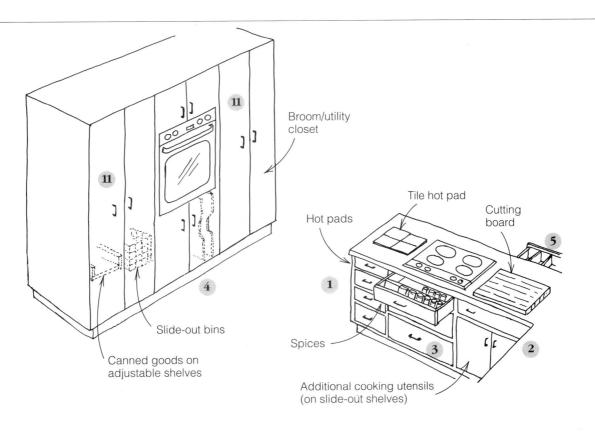

Broom/utility closet

Tile hot pad

Cutting board

Hot pads

Spices

Slide-out bins

Canned goods on adjustable shelves

Additional cooking utensils (on slide-out shelves)

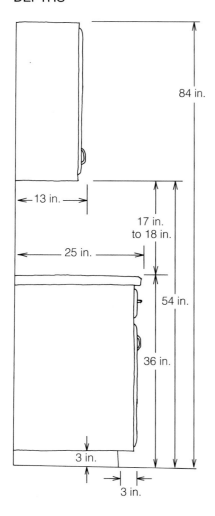

84 in.

← 13 in. →

17 in.
to 18 in.

← 25 in. →

54 in.

36 in.

3 in.

3 in.

5. A drawer accessible to the dining area holds silverware and place mats — keeping table setters out of the cook's work triangle.

6. Dishes and glassware live in an upper unit to either side of the sink.

7. A tilt-out tray in front of the sink holds sponges and scrub pads.

8. A small cabinet between the sink and dishwasher holds towels on a slide-out, multi-forked bar.

9. A pull-out door conceals a slide-out waste basket under the sink.

10. Produce not requiring refrigeration and baking staples are stored in tilt-out bins or deep drawers (glass fronts are a decorative and practical touch) near the food-preparation area. Drawers for fresh bread and other goods and for foil and plastic-wrap products are located nearby.

11. Outside the work triangle, a floor-to-ceiling pantry unit holds packaged goods; slide-out bins reduce volume but make the unit much easier to use. To the other side of the partition, storage is provided for brooms and cleaning supplies.

Counter considerations

Along with providing storage, a primary function of base cabinetry is to offer support for a kitchen's working counters. Try to design your kitchen with as much continuous counter-space as possible by locating floor-to-ceiling cabinets at ends of counter runs. If possible, keep refrigerators out of the runs as well. A counter located directly opposite or next to the refrigerator can serve as a landing area for foods going in or out.

Additional guidelines, published by the National Kitchen and Bath Association and described below, suggest the minimum size of counter you should design for each work area. Be aware, however, that in a small kitchen, some areas may have to serve dual functions. For example, the food-preparation area by the sink

might function as a cleanup area after the meal is done.

The food-preparation area should be at least 36 in. wide (narrower if providing more than one food-preparation area) and located next to the sink. There should be two areas to either side of the cooktop: one at least 12 in. wide, and the other 15 in. These counters must be the same height as the cooktop.

There should be two counter areas to either side of the sink: one side at 24 in., and the other at 18 in. Allow at least 15 in. of counter to the open-door side of the refrigerator. Or, better, allow 24 in. directly across, especially for double-door units. Any baking-center counter (preferably of marble) should be at least 36 in. wide and set at table height (29 in. to 31 in.).

STANDARD PROPORTIONS FOR KITCHEN CABINETRY

The drawing at left shows the height and depth measurements of a standard set of kitchen cabinets. These figures are not arbitrary: Research conducted over the years has shown that these are the most effective proportions for storage units and counter surfaces for a person 5 ft. 4 in. tall (average female height). Of course, since you are custom-designing the kitchen, you can make the cabinets to any proportion and place them at any height from the floor — as long as the cabinets fit the people who will use them. But you should take these factors into consideration when proportioning cabinets to your design:

Standard heights of appliances such as ranges, dishwashers and trash compactors assume a counter height of 36 in. Modifications to the appliances may be necessary if you deviate more than an inch in either direction. Prefabricated counters assume the standard cabinet depths as shown in the drawing.

Upper units must not be so deep, or located so close to the work counter, that the cook's view to the back of the counter is obstructed. Cabinets deeper than standard dimensions provide more storage area but make items stored toward the back difficult to access. All base cabinets must have a toe kick to allow a person to stand comfortably next to the counter. The drawing shows the minimum height and depth.

BASIC FLOOR-PLAN LAYOUTS

Now that I've armed you with information about work triangles, interactive cabinets and standard proportions, it's time to bring all these design elements together. To create a floor plan that best suits your needs, you must decide on the best way to relate the cabinets, appliances and work areas to one another. While there are a variety of standard layout configurations to choose from (see below), there is nothing to stop you from coming up with one totally unique to your situation — as long as you heed the design principles I've introduced you to in this chapter.

Begin planning your layout with the conventional wisdom that says you need about 10 lineal feet of cabinets (upper and base units) to meet the storage needs of an average family (a couple and 2.4 kids). When the 0.4 reaches a whole number, you will need another 3 lineal feet. Add 3 ft. for each additional family member.

If you are designing the kitchen to fit an existing space, don't let a winning design be stymied by the current placement of doors, windows or, for that matter, partition walls. The effort in changing any of these things is insignificant when compared to the amount of time and money you will be devoting to building this set of kitchen cabinets. Concentrate on developing a floor plan that best meets the needs of your family.

Single-wall layout

A layout that gathers all the appliances and cabinetry against one wall must do so for a good reason — for instance, when designing a tiny apartment kitchen where there is simply no other place to put it. Since counterspace is crucial in a small kitchen, an under-counter refrigerator is strongly recommended. If a full-height unit must be used, place it at the end of the run (see the drawing on p. 14). Do not, however, locate the range or cooktop at an end. Doing so would create an unsafe situation (see p. 4) and add unnecessary steps to the cooking process. Instead, keep it near to the sink.

Corridor layout

The corridor, or "galley," layout is another common solution for small kitchen spaces. It has a distinct advantage over the single-wall layout in that you can utilize the work-triangle principle to relate the three major appliances to one another in a more efficient way. But avoid the temptation to make the triangle too small. To create a decent-sized area for food preparation, the cooktop and sink should be separated by at least 36 in. and the opposing counters should be at least 42 in. apart. Increase the width of the corridor to 48 in. and add another 8 in. to the food-prep area if two people will work in this kitchen at the same

BASIC FLOOR-PLAN CONFIGURATIONS

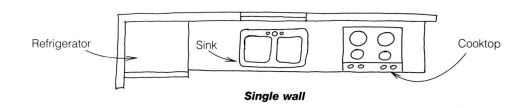

Refrigerator   Sink   Cooktop

Single wall

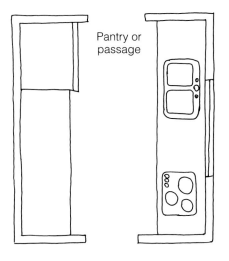

Pantry or passage

Corridor

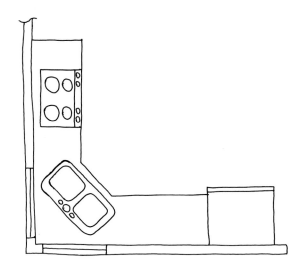

L-shape

L-shape with island

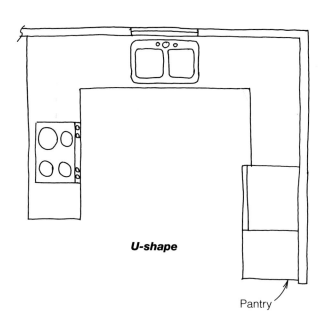

U-shape

Pantry

time. Unfortunately, unless one end of the corridor ends at a pantry, the efficiency of this layout greatly suffers from traffic passing through the kitchen. Do your best to avoid this potentially hazardous, and certainly disruptive, situation.

L-shaped layout

Choosing an L-shaped layout for a limited space usually creates a more efficient kitchen than will either the corridor or single-wall layouts. The work triangle can be kept small and free of traffic snarls, and the cook has fewer steps and can make smaller turns to navigate between the appliances. It's crucial, however, that the counters be made continuous—don't interrupt them with a passage door, a floor-to-ceiling cabinet or a refrigerator. In the layout shown on the facing page, I've placed the sink at an angle across the corner. This layout eliminates a space-wasting blind corner cabinet and creates ample counter areas to either side of this busy work area.

The L-shaped layout at bottom left on the facing page has benefited from the addition of an island cabinet. The work triangle tightens up and an excellent area for food preparation is created. A second cook can now work in this kitchen outside the primary work triangle.

U-shaped layout

If the size and configuration of your kitchen space can contain a U-shaped layout, then by all means design one for it. Of all the basic floor plans, this layout provides the most efficient and versatile kitchen. The U shape faces all the appliances, work areas and storage systems toward a central point — the cook standing in the middle of the kitchen. This layout not only makes maximum use of the work-triangle principle, but also keeps other people out of the cook's

way. You can accommodate a second cook by adding another food-prep area (and possible a small second sink) along one leg of the U or in an island cabinet.

One disadvantage of the U-shape floor plan, however, is its propensity for blind corners, which are notorious space wasters. If, however, the leg of the U is a peninsula, its corner can be accessed from outside the kitchen. Other ways to circumvent the problematic storage of a blind corner include angling the corner cabinets or installing swing-out storage fixtures.

GETTING THE FLOOR PLAN DOWN ON PAPER

Having made the fundamental decisions about the space to contain your kitchen, determining where windows, doors and walls will go (or be moved to if remodeling), it's time to choose a basic floor plan. Make a rough sketch of the layout showing the location of the counters and the primary appliances. Then sketch in the work triangle between the sink, cooktop and refrigerator. Does it fall within the guidelines suggested in the Cornell study (see pp. 8-9)?

To help you visualize your sketched layout full-size, use crayons to outline the location of all the base cabinets and major appliances on the kitchen-floor underlayment (see the top photo on p. 16). A tricky floor plan may require full-scale mock-ups in cardboard to help you fully understand how your kitchen will work. Note measurements taken from these full-size visualizations on your rough sketch. When you arrive at a layout that looks good to you, go on to create an accurately scaled plan view and set of elevations.

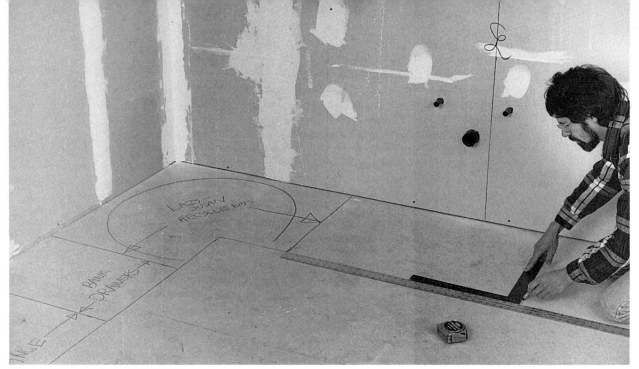

Use a crayon to draw the kitchen
layout full scale on site.

After taping down a sheet of
translucent vellum paper over a
grid sheet, use the 1 scale (1 in. =
1 ft.) of an architect's rule to
draw out the floor and elevation
views of the cabinets.
(Photo by Jim Tolpin)

Creating scaled floor and elevation plans

While a drawing board with a parallel rule or mechanical drafting arm makes scale drawing a cinch, you can get by with laying a sheet of translucent vellum over a grid sheet marked with 1-in. squares. Use the 1 scale of an architect's rule to scale out the dimensions — 1 in. equals 1 ft. Note that the 1-in. segment of the rule's scale is broken down into 12 divisions for laying out scaled inches.

Begin by drawing in the walls of the kitchen. Be sure to include the location of all doors, windows and other permanent features of the space (including heating ducts, chimneys and other fixed utilities). Double-check to make sure you have accurately scaled the length and spacing of all these elements.

At this point you must know the exact dimensions (and clearance allowances) of the appliances and hardware fixtures. Get these numbers either from the dealer's specification sheets or, better, by measuring the actual units. I have found out the hard way that a difference of less than 1 in. can throw off an entire floor plan by forcing a coveted appliance to find another location on the layout. Be sure always to include the amount of clearance to leave between the appliance and the adjoining cabinets (generally ¼ in. to ½ in.). Certain hardware fixtures, such as swing-out half-moon shelves (see pp. 156-157), require specific door openings, so be sure you make the cabinet to contain these fixtures large enough. Finally, remember to allow 1½ in. to 2 in. between a cabinet module and a meeting wall. An applied molding or the ear of a face frame bridges this gap and is scribed to the wall surface (see pp. 171-172).

Following your sketch, position the major appliances on the drawing and then draw in the outlines of the counters and the upper cabinets. Use solid lines to define the cabinet modules and dashed lines to indicate interior partitions Remember that vellum erases easily — keep at it until you feel you have it right.

When you're done with the plan view, draw face views showing each wall of the kitchen — these are your cabinet elevations (see the drawing on p. 45). Give some thought to the layout of the upper wall cabinet modules; in general, they should match up with the base units. However, factors such as window placement, oversized range hoods and pure aesthetics may dictate some deviations from this rule of thumb. Draw in the positions of all the doors and drawer faces. Indicate shelves with dotted lines. Make an X at the position of each door hinge, and an O at each knob (whenever possible, hinge doors on the side facing away from the primary work triangle).

While the completion of these scale drawings helps you take a major step toward the creation of your cabinetry, you must now move from the kitchen-layout stage to specific understanding of how traditional cabinets are designed and built. In the next chapter, I'll show you how I proportion the cabinets and their components, and introduce you to the principles of modular construction.

A GALLERY OF KITCHEN DESIGN

I have assembled this gallery of kitchens to illustrate what some cabinetmakers around the country have been custom-building into a variety of traditionally inspired homes. Most of the work is contemporary (the sink cabinet built by Joshua Pool in 1860 being the only exception), and all the kitchens contain good examples of traditional layouts and design elements. While some of the kitchens honor specific period styles, others serve to elicit what is now commonly referred to as the "country" look. To me, each of these projects has gone beyond simply fitting well with its surroundings, and has lent its home that intangible gift of "ambiance."

BRIAN VANDEN BRINK

Cabinetmaker: Jay Fischer
Designer: Karin Thomas

Many design elements converge in these cabinets to present a tasteful example of the "country" look. While the white painted surfaces set off by varnished wood edgings and the tongue-and-groove paneling are sure indicators of this style, note these more subtle details: full-inset doors and drawer faces surrounded by cock beading; brass butt hinges; and copious use of moldings (including a plinth above the kick boards). Also note how mid-stiles are used to reduce the visual size of the wider doors.

KEVIN IRETON

Cabinetmaker: Mike Hamilton
Designer: Judith Landau (of Timbercraft Homes)

These cabinets, built from old-growth fir ripped out of the same lumber from which the timber frame of the house was constructed, reflect a crossbreeding of styles: English country, and the American Arts and Crafts movement. You can see the English influence in the rounded pillars of the island, the hanging plate rack, and the pull handles carried over a recess in the drawer face. The Arts and Crafts look is carried by the strongly rectilinear cabinet face framing and the design of the window sash in the wall cabinets. This kitchen features granite and wood counter surfaces.

Cabinetmaker: Jim Tolpin
Designer: Martha Ditchfield

Although I didn't set out to build these hard-maple cabinets to embrace a particular style period, I did strive to give them a strong "country" look. To that end, I made prolific use of tongue-and-groove boards — not only to cover the exposed sides and backs of base units, but also to serve as the panels in the doors. In addition, I employed cock beading around doors and drawers and lead sash in the glassed wall cabinets. Note the unusual sink placement, which was done to take advantage of the light and view coming to the kitchen from the dining room to the foreground.

BRUCE GREENLAW

Cabinetmaker: Joseph Waltman and Co.
Designer: Mr. and Mrs. Mayer

This well-thought-out U-shaped kitchen exemplifies the concept of carrying interior architectural design elements into the cabinetry. Here the use of pine as the primary wood for tongue-and-groove panel doors, face frames and trim seamlessly blends the cabinets to the softwood logs that dominate the interior of the home. Choosing to use twigs as handles was a clever way for the designer to confirm this relationship. Also note the unusual placement of the dishwasher in the corner — yet another good way to make the most of a troublesome area.

BRIAN VANDEN BRINK

Cabinetmaker: Joshua Pool
Designer: Probably Captain Richard H. Tucker, Jr.

This dedicated sink cabinet, custom-built for this kitchen in 1860 by skiff builder Joshua Pool, features ash tongue-and-groove boards carried around the curved ends of an oak counter — a functional design element that serves to ease the flow of traffic to the passage doors on either side. Note how the curved backsplash and specially made braided rug carry the theme initiated by the rounded ends.

BRIAN VANDEN BRINK

Cabinetmaker/Designer:

Tom Hampson

Appearing through a brick-lined entry hall, a rather small set of cabinets hunker under basket-strewn exposed beams. Set on a wide-planked pine floor, the cabinets are purposely Colonial in design. The wide raised-panel doors, arched glass corner door, wrought-iron butterfly hinges and unusual slanted top storage bin by the stove all hark back to the early furniture of New England. Note the deep drawer under the drop-in range — an excellent use of an otherwise wasted space.

BRIAN VANDEN BRINK

Cabinetmaker: Kennebec Cabinets of Bath, Maine
Architect: Charles Allen Hill

These cherry wood cabinets are as close to pure Shaker in design as I've seen. The flat recessed frame-and-panel doors, the ungraduated bank of drawers, the small, square-faced drawers under the wall cabinet, the row of pegs under the range top cabinet and the use of wood knobs throughout speak loudly of traditional Shaker furniture. The presence of braided rugs and fabric-strip ladder-back stools completes the statement.

Cabinetmaker: Henry Walas
Designer: Lou Ekus

The design and construction of these cherry cabinets, running from floor to ceiling while incorporating a built-in marble counter and a slide-out cutting board, give the appearance of one single unit. However, careful lighting and the protrusion of the lower sink cabinet break up a potentially monolithic face. The mixing of pull hardware — wrought iron on the doors and wood pulls reminiscent of turn-of-the-century apothecary cabinets — draws the cabinets away from identification with any definitive style. If anything, the embossed metal ceiling and cornice molding gives an almost-Victorian flavor to the kitchen.

BRIAN VANDEN BRINK

Cabinetmaker: Crown Point Cabinetry, Claremont, N.H.
Designer: Beverly Marois

This kitchen is an excellent example of an L-shaped kitchen utilizing a working island to tighten the work triangle and to provide room for two cooks (or one cook and some loquacious company). The designer intended the cherry cabinets to reflect a traditional "country" design: note, for example, the raised-panel doors; the braces supporting wall cabinets; the corbels supporting the overhanging island counter; and the leaded glazing in the wall cabinets.

Cabinetmaker/Designer:
Rick Poore

The design and finish of this modest L-shaped kitchen helps establish the Colonial ambiance of this timber-frame house. Note the unusually wide raised-panel doors; the small wood knobs (their placement toward the middle of the door stiles is typical of Colonial furniture); and the use of a trestle table for a work island (and cat perch). True to the era, the only wall cabinet in this kitchen is a hanging plate cupboard. The finish on the cabinetry is a semi-transparent mustard paint over pine.

2
CABINET DESIGN AND CONSTRUCTION

Until the 20th century, most kitchens in American homes were outfitted with closet pantries, built-in cold larders and freestanding furniture. Tall hutches held additional food staples and stored dinnerware, while a long "harvest" table served as the food-preparation area (see the top photo on the facing page). A large stone or cast-iron sink provided a work area for cleaning up dishes and washing foods. But as the eating habits of 20th-century Americans shifted dramatically toward the consumption of packaged foods, and as postwar housing booms demanded efficient construction of "turnkey" homes, the basic concept of what constituted kitchen furnishings underwent a marked evolution.

Many cabinetmakers turned away from their traditional preoccupation with furniture making to specialize in building kitchen and bath cabinets, using plywood as their primary construction material. These cabinets replaced the need for hutches, harvest tables and pantry rooms. Contiguous runs of upper and lower cabinets, supporting a work counter of plastic laminate, ran along the walls of almost every kitchen built in 20th-century America.

Because a primary goal of kitchen cabinetmakers was (and still is) efficiency of construction, new kinds of materials, tools and techniques quickly swept through the trade. Hardwood-veneer plywoods and other man-made sheet goods became widely available, as did the tooling to cut, edge-band and join

the components made from them. Easy-to-install hardware was developed for hanging cabinet doors, supporting adjustable shelving and sliding drawer boxes in and out. With each passing year, innovative fixtures such as tilt-out sink trays and slide-out bins, baskets and shelving come on the market, each adding to the performance and versatility of the cabinetmaker's kitchens while adding little to the construction time.

All this is good news for woodworkers who wish to build their own kitchen cabinets. Sheet goods, some hardwoods, most hardware fittings and a wide selection of fixtures are now available through most large building-supply and home-center stores. Specialized tools that help the cabinetmaker cut sheet stock quickly and accurately, cut slots for

Where are the cabinets? This early American kitchen, still standing in the Jefferds Tavern in Old York, Maine, typifies the layout and furnishings of most 18th-century kitchens: huge hearth, long harvest table, walk-in pantries and freestanding hutches. (Photo by Brian Vanden Brink)

biscuit joinery, guide drill bits for the installation of certain fittings, and help with other specialized tasks are available through mail-order tool suppliers. Many jigs and fixtures that are not available commercially are easily made in the shop, as I will show you in later chapters.

Even the occasional woodworker is likely to have most of the basic tools needed for building kitchen cabinets (or "case goods"). The sidebar on p. 29 lists the hand and power tools I consider essential. I've also listed optional tools that speed up some of the processes; you may want to buy these if you think you'll continue to build case goods.

A CABINET: THE SUM OF ITS PARTS

A typical kitchen cabinet is little more than a box with one open side. You can close in the open side with a lid: a cabinet door. Or you may chose to build more boxes to slide into the first: a set of drawers. A third option is some combination of the two.

The drawing on p. 26 shows the parts that comprise a typical base and wall unit built in a traditional style. Note the extensive use of moldings, which serve to tie the cabinets to one another visually and to hide the gaps that invariably occur when joining square boxes to a nonlevel ceiling or floor, or an out-of-plumb wall. Also note that the sides of the cabinets are made up from ¾-in. plywood, even if

Innovative fixtures increase the versatility of kitchen cabinets. The sink cabinet contains a slide-out waste basket and towel rack and a tilt-out soap tray. Utility bins slide out to the right of the sink. The corner cabinet houses a swiveling, three-compartment recycling system.

TRADITIONAL FACE-FRAME CABINET

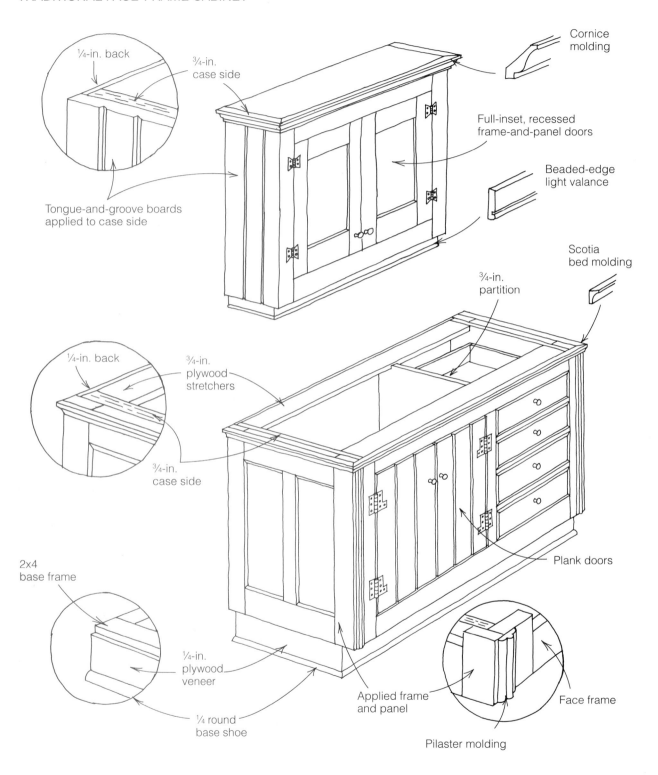

¼-in. back

¾-in. case side

Cornice molding

Full-inset, recessed frame-and-panel doors

Beaded-edge light valance

Tongue-and-groove boards applied to case side

Scotia bed molding

¾-in. partition

¼-in. back

¾-in. plywood stretchers

¾-in. case side

Plank doors

2x4 base frame

¼-in. plywood veneer

¼ round base shoe

Applied frame and panel

Face frame

Pilaster molding

they underlie an exposed end. To hide the plywood — and the screws that fasten the side to the floors and stretchers — I apply a panel. This panel may be made up of ¼-in. hardwood plywood, tongue-and-groove boards, or even a frame and panel. I make the applied panel oversize in width, final-fitting it to the wall during the installation of the cabinets.

CABINET DESIGN

As I discussed in the previous chapter on kitchen design, the overall depth and height of most cabinets are largely predetermined — both by the limits of the average person's reach and by standardized sizes of appliances and counter surfaces. Unless a cabinet must contain a specific appliance (an oven or sink, for example, requires a certain minimum width of cabinet), you can build it to any width (or "run") that best accommodates your floor plan. Of course, restricted access — a narrow door or hallway, for example — may also have something to say about how large a cabinet you can build.

Proportioning doors and drawer faces

Within a cabinet, function may predetermine some door and drawer-face sizes. For example, fixtures such as slide-out half-moon shelves demand a certain single width of door. In a pot and pan storage cabinet, the height of the drawers is largely determined by the sizes of the wares to be placed in them.

Whenever possible, I restrict the width of cabinet doors to less than 21 in., pairing narrow doors in wider cabinets. Doors wider than this usually look out of proportion and take up a lot of the cook's space when opened. On the rare occasion that a single door wider than 21 in. seems necessary, I often install an inter-

mediate stile (or "mid-stile") to break up the wide expanse of door panel (see the drawing at right). Adding a mid-stile provides the same sense of proportion that a pair of doors would lend to the cabinet. I also restrict the height of cabinet doors to 60 in. On most cabinets, a taller door looks out of proportion. Large doors also tend to sag on their hinges over time (because of their weight) and are difficult to build, and keep, free of warp.

In general, I make the height of a single drawer of a cupboard (and false front of the sink cabinet) about one-sixth the height of the total cabinet face (about 5½ in.). For visual continuity, I run this drawer height around the circumference of the kitchen — though I reduce the height of the top drawer of a bank of drawers. In a four-drawer bank, I either graduate the size of the drawers from bottom to top or I make the middle two drawers the same (see the drawing on p. 28). Let your sense of aesthetics be your guide. The width of a drawer face generally matches that of the door below; paired doors may be overlaid by a single drawer.

CABINET ASSEMBLY

Before I give you an overview of how I construct kitchen case work, I must first offer this advice: If possible, build the cabinets in your shop, not on site. Some professionals argue that novices make fewer mistakes building on site since they can measure and fit components directly to the walls of the kitchen. But if you use the story-pole method to lay out the cabinet components (see Chapter 4), you can, in effect, bring the site into your shop.

In addition, the modular construction methods that I use are simple and straightforward. First-time cabi-

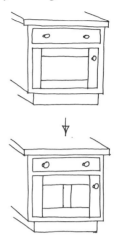

Break up a wide door by installing a mid-stile.

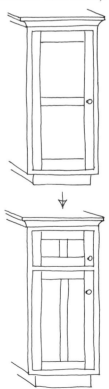

Change a full-height door to two doors (adding mid-stiles for wide doors).

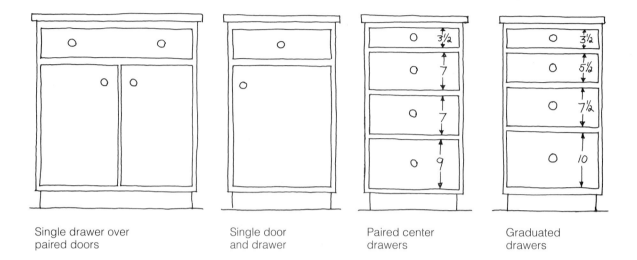

Single drawer over
paired doors

Single door
and drawer

Paired center
drawers

Graduated
drawers

netmakers should have little trouble following them, with or without a kitchen in front of them. Modular construction also restricts most cabinets to an easily managed size — there is little need to jockey massive cabinetry from shop to site. As another argument against site-built cabinets, their lack of backs (and sometimes sides) makes them difficult to remove and reuse in a subsequent remodel.

There is also the question of space. To build cabinets on site you need to set up stationary tools, leaving enough space around them to manipulate full sheets of plywood. Because much other work is involved in a kitchen installation — plumbing, electrical, painting, and so on — there may be other people, and certainly piles of materials and tools, to work around. Unless you have a huge dining room adjacent to the kitchen, you'll find it much easier to set up shop in the garage — a double-car garage is ideal, though you can make do in a single.

And finally, there is the question of time: Building a complete set of kitchen cabinets can take from two to four weeks (or longer). If you are remodeling an existing space, can your family get along without a kitchen for this amount of time?

Principles of modular construction

European-style cabinets are typically modular by design. Unlike traditional face-frame cabinets, each unit of a set of Euro-cabinets is relatively small and self-contained. Each can stand alone as a finished cabinet or be joined to others to create larger units. Many of the parts are standardized in size and mill work, so they can be used interchangeably amongst many cabinet configurations.

Since this particular attribute of European cabinets simplifies the construction of case goods without compromising their strength or quality, I now follow the principles of modular cabinetmaking to make my traditional face-frame cabinets.

TOOLS
FOR BUILDING
CABINETS

Stationary Power Tools

Table saw with accurate rip fence and sliding crosscut table

Jointer

Lightweight 10-in. or 12-in. surface planer

Drill press

Dust collector

Optional

Radial-arm saw or sliding compound-miter saw

Bandsaw

Air compressor (for applying finish and driving pneumatic fasteners)

Portable Power Tools

Drill (at least one ¼-in. or ⅜-in. variable speed, reversing drill — 9.6 volt, or greater; cordless are fine for cabinetmaking)

Power screwdriver (9.6 volt cordless impact driver recommended)

Sanders (one belt and at least one square-base orbital)

Routers (3-hp table-mounted router, 1-hp plunge router, and laminate trimmer)

Circular saw (with optional cutting guides)

Jigsaw

Optional

Spline-biscuit joiner

Random orbit sander

Pneumatic tacker, nailer

Air sprayer finish applicator

Hand-operated heat-gun edgebander

Hand Tools

Layout tools

16-ft. tape measure

24-in. framing square, 12-in. combination square

Water level (or 6-ft. bubble level), 4-ft. level

Architect's rule

Bevel gauge

Compass scribe, trammel points

Marking knife, awl, chalk, pencils and sharpener

Layout template/drill guide for shelf holes (optional)

Cutting tools

Set of handsaws for ripping and crosscutting (Japanese combination saw recommended)

Miter box (for joining moldings)

Compass saw, hacksaw

Hole saws

Set of butt chisels

Block, rabbet and jack planes

Drill bits, countersink and plug-cutting bits, router bits

Fastening tools

Set of screwdrivers

Hammers (13-oz. claw, tack and rubber mallet)

Nail set

Jig for hand-drilling pocket holes (optional)

Jig for drilling dowel holes (optional)

Holding and grasping tools

Wood vise

Pipe clamps (at least one pair each with 24-in., 36-in. and 48-in. capacities)

Pair of 5-in. C-clamps

Pliers, wrench

Socket set

Vise-grip clamp to align frame stock for pocket-hole assembly (optional)

Finishing tools

Cabinet scraper

Hand files

Glue scraper

Putty knives (for applying fillers)

Shaped sanding blocks, sandpaper assortment

Miscellaneous

Glue applicator (with optional nozzle for spline slots)

Roller for pressing down laminate

Electronic stud finder

Scissors jack (for installing wall cabinets)

Stand-mounted lights

Extension cords

Stepladder

First-aid kit

Consistency of construction I build all case units, no matter what their size, function or placement within the layout, of the same basic components (sides, floor, stretchers or ceiling, and back). I use the same techniques to join the components together — for example, screws and splines to join sides to floors and tops. Note in the drawing below that the outside faces of the side components (and thus the exposed screwheads) are never seen — they either face against another cabinet or wall or are covered by an applied panel.

Standard sizing As much as possible, I make the case components interchangeable. For example, I cut out a base unit's left-hand-side panel to a standard height and depth, drill it with shelf-clip holes, cut slots for the assembly splines and drill pilot holes for the screws — stopping at a point where this side component could still be used in any base module. In this way, I can do almost all the processes for every base side panel in one shot.

Economization of materials Because I cut the case components from 4x8 sheets, I standardize component sizes to fall within equal divisions of these dimensions (see the drawing on the facing page). For example, I keep base-unit sides and floors less than 24 in. in width, and keep the sides under 32 in. in height. I can then get six sides out of one sheet. I make upper-unit sides, floors, tops and shelves under 12 in. in width, which allows me to rip four runs out of a sheet. In general, I try to keep lengths under 32 in., 48 in. and 64 in., which not only makes for effi-

BASE-UNIT LAYOUT

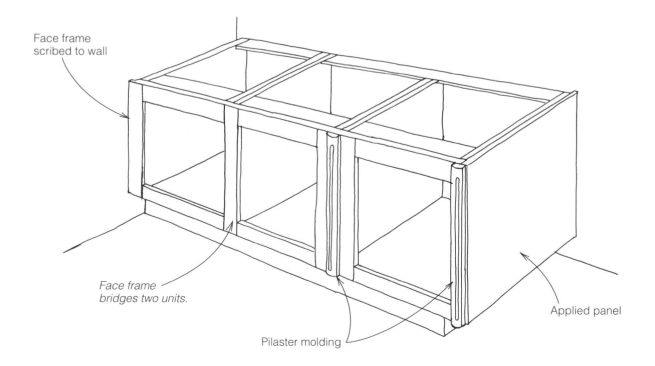

Face frame scribed to wall

Face frame bridges two units.

Pilaster molding

Applied panel

Lengths under 48 in. allow run to produce two components.

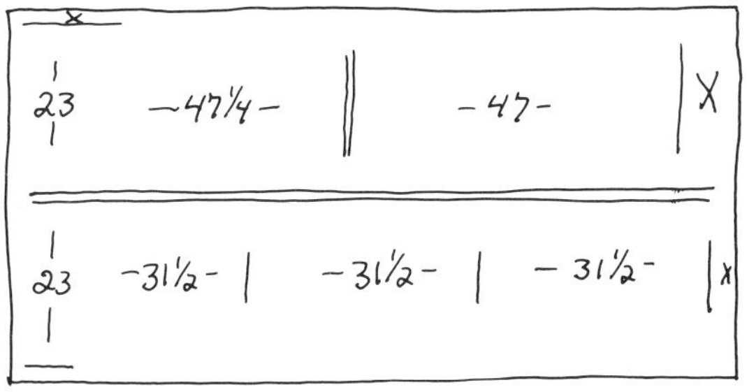

Widths under 24 in. allow stock to be divided in half.

```
x
23    — 47¼ —  ‖    — 47 —    | X
      ────────────────────────
23   — 31½ — | — 31½ — | — 31½ — | x
```

Lengths under 32 in. allow sheet to produce three pieces per run.

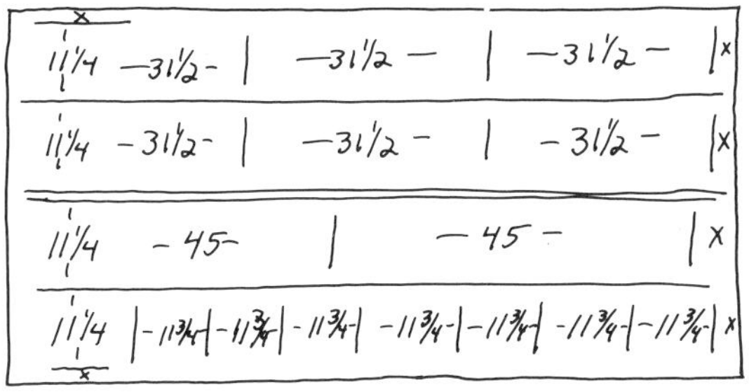

Widths under 12 in. allow sheet to be divided in four parts.

```
x
11¼ — 31½ — | — 31½ — | — 31½ — |x
11¼ — 31½ — | — 31½ — | — 31½ — |x
────────────────────────────────
11¼   — 45 —  |   — 45 —   | x
11¼ |—11¾—|—11¾—|—11¾—|—11¾—|—11¾—|—11¾—|—11¾—| x
x
```

Lengths under 12 in. allow eight pieces.

cient use of the stock but also helps me keep the modules to a manageable size.

Creation of large units from smaller modules After many years building cabinets single-handedly, I have gotten into the habit of constructing units in sizes that one person can easily lift and maneuver into place. For example, I rarely make a base unit more than 36 in. long. Instead, I create a longer unit by joining two or more modules together. Depending on the style of cabinet, I then either overlay the joined cabinets with a single face frame or use a pilaster molding to hide the seam between them (see the drawing on the facing page).

Having decided on the layout of your kitchen and settled on a style of cabinetry, there are still many more decisions to make before you can turn from paperworking to woodworking. Your next step is to choose what materials and hardware you'll use to build the cabinets. You'll also soon have to make that often excruciating choice about counters: What surface best suits the aesthetics, needs and finances of your kitchen? The next chapter will help you find answers to these questions.

3
MATERIALS

ell over twenty years ago while working for a timber-frame-home builder, I was assigned the task of building a bathroom vanity for a home we had just raised. Since the house was a close reproduction of a late-17th-century home in Sturbridge Village, Massachusetts, the owners wanted to keep the style of the bathroom cabinetry (which didn't exist of course in the original home) in sync with the rest of the structure. To that end, the builder handed me a 16-ft. long plank of perfectly clear pine over 24 in. wide (logged off the owner's property), a bag of hand-forged nails and two pairs of antique wrought-iron butterfly hinges. "Go to it, young man," he declared. And with great trepidation, I did.

As it turned out, this was my first solo cabinet job (little did the builder know!), and the last job in which the materials totally dictated the style and construction of the cabinetry. These days I choose from a wide variety of panel and solid-wood products and hardware fittings, carefully matching the materials to the functions they fill and to the style I wish to create.

SHEET STOCK

Don't get me wrong, I have nothing against using single widths of solid boards to create cabinets. The results are certainly beautiful; and as long as you follow certain assembly methods, you can generally avoid problems caused by the significant dimensional instability of wide planks. But it has been more than a

score of years since that bathroom-vanity project, and I'm still waiting to have another 24-in. wide board willingly handed over to me.

To make up the wide components of cabinet cases, I now choose from a variety of sheet stocks. If the cabinets are to be stained or finished clear, I use hardwood plywood or fiberboard veneered with a wood that matches the face frame, door and drawer parts. For paint-grade or laminate-coated cabinets, I use medium-density fiberboard (MDF) — a panel made from highly compressed wood fibers. I make drawer bottoms, recessed door panels, cabinet backs and toe-kick veneer from ¼-in. sheet stock. Finally, I use high-density particleboard or fir plywood as substrates for countertops.

Although I could edge-join solid wood to create wide panels (and sometimes do for aesthetic reasons), there are some good reasons not to. The first is that it is time-consuming to lay out, cut, join and flatten solid boards. The second is that the resulting panel will inevitably change dimension, and sometimes even warp, in response to varying environmental moisture levels. If drawer slides, shelf standards or other hardware fixtures are fastened across a solid-wood case side, there is a strong risk that the side will split or the hardware will be thrown out of whack.

To be fair, though, there are also disadvantages to working with sheet stock (and certain varieties, such as melamine-laminated MDF, may be difficult to find in some areas). The ¾-in. material is relatively heavy (a sheet of MDF weighs about 100 lb.) and awkward to handle in a small, one-person shop. Because panels can acquire a permanent sag if leaned against a wall, you should always store them flat on a level surface. As you can imagine, this doesn't make for efficient use of your valuable floor space. When working with veneered panels, your sawblades must be as sharp as possible and your machines running with minimal vibration, or you risk tearing the delicate face veneer. And finally, the fumes released when cutting many sheet goods are toxic to breathe — more than a dust mask is required to filter them. Although MDF has been the main offender in this regard, some manufacturers are now using formaldehyde-free glues, which substantially reduce the toxicity.

Applications

In the chart on p. 34, I suggest appropriate uses for a variety of commonly available sheet stocks. You'll note that I make fine distinctions in grain patterns amongst the hard-

A wide variety of sheet stocks can be used to make up cabinet case components.

wood plywoods. This distinction is one of aesthetics only. The plain-sawn veneers look very much like boards joined together to form a panel. Conversely, rotary-sawn veneer looks unlike any typical board surface — you can tell it's plywood a mile away. The lumber-core variety of plywood, in which solid wood rather than thin veneers composes the inner layers, can be used interchangeably with veneer core. Lumber core does, however, provide a somewhat more rigid sheet, making it a better choice when using a panel to span a significant distance without support (for instance, a tall pantry door).

You may be surprised at my suggestion that MDF be used to make up traditional frame-and-panel doors (as long as they're painted). In many ways, it is a superior choice to solid wood for this application. Because MDF's dimensions and flatness re-

SHEET-STOCK VARIETIES AND SUGGESTED APPLICATIONS

Hardwood Plywood (veneer core)	¾ in. or ⅝ in.	Carcase sides, tops, bottoms (rotary sawn OK) Panel doors (use plainsawn; use lumber core for tall panels) Base frame (can be used in lieu of 2x4s) Kickboards (removable toe kick with leg-leveler hardware) Drawer sides and faces Counter substrate (scrap strips can be used as first layer or under Corian)
	½ in.	Recessed panels Drawer sides (edge-band exposed edge, unless void-free)
	¼ in.	Case backs Recessed panels Toe kicks (veneered over face edge of base frame) Drawer bottoms
Medium-Density Fiberboard	uncoated ¾ in. (painted)	Panel doors (rails and stiles also) Recessed panels Drawer sides and faces
	melamine laminated ¾ in.	Carcase sides, tops, bottoms (seal all edges) Toe kicks (not recommended unless all edges sealed) (Note that you may not be able to buy this material in small quantities in some areas.)
	melamine laminated ¼ in.	Case backs Recessed panels Toe kicks (base-frame veneer) Drawer bottoms (Note that you may not be able to buy this material in small quantities in some areas.)
High-Density Particleboard	¾ in.	Counter substrate

main stable over time, the inset panel can be glued to the door frame. Gluing the panel increases the door's strength and eliminates the characteristic rattling and changing margin line of solid panels (which must be allowed to float in the frame to prevent their splitting or warping the door). In addition, MDF machines as easily and smoothly as most solid wood — and often better. The only drawback may be the relatively heavy weight of MDF doors.

SOLID STOCK

For all the advantages and versatility of hardwood-veneered plywood or fiberboard, there are many cabinet components that are best made from solid stock. These components include face frames, door rails and stiles, moldings, light valances, and raised or tongue-and-groove panels. Making these parts from solid wood allows you to shape and expose their edges without having to deal with unsightly veneer or joint lines.

Another, perhaps more subtle, quality of solid wood may encourage you to use it as much as possible: its incomparably beautiful depth of finish. To my eye, a plywood veneer never seems to achieve the depth of finish that a piece of solid wood attains. Lastly, you may find that the selection of wood available in solid stock is far greater than that available in veneered panels. Going with solid wood, even if it means making your own veneered panels for certain case components, allows you to create a truly unique set of cabinets.

When working with solid wood, you must be prepared to deal with its drawbacks. Unlike defect-free and inherently stable veneered sheet stocks, a solid piece of wood often contains defects, not all of which can be seen. This means that you not only have to work around the visible defects, but also must try to account for those you can't see. For example, you must always waste at least an inch at the ends of each board to avoid the inevitable, but invisible, drying splits. And because boards with the straightest-appearing grain patterns might curve when ripped, you must always allow plenty of material for jointing ripped components to width. As a result, working with solid wood produces significantly more waste than working with sheet stock, making it more expensive.

Using solid wood also raises the ethical question of consuming scarce resources. To assuage my own concerns about working with solid stock, I try as much as possible to use local sources of wood. Shopping locally gives me the opportunity to find lumber that has at least been logged using sustainable-yield forestry practices. In addition, I try to cut as much stock from the lower lumber grades as possible. Though there are many more knots, I find I can lay out a surprising amount of clear stock in between them — most components in cabinetmaking are relatively short. Finally, I rarely use exotic woods, though I may be more tempted now that certain suppliers buy only from South American cooperatives practicing conscientious forestry (see Sources of Supply on pp. 194-196).

In the chart on p. 36, I have listed the woods that are commonly available, relatively easy to work, stable and otherwise suitable for cabinetmaking. Note that I have grouped some wood species together (one grouping even contains both hardwood and softwood types because of the similarity of their primary characteristics and applications).

WOOD CHARACTERISTICS

Species	Figure and Coloration	Milling Qualities	Stability	Gluing and Fastening	Cost	Comments
Pines Soft maple Alder Poplar	Very little figure Homogeneous color	Excellent	Excellent	Good to excellent	Low (except for clear pine, which is high)	Often used in paint-grade work
Oaks (red, white, black) Vertical-grain fir	Moderate to high figure Varied color	Fair to good	Good	Good	Moderate	Red oak is most common kitchen cabinet wood in America
Hard maple Cherry Pecan Hickory Walnut	High figure Rich color (except for maple)	Good to excellent	Good	Good	Moderate to high	Premier cabinet woods
Exotics	High figure Rich color	Good to excellent	Fair to excellent	Poor glue characteristics (oily varieties) Good to excellent screwing	High	Used mostly as veneers because of expense, weight, susceptibility to movement

Also be aware that riftsawn or quartersawn stock of any species is more stable than plainsawn. I have left out many properties of wood that are of little concern to cabinetmaking, such as compression and tensile strengths, and so on.

HARDWARE

If you're like me and most other woodworkers I know, hardware fascinates you as much as beautifully figured wood or fine hand tools. (In my days before fatherhood, my idea of a weekend vacation was to rummage leisurely through an old hardware store.) It's likely, then, that one of the big attractions of building your own cabinets is your getting to play with a wide variety of hardware fittings. Any part of a cabinet that must be swung, slid, supported, attached or manipulated in some way is very likely to require a fitting. In this section I cover the basic types of fittings I use in case cabinetry. It's by no means inclusive of all that is out there. Information about installing and adjusting the hardware is presented in later chapters.

HINGE ATTRIBUTES AND APPLICATIONS

		Ease of Installation	Ease of Adjustment	Closing Mechanism	Cost	Comments
Surface		Easy (screws only)	No adjustment after installation	Requires catch	Low to moderate (hand-forged expensive)	Hinge of choice for certain style periods
Butt		Requires mortise	Side-to-side adjustment by shimming; up-and-down adjustment difficult	Requires catch	Low (solid brass expensive)	Avoid unless necessary for style period
Pivot		Easy (screws only) Mortise optional (except for 3rd hinge)	Some up-and-down, side-to-side adjustment	Requires catch	Moderate	Nearly invisible when installed in mortised door
Formed		Easy (screws only)	Difficult	Self-closing	Moderate	Most common face-frame hinge (though does not convey a particular period style)
European cup		Requires 35mm cup-hinge hole	Excellent (adjusts in three planes)	Self-closing	Moderate (some specialty types expensive)	Totally concealed hinge (highly recommended unless hinge needed to help define style)

Hinges

When choosing what type of hinge to use to swing the cabinet doors, you should consider the following factors: appropriateness to the style of the cabinetry, ease of installation and adjustment, closing mechanism (self or catch) and cost. My ordering of the factors is not arbitrary. I list style first because it may strictly define the type of hinge. For example, Early American pine cabinets beg for surface mounted "L," "H" or "butterfly" hinges. While these hinges are easy to install, you must accept their characteristic drawbacks: difficulty of adjustment, limited weight capacity, non-self-closure (a safety issue) and expense if hand-wrought.

If, however, the appearance of the hinge is not critical to style, then you can opt first for ease of installation and adjustment. If a fully concealed hinge works for your cabinet design, I strongly suggest using European-type cup hinges (most brands have versions designed for use with face-frame construction). Although it may be expensive, the cup hinge has almost everything else going for it. It is the easiest of all hinge types to in-

This European-type concealed cup hinge, designed to mount to the edge of a face frame, can be used on traditional-style cabinets.

stall, and it allows for the greatest range of adjustment after installation. Cup hinges are self-closing (when held within an inch or so of their closed position) and can support more weight than any other type of cabinet-door hinge, which means that you might get away with using a pair of hinges while another hinge type requires three. A variety of mounting plates allows you to control how much the door overlays the face frame.

In certain applications, such as an enclosed microwave cabinet, I want the frequently opened doors to swing totally out of the way without blocking other cabinets. I use a combination hinge and slide hardware fitting to accomplish this — a "flip-door" hinge. Note that you must fully recess flip doors into the surrounding face frames, and the other doors must follow this style so they don't stand out visually.

Drawer slides

There are many types and variations of drawer-slide hardware, each filling a specific styling or application need, but I confine my choices to just a few types. Occasionally I use side-mounted, heavy-duty, full-extension slides on drawers where loads may exceed 75 lb. (food-produce bins, for example). These fittings slide effortlessly on steel ball-bearing runners, even when loaded to capacity. Unfortunately, however, they are not self-closing. For most other purposes, I use the considerably less expensive, and easier to install, European-made corner-mounted slides. These fittings are rated at medium duty (up to 75 lb.) and are available in full and three-quarter extension models. All are self-closing.

You can, of course, build your drawer and slide-out shelf runners from wood, eliminating the need for a manufactured hardware fitting en-

Heavy-duty, full-extension slides can carry up to 125 lb. without affecting their smooth, quiet motion. Note that the lower slide features 'over-travel' — the back of the drawer box is extended beyond the face frame.

Corner-mounted slides cannot carry the weight of side-mounted slides, but they are easier to install and are self-closing. The lower slide, made by Blum, is full extension.

tirely. If you build the runners from stable hardwood, mount them properly and keep them waxed, they will provide years of trouble-free service. What wood runners cannot give you, however, is the ability to support a drawer holding over 100 lb. of produce when fully extended out of the cabinet — while still offering a silky-smooth, self-closing slide action. Throw in ease of installation and adjustment and you'll understand why I use metal drawer-slide hardware almost exclusively, even when building kitchen cabinetry for myself.

Shelf supports

When installing shelving in my cabinets, I nearly always use some type of adjustable shelf-support hardware. Admittedly, I rarely move a shelf once I've put it into use, but I've learned the hard way that it's best to leave the possibility open. Furthermore, using hardware makes it as easy to build for adjustable shelving as it is to fix it permanently into place.

For most shelving applications, I use one of a variety of brass, steel or plastic pins. Some types are designed to prevent the shelf from sliding to and fro, which is an essential safety feature if you live in earthquake country. To support a shelf, you insert the pins into holes drilled into the opposing case sides.

You need only drill parallel rows of evenly spaced holes in the areas that will receive shelves. Of course, if you are faced with drilling four rows of holes in a floor-to-ceiling pantry unit, that is easier said than done. In this case, I use shelf standards. To reduce their visibility while at the same time increasing shelf capacity, I set the standards into a dadoed groove. I also use standards in cabinets whose shelving heights might

change relatively often (for example, cabinets for dry-goods storage). Since the holes for the pins tend to increase in diameter with constant usage (resulting in loosely fitting pins), standards provide a stronger and more durable option.

Specialty case-goods hardware

In recent years European hardware manufacturers have made deep inroads in the supply of fittings to the American cabinetmaking industry. Although designed originally for use within the automated 32mm system of cabinet construction, much of this highly innovative hardware has trickled down to the home-shop woodworker. Today, nearly every mail-order hardware outlet carries a wide range of European hinge and slide hardware, as well as specialty support and installation fittings.

In this book, I'll suggest using many of these fittings in building your own kitchen cabinets (you may find applications in case-furniture making as well). While the use of European-style hardware revises many of the time-honored ways of constructing cabinets, it does so without sacrificing appearance or strength — in some cases it adds to both.

Adjustable leg levelers No more time wasted building and leveling base frames! That was the promise that sold me when first introduced to the concept of using adjustable plastic feet in lieu of a wooden support frame. For the most part, the promise has held true. Although I still go with a built-up base frame for many of my traditional kitchens, leg levelers give me a viable alternative for setting lower base cabinets.

Not only does this hardware save a significant amount of materials and

Adjustable shelf-support hardware can be mounted in shelf standards (left) or in holes in the case sides. Note the unusual design of the top hole-mounted pin — the protrusion above the pin's ledge prevents the shelf from lifting or sliding.

labor by eliminating the need to build a frame, it also reduces numerous hassles encountered during installation (see Chapter 12). I've discovered another benefit as well: Because the underside of the base cabinets remains accessible (note the removable kickboard in the photo below), any post-installation of flooring, plumbing or wiring can proceed unhampered.

Drawer-face adjustment cams
One of the more frustrating jobs during final assembly is attaching the drawer face to the drawer box. Even the slightest amount of misalignment can be noticed by the observant eye. In frameless construction there is even less room for error, and an uneven margin line screams for attention. The use of adjustment

cams (see the photo at right below) allows you to shift the position of the drawer face up to $3/32$ in. in any direction. When cinched down, the adjustment cams provide an attachment as strong as my former method of permanently fixing the faces to the boxes with screws.

RTA fasteners Another fitting to come out of the European hardware system gives me a radically different option for assembling the basic components of a cabinet: RTA (ready-to-assemble) fasteners, also known as knockdown fasteners. These fittings are a godsend in situations where an assembled unit is too large to bring into the kitchen, since RTAs allow me to transport the cabinet flat. A screwdriver is all that is necessary to assemble the unit. And because RTA

Adjustment cams simplify the task of attaching a drawer face to a drawer box. (Photo courtesy Blum)

Kickboards fasten to adjustable leg levelers with plastic clips. Note the spline biscuit, which helps keep the corner joint true and secure.

fittings need no glue for strength, you can disassemble the cabinets at any time — have kitchen, will travel. (Don't laugh: In Europe, when people move, they often take their kitchens with them!)

Knobs and pulls

As I've already shown in the chart on pp. 6-7, the style of your cabinets can be greatly influenced by your choice of handles. Remember, however, that safety concerns and usage by mobility-impaired persons could also influence your decisions. For example, a bailed pull is safer than a pedestal knob if children are around (they can't catch or cut themselves on it), and it's much easier to grasp with arthritic fingers.

You can design a traditional-looking set of cabinets without knobs or pulls by profiling the edges of full-overlay doors and drawer faces to provide pull surfaces. Another alternative is to use push latches. This hardware holds the door firmly closed, yet springs the door open when given a slight push.

Nothing botches up the look of a set of cabinets as much as misaligned or misplaced handles, so take the time to decide on the most pleasing arrangement. Try using double-stick tape to position the hardware temporarily to help you visualize the overall picture. Finally, be sure to use an alignment jig to predrill the attachment screw holes (see pgs. 98 and 112-113).

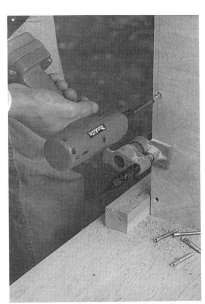

RTA fasteners allow quick assembly (and disassembly) of individual cabinets.

The style of a kitchen cabinet can be greatly influenced by the choice of knobs and pulls.

COUNTER-SURFACE MATERIALS

	Scratch Resistance	Heat Resistance	Stain Resistance	Presence/ Visibility of Seams	Ease of Cleaning
Wood (e.g., hard maple)	Good	Poor	Poor	Potentially seam free except at corners Moderate visibility	Fair
Plastic laminate (e.g., Formica)	Poor	Poor	Good	If surface ≥ 5 ft. x 12 ft. Low visibility	Good
Solid resin (e.g., Corian)	Poor (but doesn't show)	Good	Excellent	If surface ≥ 3 ft. x 12 ft. Low visibility	Good
Glazed tile	Excellent	Excellent	Excellent (though grout may stain)	N/A	Excellent
Stone (granite and marble)	Excellent	Excellent	Excellent (except hot oil)	If surface ≥ 5 ft. x 9 ft. Moderate visibility	Excellent
Metal (stainless steel)	Excellent	Excellent	Excellent	Low visibility	Excellent

COUNTERTOPS

One of the most important decisions you must make about your kitchen is the choice of material for the countertops. Because these surfaces lend a huge amount of visual impact, must serve a host of demanding functions and can be very expensive, give yourself plenty of time to consider all the options.

In the earliest American kitchens, counters were often made from wide slabs of pine. Though the wood burned under hot iron pots, stained easily after food spills, and deteriorated in areas that trapped water, it served the basic functions of a Colonial kitchen well enough. For those trying to recreate the feel of this era, these failings only serve to lend a distinctive and authentic charm.

But for those not willing to live with such marks of distinction (or not willing to plane them off every few years), there are now a number of more durable materials available. These include plastic laminate (melamine resin over kraft paper), solid surface (cast plastic), glazed tile, stone (granite and marble) and stainless steel. The most common choice, though a bit overrated in durability, is plastic laminate. It's the least expensive counter surface, and the easiest to install yourself without special tooling or extraordinary skills — possibly easier than laminating up a solid-wood counter. Later in this book (see pp. 184-193), I'll show you how to construct and install a laminate counter with a wood backsplash. To install other counter materials, seek out the advice, if not the services, of a trained professional.

Ease of Repair	Relative Cost	Comments
Good	Low to moderate	Adds much character and utility to an early, traditional-style kitchen
Poor	Low	Failings usually outweighed by low cost and breathtaking variety of colors
Excellent	Moderate	Available as combination sink/countertop
Good	Low to moderate	Use epoxy grout to reduce staining
Poor	High	Superb choice for baking center (rolling dough)
Good	Moderate to high	Use only 400 series or better stainless

In the chart above, I have listed the major attributes of the most popular counter materials. Carefully balance your needs for a material's particular strengths against your aesthetic sensibilities and budgetary limits. Consider mixing counter surfaces, making the most out of the virtues of each type of material for specific work areas. For instance, you could choose the absolute waterproofness and stain resistance of stainless steel for the cleanup area, and the superb heat resistance of tile for the cooktop area. Choose marble, though extremely expensive (but incomparable for rolling out dough), for the relatively small counter in the baking center. The rest of the counters might then be of laminate in a color that complements and unifies the appearance of the other surfaces. To save money, you could simply laminate the entire counter area and use movable wood cutting boards in the food-preparation area and trivets by the cooktop.

With the choice of materials out of the way, you're finally ready to order materials and to organize the cutting up of the stock — the last step before getting down to woodworking. In the next chapter, I'll show you how to develop the various bills of materials so you can get your orders in to your suppliers. Then I'll introduce you to the use of story poles, on which you'll define the specific dimensions of your cabinetry — and from there develop the master cutlists.

4

BILLS OF MATERIALS AND CUTLISTS

Working up a bill of materials for wood, hardware and other supplies, and then developing master cutlists for all the components, is the final bit of paperwork you'll have to do prior to woodworking. Anxious as you may be to roll up your sleeves and start cutting up wood, take your time here. The information you gather must be accurate and it must be complete — you are creating a bridge between the dream and the reality of your kitchen. Once the kitchen is built, this is one bridge you can burn behind you, as long as you carry everything you need over it.

MAKING UP THE BILLS
In the drawing on the facing page, I have drawn the floor plan and elevations of a small L-shaped kitchen. (Refer to pp. 15-17 for information about developing working drawings.) From this scale drawing showing the top, face and side view of the cabinets, I can work up order bills for the materials I'll need to build this kitchen: sheet stock, solid stock, hardware and fasteners, and miscellaneous supplies.

Sheet-stock bill
Along the left-hand side of the sheet-stock bill (shown on p. 46), I list all the types of sheet stock to be used in this sample kitchen. You'll see that I've called for some sheet stock to be "A-C" (one good side), while others of the same species and thickness are to be "A-A" (two good sides). If my local supplier tells me that I cannot get the A-C, then I'll add these to the A-A count. When ordering mela-

mine, the "A" side is a white plastic face, while the "B" side is a dull, thin paper. Note that particleboard should be of a hard industrial grade — "H.D." (high density).

To determine the amount of square footage required of each type of sheet, I measure and multiply the widths and lengths (rounding up to the nearest foot) of each component to be made from this stock and add them up. Whenever possible, I simplify the count by multiplying the square footage of similar components such as case sides, or drawer bottoms within the same bank of drawers, by their number.

To find the number of sheets necessary to accommodate the sum total of square footage, I divide the result by 32, the number of square feet in a

SCALE PLAN AND ELEVATIONS OF L-SHAPED KITCHEN

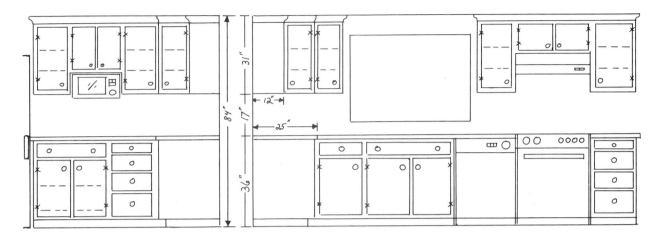

West-wall elevation

North-wall elevation

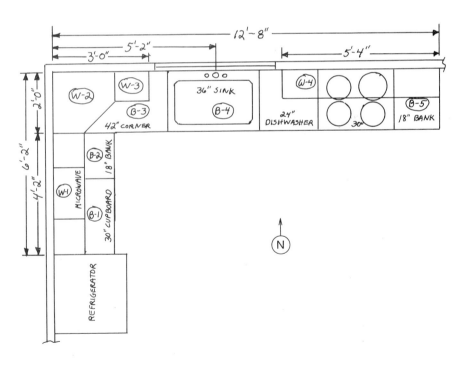

Floor plan

4x8 panel. I usually round off the result to the next highest number of sheets (to allow extra material for saw cuts, and scrap to replace a miscut piece or two). If I want an exact accounting of the waste, I wait to finalize the sheet count until after I've worked up the graphic layout of the sheet cuts (see p. 57).

Solid-stock bill

My bill of solid stock (shown at bottom) lists the wood needed in two ways: by square footage and by lineal footage. Under square footage, I list the lumber by species and thickness in a vertical column, specifying the amount needed under five headings in a spreadsheet to the right. I list stock to be ordered by the lineal foot — my supplier sells drawer sides and stock moldings by lineal rather than board footage — in a second spreadsheet as shown. There is no need to be more specific about component sizes at this point, since the master cutlist I will develop later defines the dimensions and amounts needed of each component.

To arrive at square-footage figures for narrow components such as rails and stiles, I multiply the width of the component (using decimal fractions of a foot) by the total length required throughout the cabinets. In the bill shown below, I arrived at the face-frame square footage this way:

0.19 (2¼-in. rails) x 16.5 lin. ft. = 3.1 sq. ft.
0.15 (1¾-in. stiles) x 49.5 lin. ft. = 7.4 sq. ft.
0.10 (1¼-in. rails) x 42.0 lin. ft. = 4.2 sq. ft.

Adding the three results gives me the total square footage of material consumed by the face frame: 14.7 sq. ft. of 4/4 oak.

SHEET-STOCK BILL OF MATERIALS

TYPE AND THICKNESS	GRADE/CORE	APPLICATION	SQUARE FT.	SHEETS NEEDED (32 SQ. FT. = 1 SHEET)
¾" MAPLE	A-C or A-A (ROTARY-SAWN)	CASE COMP.	147	5
¼" RED OAK	A-A (PLAINSAWN)	RECESSED DOOR PANELS APPLIED END PANELS	48	2
¼" MELAMINE	A-B	DRAWER BOTTOMS CASE BACKS	105	4
¾" PARTICLE-BOARD	H.D.	COUNTER SUBSTRATE	28.5	1

SOLID-STOCK BILL OF MATERIALS

SPECIES (AND THICKNESS)	SQUARE FOOTAGE					LINEAL FOOTAGE			
	FACE FRAMES	DOOR FRAMES	DRAWER FACES	MISC.	TOTAL BD. FT.*	½ MAPLE (DRAWER SIDES)		STOCK MOLDINGS	
RED OAK (4/4)	15.0	17.0	10.75	12.0	63.0	x 5 IN.	15	2¼ IN. CORNICE	18
MAPLE (6/4)				(BREADBOARD) 24 x 24	5.0	x 3½ IN.	14	¾ IN. SCOTIA	20
						x 6½ IN.	28	¾ IN. QUARTER ROUND	16
						x 8½ IN.	14		
				*INCLUDES 15% WASTE					

To find the total amount of 4/4 oak that must be ordered, I add this face-frame square footage to that of any other components made from this thickness of stock. Then I add 15% to this amount to allow for waste, and convert the sum total of square footage to board footage. In this case, because 4/4 stock is 1 in. thick, the board footage equals square footage. In the case of 6/4 stock (1½ in.), I find the board footage by multiplying the sum total of square footage by 1.5.

Hardware and fasteners bill

To ensure accuracy when taking the counts of hinges, slides, pulls and leg levelers from the scaled drawing, I mark these fittings where they appear on the elevation or plan views (see the drawing on p. 45). I place a small check next to the mark as I add them up.

To count shelf-support pins, I multiply the number of shelves (indicated by dotted lines on the plans) by four. I count drawer-face adjustment cams by counting up the drawer faces and

HARDWARE AND FASTENERS BILL

ITEM	TYPE/SIZE	ORDER NUMBER	QUANTITY	PRICE
HINGES	3/8 FORMED OFFSET	A0 3428 BB	15 pr.	1.92
HINGE PLATES	N/A			
SLIDES	22" FULL EXT.	430 E5500V	2 pr.	19.83
	22" THREE-QUARTER EXT.	230 M 5500	10 pr.	4.46
	SOCKETS	603720. UH	10 pr.	.78
PULLS/HANDLES	PORCELAIN KNOBS (1¼ in.)	A 76244 ALB	28	2.21
LEG LEVELERS		BLUM	20	2.56
SHELF SUPPORTS	STANDARDS	N/A		
	PINS	SPOONS # 30692	48	.09
FASTENERS	DRAWER-FACE ADJUSTERS	BLUM B 295.100	20	.32
	BISCUITS/DOWELS	#20 BISCUITS	25	.14
	RTA FASTENERS	HAFELE 7×50 264, 42, 197	100	.14
FIXTURES	SLIDE-OUT TOWEL BAR	KV 079 ANO	1	15.80
	TILT-OUT TRAY - 31 in.	FE SFT 31	1	9.27
	HALF-MOON SLIDE OUTS	FE HM 28G	2	48.08
	SPICE DRAWER INSET	V 50 21S	1	44.19

multiplying by two. To find the number of spline biscuits I'll need for joining the case sides, I multiply the number used per joint (5 for base units and 3 for wall units) by the number of joints present in the kitchen. Finally, I make a list of all the special fixtures, such as tilt-out sink trays, lazy Susans or slide-out baskets, being sure to specify sizes.

Bill of supplies

The bill shown below lists the supplies that I predict I'll consume in the process of building, finishing and installing the sample kitchen. To avoid having to stop in the middle of the finishing process (which can be disastrous to the outcome), I always buy more finish material, filler putty

and caulk than I think I'll use. My supplier lets me bring back any unopened containers.

Ordering materials

Because of the amount of material you need to build a complete set of kitchen cabinets, you have to order some, if not all, of the stock and hardware items ahead of time from your local building-goods supplier and mail-order houses.

When ordering sheet stock, be sure to specify, in addition to species and thickness, the grade of each face and the type of core and veneer (see p. 33). Although "shop grade" sheets (non-graded because of damage) are considerably cheaper, don't order them sight unseen because the defects may be so extensive that the sheets are largely unusable.

The only sure way to get high-quality lumber is to hand-pick your boards by going through the stacks at your supplier's yard. You may even be able to save some money by finding a lot of usable boards in cheaper, lower-graded lumber. Unfortunately, many yards either forbid customers to go through the piles, or they charge extra for this privilege, thereby canceling out the savings. If you can't go through the piles, be sure to order only FAS lumber. This grade guarantees a knot-free face over about 90% of the board, though it doesn't guarantee that the board is free from cup or warp. To cover your order, then, add at least 15% to your estimate to account for ungraded defects.

Unless you have a planer powerful and durable enough to surface rough lumber, you are better off having the supplier plane the boards for you. If you do have a planer, tell the supplier to leave the last $1/16$ in. for you to remove. In this way you can clean

BILL OF SUPPLIES

ITEM	SIZE / COLOR	QUANTITY
SCREWS	2½ IN. DRYWALL	1 LB
	1 ⅝ IN. "	1 LB
	1 ¼ IN. "	1 LB
GLUE	YELLOW GLUE	1 PT
EDGE BANDING	N/A	
DOOR AND DRAWER BUMPER PADS	⅜ IN. DIA. CLEAR	52
SCREW COVERCAPS	TITUS (WHITE)	2 DOZ.
BRADS/NAILS	¾ IN. #17	1 PACK
	1 IN. #17	1 PACK
FINISH MATERIALS	PENETRATING OIL	1 GAL.
SANDPAPER STEEL WOOL RAGS	80-120-180-220 0000	1 ROLL @ 1 PACK 1 BAG
CAULK FILLER PUTTY	COLORED - CLEAR COLOR: WHITE OAK	1 TUBE @ 1 JAR
SHIM STOCK	DRY PINE OR CEDAR	1 BUNDLE

up their job (their blades are rarely sharp) and bring all the stock to the exact same thickness.

You can often save money on hardware by ordering full boxes. Hinges and drawer slides, for example, are usually offered at a substantial per-unit deduction when sold in bulk. To take advantage of this, find another person or two to share in the hardware order. As an alternative, you may be able to buy your hardware through a friendly local woodworking business. Even with their markup they may be able to give you a much better price than a lumberyard or home center can.

STORY POLES

When I started building kitchens, I spent untold hours with a steel tape measuring the space for which I would be building and installing the cabinets. The drawings I brought back from the site were filled with a jumble of lines, arrows and notes indicating sizes of walls, positions of window and door openings, locations of outlets and plumbing, and a host of other dimensions and special conditions. These drawings were rich in information but short on clarity, and more than a few misbuilt cabinets never found a home.

Then an elderly cabinetmaker took me under his wing and taught me how to use story poles. Now I return from the site bearing only a small bundle of sticks—and the confidence that comes with having created a full-scale, and blessedly infallible, rendering of the kitchen walls.

Transferring wall features to story poles

To prepare story poles on which to record the features of the space that will contain the sample L-shaped kitchen, I cut out some straight

Using a reservoir-type water level enables the installer to mark a level reference line around the perimeter of the kitchen single-handedly.

lengths of ¾-in. x 1½-in. pine (or any other light-colored wood). I make two poles long enough to span the horizontal runs, and cut a third to a length just shy of the distance between the floor and ceiling. If a run of cabinets in your kitchen is to fit between two walls, cut out two poles for that run, each about 1 ft. longer than one-half the span. On site, slide the poles by one another until they touch the walls, then nail them together.

I wait to record the features of the kitchen walls on the poles until all door, window, plumbing and electrical work has been roughed in and the drywall hung. In this way, I can be sure that I know where everything is that might affect the cabinet layout. When all is ready, I begin by striking a level reference line at a comfortable working height (about 40 in. for me) around the perimeter of the kitchen. A builder's sight level or a reservoir-type water level makes short work of this task. I then draw plumb lines to the reference line from all the utilities and edges of

Draw plumb lines from the pipes to the reference lines.

STORY POLES IN POSITION FOR TAKING SITE MEASUREMENTS

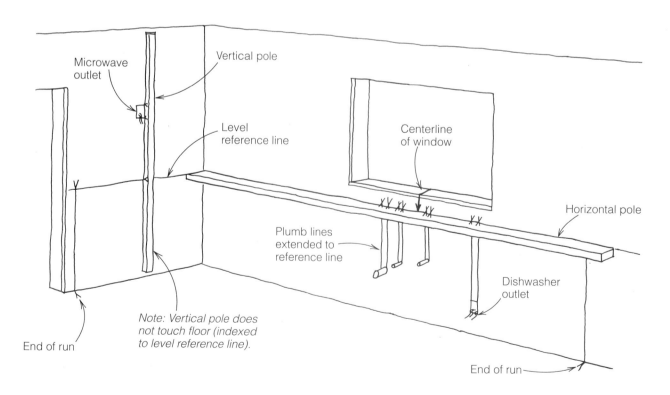

Microwave outlet

Vertical pole

Level reference line

Centerline of window

Horizontal pole

Plumb lines extended to reference line

Dishwasher outlet

End of run

Note: Vertical pole does not touch floor (indexed to level reference line).

End of run

Holding the story pole to the reference line, transfer the intersection points to the stick.

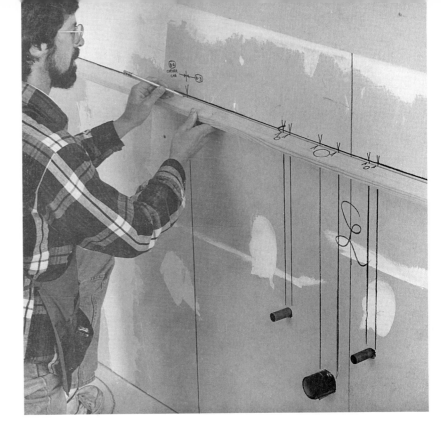

rough openings that I wish to record (see the photo on the facing page). Working to an established reference line ensures a more accurate story-pole layout since it eliminates errors otherwise introduced by running the poles at varying heights to an out-of-plumb wall.

The next step is to transfer the site measurements I've brought to the reference line to the story pole. To do this I hold the pole firmly to the line (pressing one end tight against the wall corner) and then transfer the intersection points to it. I make a tick mark at each point with a fine pen or sharp pencil and note what the mark indicates. I then use a small square to extend the mark across the pole. Before removing the pole from the wall, I note (by compass direction) what wall this pole is recording — my floor-plan drawing indicates which wall is north. Depending on the situation, I'll make other marks and notations on the pole. For example, I marked the center of the window opening in this example because the sink is to be centered there (see the drawing on the facing page).

To develop the vertical dimensions of the cabinets and to record the height locations of the wall features, I hold a story pole plumb between the floor and ceiling. Note in the drawing at right that the stick does not touch either — you cannot depend on these surfaces to be flat or level. The only way to ensure that the marks will be consistently accurate around the room is to reference the vertical story pole to the level reference line.

RECORDING HIGH AND LOW POINTS ON VERTICAL STORY POLE

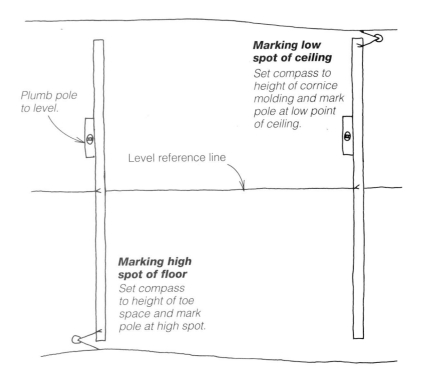

Plumb pole to level.

Marking low spot of ceiling
Set compass to height of cornice molding and mark pole at low point of ceiling.

Level reference line

Marking high spot of floor
Set compass to height of toe space and mark pole at high spot.

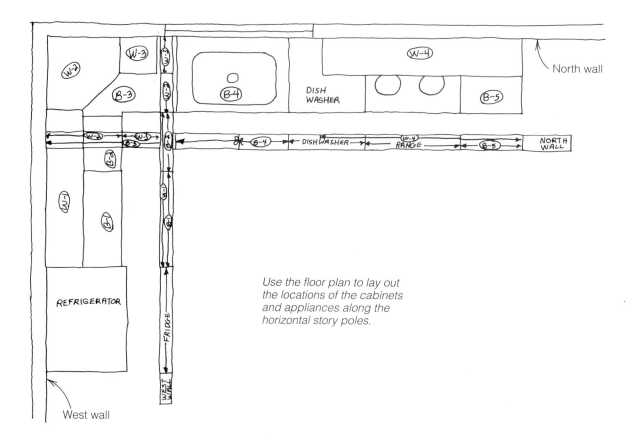

Use the floor plan to lay out the locations of the cabinets and appliances along the horizontal story poles.

Checking with a level attached to a long straightedge (or ideally with a builder's level), I find the high point of the floor and the low point of the ceiling or soffit along the wall. I then bring the story pole to these places and mark the high and low points on the stick as shown in the drawing on p. 51. I choose 3½ in. for the toe-space height, which allows me to use 2x4 stock for the base frame. I get the cornice-height setting by measuring a sample piece of molding. As I explain below, you will need this information to determine the heights of the cabinets.

Laying out the cabinets on the poles

The poles now have a story to tell. Everything I need to know about this space is recorded on them. I can take the story poles back to my shop and continue to work with them, defining the exact locations of the appliances and the sizes and position of each cabinet module.

Using the floor-plan drawing as a general outline, I lay out the base cabinets for each wall along their corresponding story poles. I account for appliances (and their clearance spaces) by referring to the manufacturer's specification sheets (the dealer usually has this information). Note that a portion of the poles shows the side profile of both a base and a

LAYOUT OF FACE FRAME AT CORNERS AND WALLS

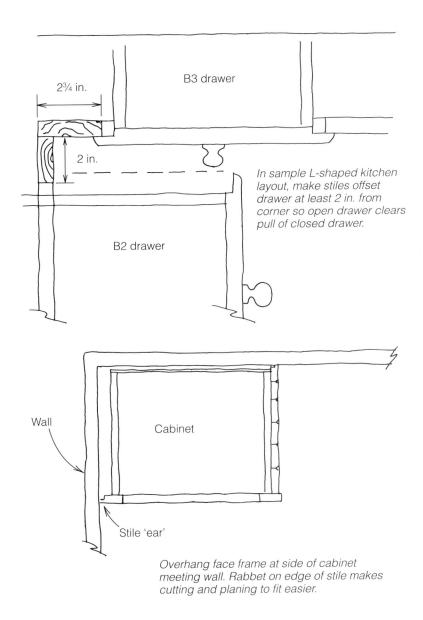

2¾ in.

B3 drawer

2 in.

In sample L-shaped kitchen layout, make stiles offset drawer at least 2 in. from corner so open drawer clears pull of closed drawer.

B2 drawer

Wall

Cabinet

Stile 'ear'

Overhang face frame at side of cabinet meeting wall. Rabbet on edge of stile makes cutting and planing to fit easier.

wall cabinet. I use the poles to lay out the depth of these cabinets.

Give special attention to the corners where base units meet — you must ensure that any extended drawers clear protruding handles. Because you have to make face frames a little wider in this situation, door and drawer widths are consequently a little narrower than the overall size of the cabinet would at first indicate. Where a cabinet meets a wall, extend out the face frame — called an "ear" — so that it can later be scribed to fit the surface of the wall. Toward the opening of the cabinet, either overhang the face frames ½ in. or more past the case sides (to allow the use of back sockets for drawer

LAYOUT OF CABINETS ON VERTICAL STORY POLE

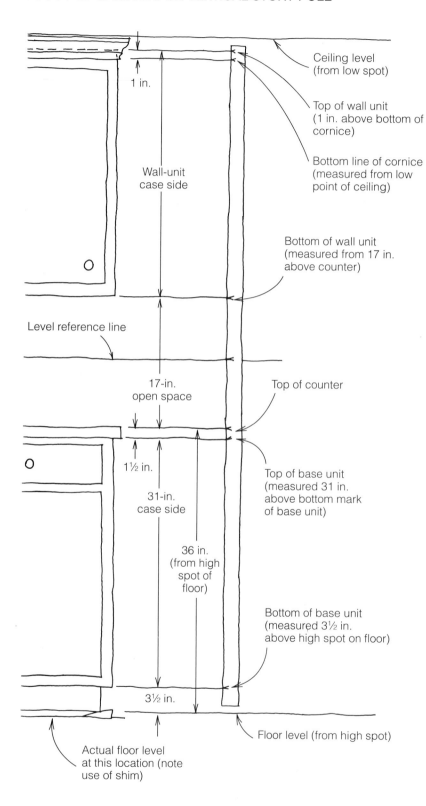

Ceiling level
(from low spot)

1 in.

Top of wall unit
(1 in. above bottom of
cornice)

Bottom line of cornice
(measured from low
point of ceiling)

Wall-unit
case side

Bottom of wall unit
(measured from 17 in.
above counter)

Level reference line

17-in.
open space

Top of counter

1½ in.

31-in.
case side

Top of base unit
(measured 31 in.
above bottom mark
of base unit)

36 in.
(from high
spot of
floor)

Bottom of base unit
(measured 3½ in.
above high spot on floor)

3½ in.

Floor level (from high spot)

Actual floor level
at this location (note
use of shim)

slides), or make the frames flush (so the slides can mount directly on the case sides).

Once I've marked the poles with the positions of the outside dimensions of the base units, I then proceed to lay out the wall cabinets. I flip the sticks a quarter turn (giving myself a clean surface to work on), and bring around lines from any base units that align with the wall cabinets above them. In this kitchen (in common with many other cabinet designs), the wall cabinets are oriented directly over certain base units.

When I've laid out all the cabinets on the horizontal poles, I go back over the layout, double-checking to be sure that the layout closely approximates that of my scale-plan-view drawings. Some discrepancies in cabinet sizing and positioning must be accepted, but because of its accuracy, the full-scale story-pole layout takes precedence. Finally, I check the positions of the utility openings to be sure that they fall (with room to spare for cover plates) within the walls of the appropriate cabinets.

To develop the vertical dimensions of the cabinets, I lay out a side profile of the base and wall cabinets along the vertical story pole. Because I have defined the high point of the floor and the low point of the ceiling, I can find the cabinet side heights by deduction. A base-cabinet side is the distance between the underside of the countertop (which I set at 34½ in. above the high point of the floor) and the toe-space mark (here 3½ in. above the floor's high point). A wall-cabinet side is the distance from a predetermined point behind the cornice molding (here 1 in. above the bottom edge of the molding) to the top of the open space (I generally allow 17 in. above the counter surface). A floor-to-ceiling-

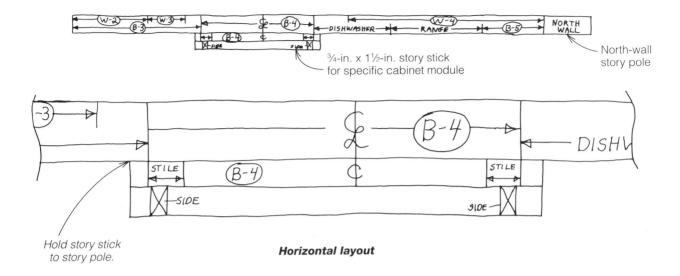

North-wall story pole

¾-in. x 1½-in. story stick for specific cabinet module

Horizontal layout

Hold story stick to story pole.

CREATING MASTER CUTLISTS

With the site story poles completed, I have a precise layout of the outside dimensions of each cabinet module for this L-shaped kitchen. The pair of horizontal poles gives me the cabinets' width and depth, and the vertical pole their height. But to create master cutlists, I now need to know the precise dimensions of the components: length of floors and ceilings, face-frame rails and stiles, drawer faces and doors. To do this

unit side is the distance from the top of the wall-cabinet side to the bottom of a base-unit side.

Note that although the floor of the base units and the top of the wall cabinets are shown on the vertical story pole, the top edge of the cornice molding and bottom edge of the kick board are not. As you might remember, the pole was cut shy of touching either the floor or ceiling of the room.

quickly while nearly eliminating the chance for errors, I make up a second set of story poles — this time to represent each cabinet module. (I refer to these shorter-length poles as "story sticks," to distinguish them from the full-length site story poles.) After laying out the components on the module story stick, I go on to make a card for the cabinet, drawing a view of its face and listing the components. I then use these cards to compile the master cutlists for the sheet and solid stock.

Creating a module story stick

To make up a story stick for a specific cabinet module, get out the site story pole showing the cabinet and hold a second stick tight against it. I use a 1½-in. wide strip of ¾-in. plywood cut an inch or so longer than the width of the cabinet. I draw a line down the length of the stick to divide it into two parts. Along the edge against the site pole, draw the outside dimensions of the cabinet, then develop the layout of the face

SAMPLE SOLID-STOCK CUTLIST

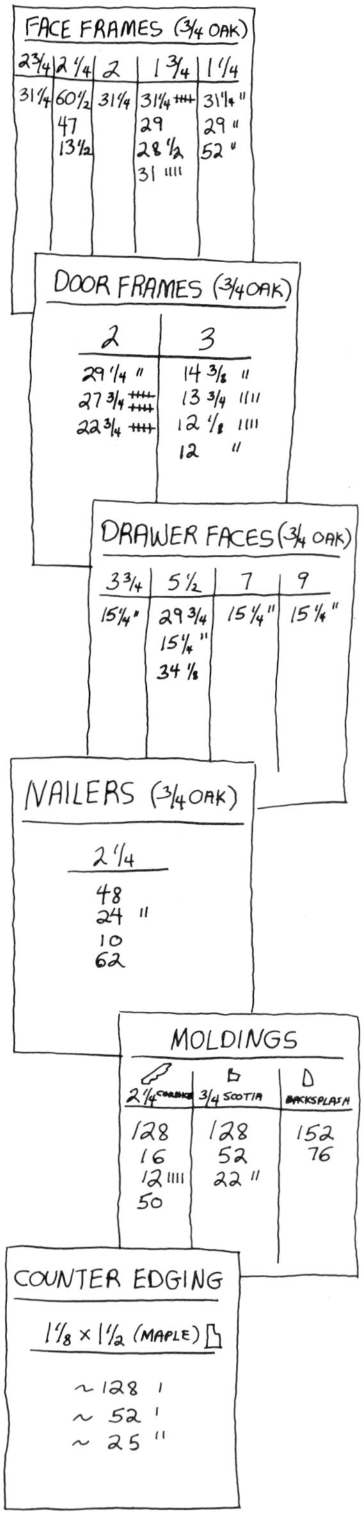
FACE FRAMES (3/4 OAK)
2 3/4 | 2 1/4 | 2 | 1 3/4 | 1 1/4
31 1/4 | 60 1/2 | 31 1/4 | 31 1/4 | 31 1/4
47 | 29 | 29
13 1/2 | 28 1/2 | 52
31
DOOR FRAMES (3/4 OAK)
2 | 3
29 1/4 | 14 3/8
27 3/4 | 13 3/4
22 3/4 | 12 1/8
12
DRAWER FACES (3/4 OAK)
3 3/4 | 5 1/2 | 7 | 9
15 1/4 | 29 3/4 | 15 1/4 | 15 1/4
15 1/4
34 1/8
NAILERS (3/4 OAK)
2 1/4
48
24
10
62
MOLDINGS
2 1/4 CORNICE | 3/4 SCOTIA | BACKSPLASH
128 | 128 | 152
16 | 52 | 76
12 | 22
50
COUNTER EDGING
1 1/8 x 1 1/2 (MAPLE)
~128
~52
~25

frame. On the opposite side of the stick, on the other side of the line, draw in the side and partition components. (Check your sheet stock — don't assume that ¾-in. plywood is really ¾ in. thick.) This split-stick method allows you to see clearly how the face frame relates to the sides and any partitions. (For a more detailed discussion of laying out the face frames, see pp. 66-68.)

With the face frame laid out, continue the story-stick layout by marking the position of doors and drawer faces relative to the face frame. Flip the stick over to lay out height dimensions. Refer ahead to Chapters 7 and 8 for details of laying out these components on the module sticks.

Module cards

Using the unruled side of a 5x8 index card, I make up one card for each cabinet module. On one half of the card, I draw in a front view of the cabinet and a sketch of the face frame. On the other half, I list the sizes and numbers of all the components, gleaning the information from that module's story stick. The mark in the upper-left-hand corner of the card (here B-4) corresponds to the symbol I've given this cabinet on my original floor-plan drawing (see p. 45).

Solid-stock cutlist

To create a solid-stock cutlist for this sample kitchen, I go through the module cards, noting all the types and widths of solid-wood components that are to go into the cabinets. I then compile this information as a series of titled columns and subcolumns. For example, in the cutlist at left I've established five columns under face-frame components in which to list the five widths: 2¾ in., 2¼ in., 2 in., 1¾ in. and 1¼ in.

Once the columns are established, I go through the module cards again, writing in the lengths specified for each component under the appropriate column heading. As each becomes listed, I lightly cross it off on

SAMPLE MODULE CARD

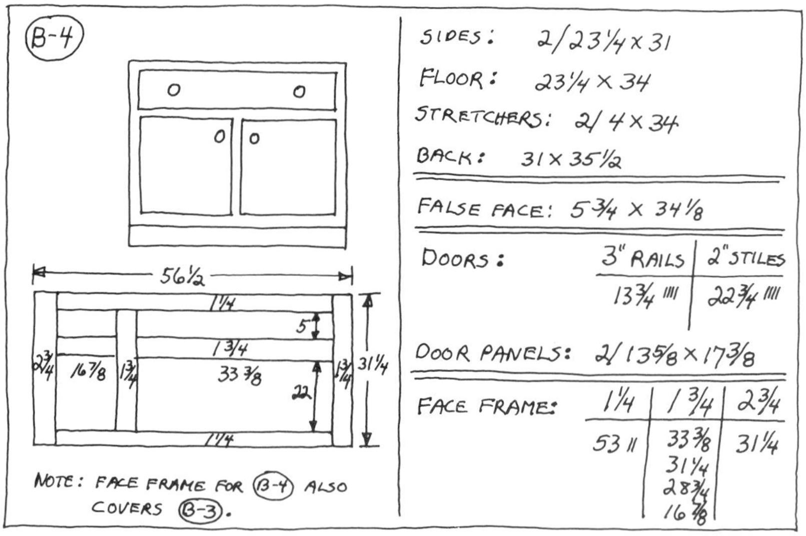
B-4
56 1/2
1 1/4
5
1 3/4
2 3/4
16 7/8
1 3/4
33 3/8
22
1 3/4
31 1/4
1 1/4
NOTE: FACE FRAME FOR B-4 ALSO COVERS B-3.
SIDES: 2/23 1/4 x 31
FLOOR: 23 1/4 x 34
STRETCHERS: 2/4 x 34
BACK: 31 x 35 1/2
FALSE FACE: 5 3/4 x 34 1/8
DOORS: 3" RAILS | 2" STILES
13 3/4 | 22 3/4
DOOR PANELS: 2/13 5/8 x 17 3/8
FACE FRAME: 1 1/4 | 1 3/4 | 2 3/4
53 | 33 3/8 | 31 1/4
31 1/4
28 3/4
16 7/8

the module card. Instead of assigning a number to components listed of the same size — which could easily be confused with a measurement number — I make tick marks to the right of the length dimension. Later, when I lay out these components on the wood, I'll make tick marks to the left of the length dimension as each is accounted for in the layout. When the tick marks equalize, I cross off this dimension.

Sheet-stock cutlist

I develop the sheet-stock cutlist in a similar fashion, creating a sheet of columns and subcolumns of components by type and width, and then listing lengths. Once this compilation is done, I go one step farther and make up a graphic representation of how the components are to be cut out of the 4x8 sheets. Doing this layout work now saves me an enormous amount of time during the cutting process.

To speed up the process, I search through the columns for the largest components and lay them out first, working my way down to the smallest. I group together like-sized parts whenever possible, and arrange them so that my first cut into the panel can be a full-length rip, which will lighten the sheet for me as I continue to process it.

I try always to lay out the highly visible door and applied side panels with the figure of the grain in mind, shifting the cutlines if necessary to take advantage of particular grain patterns. In general, I assume that the length of the components runs with the grain of the plywood. If, however, a more economical layout will result from breaking this rule, I'll do so as long as the panel is not conspicuous.

As the components find their homes on the graphic-panel layouts, I tick them off on the column listing. Then I label the components on the layout with their module symbol. I do this by going through the module cards and finding an appropriately sized panel on the graphic layout for the component listed on the card. As I assign the component to its panel on the layout, I mark it with the module symbol and then check the component off the card. This serves as a double-check — when the tick marks on the column listing equalize and all the components listed on the module cards are checked off, I know that I've accounted for all the sheet-stock components.

With the solid-stock master cutlist compiled and the sheet stock graphically laid out, the time has finally come to make some sawdust. In the next chapter, I'll show you how to lay out the components on the stock and then cut the stock to size.

SAMPLE SHEET-STOCK CUTLIST

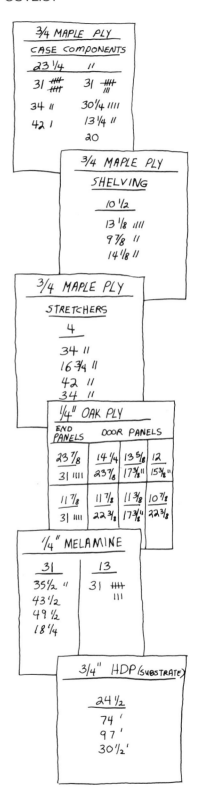

5

CUTTING STOCK TO SIZE

To ensure that the cabinets go together smoothly and be of the correct dimensions, you must carefully lay out the components on the stock in accordance with the master cutlists — and then you must accurately cut them out. Because solid hardwood stock comes in random widths and lengths and invariably harbors some defects, it's necessary to juggle the layout of the components on each board, avoiding the defects and making the most economical use of the remaining usable space. The fixed dimensions and absence of defects in sheet stocks, however, allow you to lay out the components directly from the graphic cutsheet you developed earlier (see p. 57).

Once you have committed the stock to a layout of components, the next

step is to cut them out. Because sheet stock is inherently stable in dimension, you can cut panel components directly to their finished sizes. I suggest using either a table saw or a guided circular saw to do this. Solid stock, which is notorious for taking a curve when ripped into narrower widths, requires a two-step process: first cutting the components to an oversized width and length, and then jointing and recutting them to their final dimensions.

SHEET-STOCK LAYOUT AND SIZING

Before laying out the components on a sheet, first check both sides of the panel for any shipping damage (or for defects if it's shop-grade stock). If necessary, redraw the layout so bad spots occur in areas that

won't show — most case components (with the exception of some partitions) are visible from only one side. I generally don't bother to transfer the layout from the graphic cutsheet onto the stock, but instead keep the cutsheet close at hand on a clipboard, referring to it as I make each cut. But if you feel uncomfortable cutting into expensive sheet stock, go ahead and chalk the layout onto the sheet. In addition to giving you the security of working with the layout drawn on the actual sheet, you get another chance to double-check your graphic cutsheet. Remember to add room for saw kerfs as you transfer the layout.

Ripping to width
The tool of choice for ripping sheet stock is a table saw outfitted with the following: a blade capable of pro-

Transferring the layout from the graphic cutsheet onto the panel stock reduces the risk of cutting error.

Make the first rip cut of the panel on the table saw with hold-downs and outfeed support in place.

ducing a splinter-free cut, an accurate and secure rip fence, hold-downs to keep the stock riding tight to the fence, and a support to catch the panel on the outfeed side of the saw (see the photo at right).

Begin the cutting process on each sheet by ripping out a full-length run of components. Choose a cutline near the center of the panel, adding at least ¼ in. to the specified width. Make the cut and then use the sawn edge, which is cleaner than the factory panel edge, to reference subsequent rip cuts to their exact width. Turn the full-length run edge for edge, set the rip fence to the exact width, and make the cut.

You can also rip sheet stock using a circular saw and a shopmade guide.

Instead of a table saw, you can use a shopmade jig (as shown in the photo at left) to guide a circular saw. Support the stock on a pair of shopmade lifts (see p. 121), and be sure to align the edge of the guide directly over the cutline marks and clamp it securely to the panel.

Crosscutting to length

Having produced full-length runs cut to an exact width, your next step is to cut the individual components to length. Again I suggest using the table saw, this time outfitted with a shopmade sliding crosscut box (see the drawing below) or a commercially-made sliding side-extension table (see the photo on the facing page). To use the shopmade fixture safely,

TABLE-SAW SLIDING CROSSCUT BOX

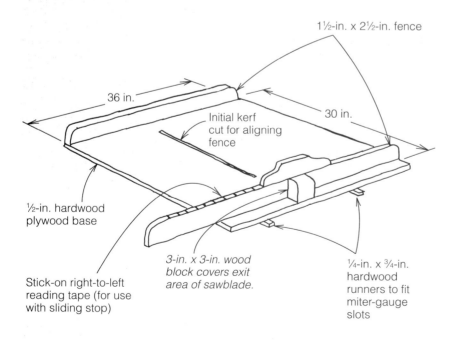

36 in.

1½-in. x 2½-in. fence

Initial kerf cut for aligning fence

30 in.

½-in. hardwood plywood base

3-in. x 3-in. wood block covers exit area of sawblade.

¼-in. x ¾-in. hardwood runners to fit miter-gauge slots

Stick-on right-to-left reading tape (for use with sliding stop)

Construction sequence

1. Attach runners to base: Lay runners in miter-gauge slots, apply double-stick tape, and lay down base oriented to front edge of table-saw table. Lift off and screw runners to base.

2. Slide base in slots; adjust for smooth glide by scraping edge of runners with cabinet scraper.

3. Run sawblade up into base, and slide box to create kerf in middle 2 ft. of base.

4. Orient fences with square to kerf; use one screw at each end.

5. Test-cut scraps, shift fence with square cut produced, and add screws to lock in place.

you must provide some form of support (either a table or a roller stand) ahead of the saw to support the fixture's weight.

You can, however, also do a good job with a circular saw, as long as you equip it with a sharp blade designed for cutting sheet stock and use a jig to guide the saw (the same jig shown in the photo on the facing page). Again, support the stock on a set of shopmade lifts to prevent tearout as the pieces are cut free from the full-length runs.

Don't depend on the factory edge at the end of the sheet to be square to the rip cuts. Instead, cut the first component out slightly oversize and then recut it to length by measuring over from the crosscut, removing the factory edge. On the table saw, you do this by sliding the piece along

the fence of the crosscut box or sliding table. If you're using a circular saw, the method is a little different. Secure the cutting guide about ¼ in. in from the factory edge and make a fresh cut square to the side edge; then measure from here to mark and cut the exact length of the component.

As you cut the components to length from the ripped runs, refer to the graphic cutsheet and mark the module and function symbols along a side and an end edge (S for side, F for floor, P for partition, etc.), as shown in the drawing on p. 62. I like to use a felt-tip marker pen because the marks are large and easy to read even with the panels stacked in a pile. As you mark each component, check off the circled module-symbol mark on the cutsheet. When all the symbols have been checked off, you

Crosscut components to length on the table saw using a sliding-table accessory (shown below) or a shopmade sliding crosscut box (shown in the drawing on the facing page).

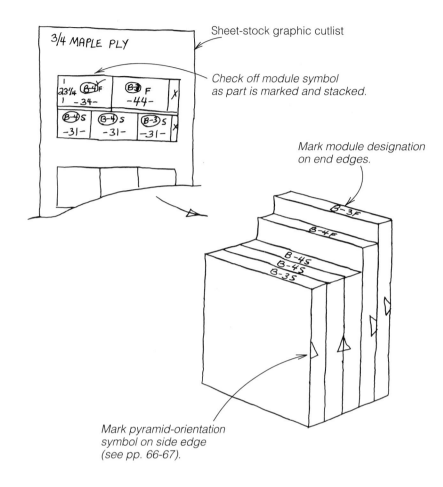

Sheet-stock graphic cutlist

3/4 MAPLE PLY

Check off module symbol
as part is marked and stacked.

Mark module designation
on end edges.

Mark pyramid-orientation
symbol on side edge
(see pp. 66-67).

SOLID-STOCK LAYOUT AND SIZING

Prepare to lay out the components on the boards by setting up a pair of sawhorses to support the stock. Take the time to level the beams — they should be parallel so that any twisted boards will expose themselves by rocking. Such stock must not be used for door parts or other components that must be free of twist.

Assuming your supplier gave you boards slightly oversized, plane the boards to their final thickness dimension (using freshly sharpened blades to reduce the amount of sanding you'll have to do to eliminate the planer marks). Then bring the boards one at a time to the sawhorses and carefully look each one over. Set them down with the worst face up so that you can see the defects that you will have to work around. If a defect shows only on the bottom side, transfer its position to the top with a chalk mark. Inspect the ends of the board for drying splits; even if you don't see any make a habit of "wasting" at least an inch. If the board rocks when you set it down, chalk a note on the board that only short or non-critical components are to be laid out here.

have produced all the components that were intended to come from that sheet.

Collate the panels by module and set them out of the way against one wall of the shop. You won't need to deal with them again until after you've cut out, milled and assembled all the solid-stock pieces into face frames, doors and other components.

Now begins the juggling act. Your challenge is to arrange and group together the components from the master cutlist in ways that make the most efficient use of the board while avoiding knots, splits and other defects. In general, I lay out the largest components first, working my way down to the smallest (though there are several exceptions to this rule). Note in the drawing on the facing page that the board with a curved edge is laid out with groupings of short pieces in order to reduce waste. You must also be aware of

EFFICIENT BOARD LAYOUTS

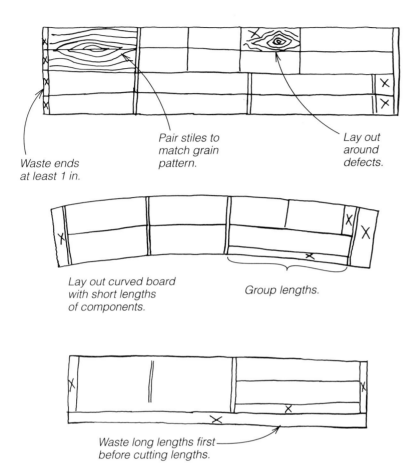

Waste ends at least 1 in.

Pair stiles to match grain pattern.

Lay out around defects.

Lay out curved board with short lengths of components.

Group lengths.

Waste long lengths first before cutting lengths.

components that are adjacent to one another in the cabinets, such as the meeting stiles of a pair of doors or a pair of drawers in a wide cupboard. You want to provide these pieces with a pleasing grain match. Because doors are the most visible components of your cabinets, and because they must stay flat over a lifetime of use, reserve your best boards for their rails and stiles. Finally, whenever possible, arrange the layout so that the scrap is offcut in long lengths rather than in less useful short, wide pieces.

Use a piece of chalk or a lumber crayon to mark out the pieces on the

stock. Be sure to add $\frac{1}{2}$ in. to the length measurement to account for the crosscut kerf and at least $\frac{3}{16}$ in. to the width to account for ripping and jointing the edges. As each piece finds a home on the boards, pencil in a tick mark to the left of the length callout on the master cutlist. When the tick marks on the left equal those on the right, all the pieces of this width and length have been accounted for.

Cutting the components to size

Begin the cutting process by crosscutting any boards laid out with components grouped to the same

ORIENTATION OF STOCK FOR JOINTING

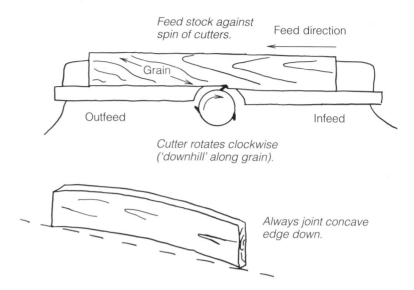

Feed stock against spin of cutters.

Feed direction

Grain

Outfeed

Infeed

Cutter rotates clockwise ('downhill' along grain).

Always joint concave edge down.

length. On boards where crosscut groupings don't allow you to work this way, rip out full-length runs to rough width, adding to the ³⁄₁₆-in. margin you provided on the layout if the stock has a strong tendency to curve as it is ripped. This may, unfortunately, require you to redo the layout (and to eat up more stock). Continue to rough-rip until all the runs for the project have been cut out.

To make the next step go smoothly, collate the ripped runs by ordering them into piles containing similar-length components. Then crosscut the components out of each run to the rough-length layout marks; a circular saw works well for this task. Again collate the piles, this time placing similar widths as well as lengths together. Then bring the piles to the jointer in preparation for the next step: jointing an edge.

Always joint the board with the concave side down; otherwise the board will rock on the bed of the machine and never achieve a straight edge. As you sight along the edge of each

piece to check for the curve, also note the grain direction. Because of the rotation of the jointer's knives, you want to run the stock through the machine with the grain going "downhill," as shown in the drawing above. Set the jointer to plane about ¹⁄₆₄ in. at a pass and run the stock through, removing only enough material to make the edge straight. Stack the jointed boards so all the flattened edges face the same way, keeping similar widths collated together.

After jointing all the pieces, bring the stock to the table saw and rip the components again—this time to ¹⁄₆₄ in. over their final width dimension. Make sure the rip fence is adjusted parallel to the blade and that the hold-downs are set to keep the jointed edge snug to the fence. After ripping, restack the piles, bring them back to the jointer, and plane ¹⁄₆₄ in. from the sawn edge (test-plane a scrap first to ensure that they are the desired dimension). The boards should now be perfectly straight and of the specified width.

Two ways to cut components to exact length are to use a sliding table (left) or a circular saw guided by a crosscut jig (below).

Finally, using the shopmade crosscut box or a sliding table, cut the pieces to their exact length after first squaring one end. A sliding stop set to length allows you to make multiple cuts without remeasuring. Note in the photo above that the fence on the Excalibur sliding table adjusts and locks to angles up to 45°. Alternatively, you can crosscut the pieces using a chopsaw (preferably fitted with a fence and stop system), or a circular saw guided by a crosscut jig. Arrange the pieces in their final resting place in piles collated by similar widths and lengths.

In the next three chapters, I'll show you how to mill and assemble this stock into face frames, doors, drawers and slide-out shelves. It's best to take care of building these components now before filling up your shop with space-eating cases.

6

FACE FRAMES

Face frames are an essential feature of most traditional styles of cabinetry. Though their presence reduces direct access to the interior of the cabinets (up to 20% less access compared to contemporary European-style frameless cabinets), face frames do add considerable strength to a case and provide another way to join smaller cabinet modules together seamlessly. In this chapter, I show you how to make the joints and assemble the frames. I offer you three joinery options: spline biscuit, pocket screws, and dowels. In the interest of getting your kitchen up and cooking as quickly as possible, I leave mortise-and-tenon joinery to the furniture makers.

LAYING OUT THE FRAMES

Begin by creating a space in your shop to lay out (and later assemble) the face frames. A clean piece of plywood or particleboard supported flat and level by three or four 2x4s set across a pair of sawhorses is sufficient. (I use an old solid-core entry door across a pair of knockdown lifts — see p. 121.) Locate this work table so you can get at all four sides.

Refer to the 5x8 module cards (see p. 56) to collate sets of frames from the stacks of solid stock previously cut to width and length. Bundle the pieces together and write the module symbol on the top board. Then choose one module frame — start with an easy one — and bring it to the work table. Lay the frame out as

shown on the card for this cabinet, inspecting each board before you set it down. If the board is bowed slightly, put the curved side up unless you are overruled by an unsightly defect. Now mark the faces of the parts with portions of a pyramid, as shown in the drawing on the facing page. With a little practice, you'll find that this marking method is quick and foolproof.

To mark the exact location of the face-frame joints, I use the module story sticks I introduced you to in Chapter 4. Note in the drawing how I set the horizontal stick (developed for this cabinet module from the site story pole) against the edge of the rail. I mark the position of the mid-stiles directly from the stick. In a similar fashion, I use the vertical stick to mark the drawer mid-rails along

LAYING OUT THE FACE-FRAME JOINTS

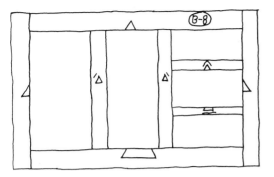

Portions of pyramid marked on face-frame components indicate location and orientation in frame assembly.

Face frame (rough layout)

An old door frame sheeted on either side with ¼-in. plywood makes a good work table for assembling face frames. The table is supported on knockdown lifts, shimmed where necessary to create a flat and level surface.

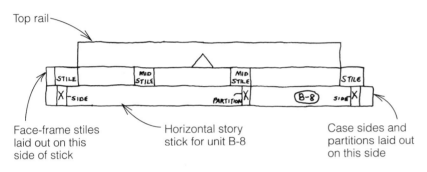

Top rail

Face-frame stiles laid out on this side of stick

Horizontal story stick for unit B-8

Case sides and partitions laid out on this side

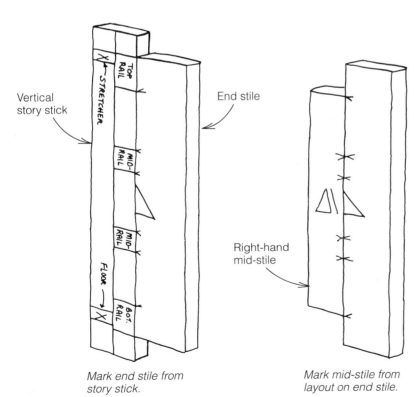

Vertical story stick

End stile

Right-hand mid-stile

Mark end stile from story stick.

Mark mid-stile from layout on end stile.

the right-hand end stile. Continuing the layout, I use this marked stile to transfer the corresponding marks to the mid-stile (and the top rail to mark the bottom rail). I find this method of layout almost foolproof — error caused by inaccurate measurement against a steel tape or rule is virtually eliminated.

With the face frame laid out, you now have the choice of continuing on to mill and assemble this frame, or setting it aside while you dry-fit and mark the others. I opt for the latter, finding it generally more efficient to complete a similar operation on all portions of a project before moving on to the next.

JOINING THE FRAMES

Woodworking books describe innumerable ways to fasten the end of one piece of wood to the side of another. But in cabinetmaking, where the face frames of one kitchen may require the builder to make 50 or more of these joints, highly efficient methods of joinery have evolved, few of which would be seen in furniture construction.

Rather than shaping the wood itself, cabinetmakers insert dowels, spline biscuits or pocket-hole screws across a simple butt joint. Although there are pros and cons for each of these methods, all provide ample holding power. If you have any doubts, make up samples of each of these joints and see for yourself what it takes to break them apart.

Dowel joinery

For many years dowel joinery has reigned supreme among cabinetmakers for joining together not only face-frame stock but also most case components. Using fast-acting jigs to guide the drill bit, dowel joinery goes relatively quickly. But I personally find it a bit slower, and more physically demanding, than either making slots for biscuits or drilling pocket holes for screws. Also, in my experience, dowel joinery produces the weakest joint of the three methods discussed here. While dowel joints are certainly viable for a face frame, which gains additional support through its attachment to a case, I shy away from using dowels to join unsupported frames (such as doors). There simply isn't enough non-end-grain gluing surface around a dowel to make it strong; over time as the wood fibers change shape, or as a result of an intense strain, these joints tend to give out.

If I'm making a dowel joint, I use a self-centering jig to hold the drill bit at the proper angle and location (see the photo at right on the facing page). Once aligned to a centerline mark (indicating the centerline of a desired dowel hole), the jig acts as a vise, gripping the sides of the stock while holding a pair of drill guide bushings over the edge or end of the stock to be drilled. The doweling jig self-centers the bushings between the jaws, allowing the user to set up and drill a pair of dowel holes quickly. A stop collar on the drill bit controls the depth of the hole.

Troubleshooting Making a mistake when dowel-joining frame components can be devastating. Once a joint is hammered together it is nearly impossible to pull apart without marring the visible face or edge of the wood. Nip mistakes in the bud by setting up the doweling jig and producing several test joints in scrap pieces of frame stock. Check for the following problems and make the necessary corrections:

Face frames can be joined quickly and efficiently with dowels (top), spline biscuits (middle) or pocket-hole screws (bottom).

Use a self-centering doweling jig to drill side-by-side holes for dowels in the face-frame stock.

PARTS WON'T COME COMPLETELY TOGETHER   The holes are not deep enough; reset the stop collar on the drill bit.

FACE OF JOINT IS NOT FLAT   The holes were drilled at an angle to the face. Use a mirror or a watchful partner to help you keep the drill at the proper angle (the jig's bushings help, but their lack of height and loose fit to the bit prevent them from over-riding a poor drilling technique).

DOWELS DON'T MATCH UP WITH HOLES   The jig was not set precisely to the centerline layout marks, or it was not clamped tightly enough and moved. Also, the drill may not have been held perpendicular to the edge and the dowel holes were not made parallel. Check the setup and your drilling technique.

DOWELS ARE TOO TIGHT IN HOLES The dowel stock probably swelled from exposure to ambient moisture. (To prevent swelling, keep dowel pins in resealable plastic bags.) If dowels fit too tightly, there is no room for glue and the joint will be weak. Dry out the dowels in an oven set to about 200°F, and check-fit in a test hole every 20 minutes. (Don't use a microwave — tests have shown that wood is weakened significantly when dried by microwaves.) The fit should be loose, but not wobbly. The addition of glue will swell the dowels tight.

JOINT FALLS APART WITH TAP OF HAMMER You didn't use enough glue. Apply glue to the hole, dowel and meeting faces of the boards, using a cotton swab to coat the inside of the hole evenly. Use loose-fitting, fluted dowel pins; otherwise the dowel pushes the glue in the hole to the bottom and leaves the glue applied to the pin at the surface.

Spline-biscuit joinery

Joining wood with compressed hardwood wafers let into slots is a viable alternative to mortise-and-tenon joinery. When done correctly, a biscuit joint is at least as strong as a similar-sized mortise and tenon, and decidedly stronger than a dowel joint. You can produce a spline-biscuit joint ten times faster than you can a mortise and tenon, and perhaps twice as fast as you can make a dowel joint. Spline-biscuit joinery also provides you with a great excuse for buying

yourself another nice hand power tool — you'll need a biscuit joiner to make the slots.

While each brand of joiner varies somewhat in the way its cutter is set to depth and aligned to the layout mark, each makes the slot by plunging its cutting wheel into the edge of the board. Familiarize yourself with your machine by making a number of sample joints. On my machine (as on many others), when I slot into the ends of narrow boards, the pins that keep the machine from sliding sideways have nothing to grab on to. To prevent this unwanted motion, and to make the machine safer to use, I make up a jig to hold the stock in place and provide a grip for the pins (see the drawing below).

Lay out the joints by indicating on the face of the frame components where you wish to slot for the biscuits (mark the centerlines). Note, however, that since the slots are 2¾ in. long (for the largest #20 biscuits) they will show through the edges of stock less than 2⅞ in. in width. If the component is a top or bottom rail, this isn't a problem. Just move the centerline so that the slot comes out where it won't be visible — at the top or bottom edge of the frame. To biscuit-join narrow mid-rails or mid-stiles, use a smaller biscuit (though even the #0 requires a 2⅜-in. slot). You'll have to use dowel or pocket-screw joints for stock less than 2⁷⁄₁₆ in. in width.

To cut the slot, hold the stock (outside face up) securely to the stop on the jig. Orient the centerline etched on the face of the biscuit joiner to the centerline mark you made on the edge or end of the stock. Keeping the base of the joiner tight to the jig table, turn on the machine and plunge the cutting wheel into the stock.

SPLINE-BISCUIT JOINING JIG

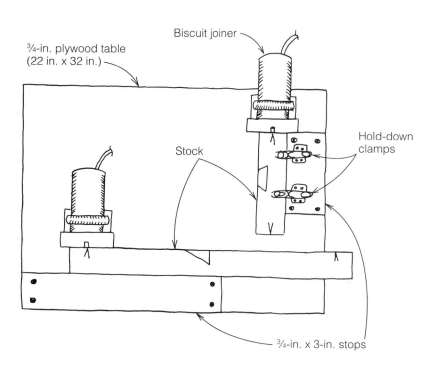

¾-in. plywood table (22 in. x 32 in.)

Biscuit joiner

Hold-down clamps

Stock

¾-in. x 3-in. stops

Use a shopmade jig to hold stock for biscuit slotting. Hold-down clamps prevent the stock from moving as you slot the ends of a rail. When slotting into the sides of the stiles, hand pressure against the back stop is adequate to hold the stock in place.

Go through the slotting of the face frame piece by piece. Make all the required slots in one component, set it back in position, and then go on to mill another. When done, double-check to be sure that a slot has been made at each centerline mark before rebundling the parts.

Troubleshooting Assuming you have set up your machine to cut the proper depth of slot for the biscuits you intend to use and are familiar with aligning your tool to the center-line marks, you should have little trouble making these joints. However, problems do creep in:

PARTS WON'T COME COMPLETELY TOGETHER The slots aren't deep enough. Check the adjustment on the machine. Also check to be sure that the joiner's inner workings haven't become clogged with sawdust, which is a common problem with some machines.

PARTS CLOSE BUT WON'T COME INTO ALIGNMENT AT CENTERLINE Either the layout marks are off (check by dry-fitting the frame together) or you are using poor machining technique. You must index the tool firmly to the stock throughout the cut. Otherwise it may cut the slot slightly to one side on the first cut and to the opposite side on the second, throwing off the joint.

BISCUITS ARE DIFFICULT TO INSERT INTO THE SLOTS   Unless you keep the wafers in resealable plastic bags, they can take on moisture from the air and swell. As with dowels, use an oven to bring them back to their original size. Be aware that adding glue to the biscuits makes them swell quickly, so don't wait more than 10 to 15 seconds before inserting them.

JOINT FALLS APART WITH TAP OF HAMMER   If you look at the biscuits in the separated joint, you're likely to find that there is little glue on them. Be sure to get the glue deeply and evenly distributed into each slot. A glue bottle with a nozzle specially designed for biscuit joinery makes this work go quickly and surely, although you can get by (albeit slowly) using a cotton swab.

Pocket-screw joinery

Cabinetmakers may have strong objections to using screws to hold together a joint, but I find that screws work very well. My tests show that they are as strong, if not stronger, than dowel, biscuit or even classic mortise-and-tenon joints. Admittedly, though, I hold them under the same suspicion as dowel joints, and I don't use them in unsupported structures (or in furniture in general). Because wood shrinks and expands seasonally, including the minute area around each screw thread, I suspect that these joints have a strong potential for loosening up over time. For backup, then, I always glue as well as screw these joints together. (Even though one surface is admittedly all end grain, the large surface area makes for a relatively effective glue joint.) It also helps to remember that kitchen cabinets are not heirloom furniture — in most homes they get replaced about every 15 years.

For me, the main advantage of pocket-screw joinery is its ability to draw joints together and keep them that way while the glue dries. This joinery method, then, completely eliminates the need to use clamps to hold the assemblies together during the construction process, which gets me around many clamp-induced alignment problems, and, more important, saves an immense amount of assembly time.

There is, however, one aspect of pocket-screw joinery that can take a little getting used to: The frames must be laid out and marked with the outside face down. You have to dry-fit (and later assemble) the frame in its mirror image. Besides marking the locations of the components, note in the photo at left that I am marking the butt ends of the components to be joined. Marking the butt ends shows me where to drill the pocket holes.

With the face frame outside face down on the table, mark the butt ends of a frame for pocket-screw countersunk holes.

Drill the pockets by using a specially designed face-frame bit (available from Kreg Tool Co., see the Sources of Supply on pp. 194-196) guided at a 22½° angle into the wood. The tip of the bit is specially ground so that it can grab the wood at this severe angle without slipping. An integral countersink forms the pocket hole that receives and buries the screw head. (As I discuss on p. 76 in assembly procedures, use only screws designed for this purpose. Unlike typical self-tapping wood screws, these have a flat, rather than a cone or "bugle," shaped head. Using screws with bugle heads tends to split out the pocket holes.)

I guide the drill bit into the butt ends of the components to be joined in one of two ways: with a shopmade jig set up on the drill press, or with a commercially made hand-held jig (available from Kreg Tool Co.). The drill-press jig is fast and accurate, though it is a bit awkward to use when drilling the ends of long, narrow lengths. The hand-held guide is a little easier to handle in this situation, since you can clamp the stock to the workbench and then clamp the jig to the wood. Lacking a drill press, the hand-held jig is essential — you cannot do this operation by eye.

Troubleshooting When making up your sample joints, look for and correct these problems:

SCREW TIP BREAKS THROUGH THE OUTSIDE FACE With the commercial hand-held jig, this problem won't surface unless you're using stock that is too thin for the design of the jig or screws that are too long.

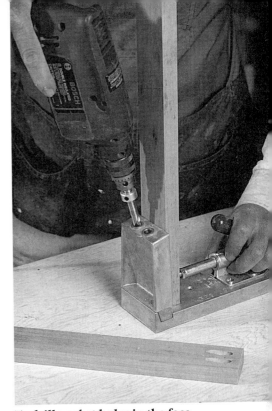

To drill pocket holes in the face-frame stock, use a hand-held jig (above) or a shopmade jig set up on the drill press (shown in the drawing at left) to guide the drill bit into the butt ends of the components.

DRILL-PRESS POCKET-HOLE JIG

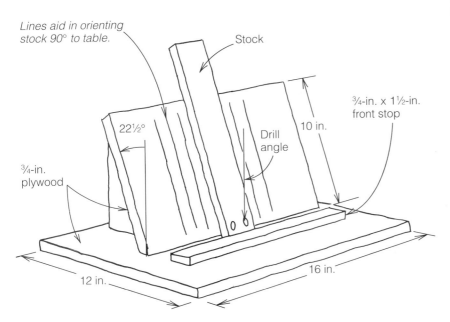

Lines aid in orienting stock 90° to table.

Stock

22½°

Drill angle

10 in.

¾-in. x 1½-in. front stop

¾-in. plywood

12 in.

16 in.

Check the manufacturer's recommendations. If you are using a shop-made jig, check the angle setting of the stock support (it should hold the stock at a $22\frac{1}{2}°$ angle to the drill bit). Adjust the position of the jig on the drill-press table to change where the drill enters the wood, and adjust the depth of the countersink (it should be just deep enough to bury the head of the screw flush to the surface).

PARTS DRAWN OUT OF ALIGNMENT (FACES NOT FLUSH) WHEN SCREWS DRIVEN HOME   Because the screws enter at an angle, they have a tendency to slide the adjoining pieces by one another, resulting in a slight ridge at the joint. You can counteract this tendency by clamping the pieces securely to a table before running in the screws (or by using a specially designed Vise-Grip clamp supplied by Kreg for use with their jig).

ASSEMBLING THE FRAMES

Once you've prepared the joints (holes for dowels, slots for biscuits or pocket holes for screws) in all the appropriate locations on the frame components, you are ready for the next step: assembling the frames. The process begins by bringing up one module's bundle of parts to the work table and orienting them according to the pyramid symbols you made earlier (remember that pocket-hole joinery requires the frame to be assembled outside face down). Double-check to be sure all joints have been made, and then count out into a small tub the number of dowels, wafers or screws required. Finally, see that all the tools you'll need (framing square, clamps, soft mallet, drill-driver, glue bottle, rags) are set on the table. From here on the steps vary according to the type of joinery.

Dowel or spline-biscuit assembly

Work from the innermost joints out to the four corners. Apply glue to the dowels or wafers and to their corresponding holes or slots (and to the meeting surfaces of the wood). Slide the fittings in place (they should fit in without hammering), and draw the pieces of wood together with hand pressure. Work quickly to keep ahead of the drying of the glue (if you're using common aliphatic-resin yellow glue at room temperature, you have about 20 minutes before surfaces get resistive).

When all the pieces are joined, lift the assembly from the table, wipe off the excess glue with a damp rag, and set the frame across two leveled plywood support stands. Apply pipe clamps under the top and bottom rails. Tighten the clamps just enough to close the joints firmly — a bead of glue will probably appear. Now, measuring from corner to corner with a tape measure, check the frame for square (the measurements should be equal). To adjust the frame, back off the clamps and reset them at a slight angle in the direction of the long diagonal. Retightening the clamps acts to shorten this diagonal, drawing the frame into square. Apply additional clamps where necessary to draw and secure other joints in the frame.

When the glue has dried, unclamp the frame. If your design calls for a quirk bead along the edges of the rails and stiles surrounding door or drawer openings, cut and install this molding now, making miter joints at the corners (see the bottom photo on the facing page). Use glue and brads to secure the quirk bead in place. Be sure that the molding is set back slightly from the face of the rails and stiles to protect it from being sanded during the face-joint-flushing process.

When assembling a face frame with pipe clamps, use plywood supports to hold the assembly flat and level. Check the frame for square by measuring from corner to corner.

Install quirk-bead molding to the inside edges of the face frame with glue and brads.

Use a C-clamp to hold the face-frame components secure as you drive in the pocket screws.

SURFACING THE JOINTS

No matter which method of joinery you choose — dowels, biscuits or pocket screws — it is unlikely that the joints will come out perfectly flush. More than a light sanding is almost always necessary on at least some of the joints.

Don't start surfacing the joints until the glue has had a chance to dry thoroughly. Wait a minimum of one day, more during periods of high humidity. Waiting for the glue to dry is especially important with spline-biscuit joinery, which uses the most glue of the three methods. Here's why: The moisture in the glue is absorbed into the wood, slightly expanding its thickness. After a day or so, the moisture leaves the wood, allowing it to return to its original size. If you had surfaced the wood across the joint while it was in a swollen state, the flush joint you created would regain a ridge, which makes more work and could result in a noticeably thinner frame around the area of the joint.

Pocket-screw assembly

With the frame laid out outside face down on the table, begin screwing components together at the innermost joints. Because the board that receives the screws must be clamped securely to a flat surface, you may have to slide parts of the frame to the edge of the table to accommodate the C-clamps (see the photo above). Alternatively, use a Vise-Grip clamp to hold the components secure. If you use the pan-headed, self-tapping screws designed specifically for pocket-hole joinery, you generally don't need to drill pilot holes prior to running in the screws. But don't forget to coat the meeting surfaces of the wood with glue before bringing the pieces together.

Once all the frame joints have been screwed together, turn the assembly over, wipe off excess glue and check for square. Make any necessary adjustment by applied angled clamping pressure as described above; remove the clamps after the glue has set. Again, if called for, install quirk moldings at this time.

I use one of two different methods to flush-surface the face of joints: planing followed by scraping, or belt sanding followed by orbital sanding. If the wood responds well to planes (it forgivingly resists tearout when planed across or against the grain), I choose the first method. It's at least as fast and effective as power sanding, and certainly a lot quieter.

I begin by clamping the frame to the table, fixing the clamps at least 12 in. away from the joints to be surfaced. With a sharp blade installed at a fine setting in a block or #3 smoothing plane, I make a series of passes at about a 45° angle to the joint line. I stop as soon as the ridge disappears and change over to a freshly burred cabinet scraper, continuing to remove any marks left behind by the plane. (I skip planing and rely on the cabinet scraper alone with woods that tend to tear out.) A light sanding with 180-grit paper on an orbital or a random orbit sander finishes up the job.

To surface the joint with the sander method, I install an 80-grit belt on a belt sander and run it carefully across the joint — as with the plane, at about a 45° angle. I avoid bearing down on the sander because this increases the rate of wood removal and may rock the machine out of flat. As soon as the ridge disappears I stop the machine and switch to a finer belt (120 for soft woods, 100 for hard). This time I run the machine parallel to the grain of the rail, crossing over the joint into the grain of the stile. Then I reorient the sander 90° to run it parallel to the grain of the stile, without touching the rail. I stop as soon as the scratch marks from the 80-grit sanding have been

removed. I finish up the job with a random orbit sander fitted with 150, and then 180 or 220 paper.

After assembling and surfacing each frame, use a router to create a slight chamfer around all the inside edges. Also rout chamfers on any outside edges that require them (exposed ends and bottoms, for example). Finally, rout a rabbet into the back of any stile "ear" that will abut a wall to make it easier to scribe-cut the frame to fit. If you wish, you can apply finish to the frames now, or wait to finish them with the doors and drawers. (I finish the frames now, unless I intend to face-screw them to the cases, which requires filling the countersunk screw holes with wood bungs.) Set the completed frames aside against a wall of the shop, and shield them from the harsh reality of your shop behind a scrap of plywood. You won't be needing them until you have milled and assembled the doors and drawers and put together the cases.

Use a cabinet scraper across the surface of each joint, then sand lightly with 180-grit paper.

BELT SANDING ACROSS FRAME JOINT

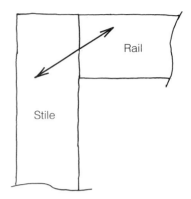

Rail

Stile

1. 80 grit at 45° angle

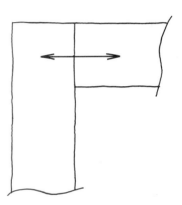

2. 100 or 120 grit across joint parallel to grain of rail

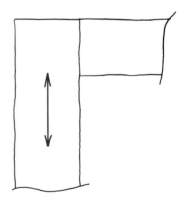

3. 100 or 120 grit parallel to grain of stile (avoid sanding rail)

7

DOOR CONSTRUCTION

hoosing what type and style of doors to build is one of the most important decisions you'll make about your set of kitchen cabinets. Doors largely define the look, quality and overall "feel" of the cabinetwork. The sheer volume of their presence (and, of course, their function) demands that they be seen, touched and manipulated by everyone who uses the kitchen.

What this means to you who must build them is that you must first carefully select a style that goes well with the period of your home and furnishings (see pp. 5-7), and, second, build the doors well. In this chapter, I show you how to construct the two most typical types of traditional cabinet doors: plank and batten, and frame and panel. None

of the processes for selecting the stock, milling the pieces or assembling the frames, panels or planks is particularly difficult. Just take your time to understand the procedure, and then proceed slowly and deliberately. Don't hesitate to make as many sample cuts and assemblies as you need to feel comfortable with the process.

PLANK-AND-BATTEN DOORS

In the earliest kitchens of America (and to this day in cabinetry featuring the "country" look), cupboard doors were often made by simply hinging a plank onto the face of the cabinet. If more than one board was necessary to span the opening, the cabinetmaker would hold them together by applying strips of wood

across the back of the planks. The usual arrangement of the strips was in the form of a Z, the diagonal strip acting as a brace to keep the door from sagging.

Although I often employ a Z-brace to join planks together, I sometimes use only the upper and lower horizontal strips. I do this when I wish to reduce the weight of the door, or when the diagonal strip would interfere with the shelving (a potential problem if the doors are fully recessed into the face frame). To gain diagonal strength, I let the strips into a groove dadoed across the back of the boards. I explain how to make Z-braces and let-in braces below.

As shown in the top drawing on the facing page, plank-and-batten doors may be mounted to the face frames in one of three styles: full recess, lipped (also known as "half overlay") or full overlay. I generally don't recommend a full-recess mounting for plank-and-batten doors. Because the wood shrinks and expands significantly in width from season to season, the margin of gap between the edge of the door and the frame constantly changes. In periods of high humidity the door may swell enough to rub or even to stick shut. To hide this wood movement, I prefer to use a lipped door rather than a full overlay, so you don't see the full thickness of the door from the side. You must decide on the style and size of overlay before laying out the cabinet doors on the module story stick, because the choice affects the overall size of the doors.

Selecting and laying out the planks

Develop the exact dimensions of the cabinet doors for each module similarly to the way you worked up the face-frame dimensions, laying out the components on the module story stick (see pp. 66-68). In the drawing below, I have laid out a door with a ⅜-in. lip on the sink-module story stick. Note the simple relationship of the door to the face-frame layout: The lines marking the door edge occur ⅜ in. to the outside of the face-frame marks.

When laying out the cutlines of the planks on the board stock, remember to add at least ½ in. to their length. Add enough extra to the width of each plank so that after joining and assembly the door is about ¼ in. oversize in width. You'll cut the door square and to its finished dimensions after assembly.

As you lay out the stock, check as usual for defects. Lay out around splits, loose knots, sapwood and wild grain. Note that defects that occur on only one side of a board can be hidden on the inside of the door. Cull out boards that have even a slight amount of warp, since their cumulative effect when assembled renders them unusable.

Milling the edges

Begin by cutting out the planks to rough length. If the stock is not already milled with a tongue-and-groove or ship-lap joint (available in softwoods at many lumberyards), set up to do this now. I suggest making the tongue-and-groove joint by cheating a little and substituting a spline made from ¼-in. plywood for the traditional integral tongue, as shown in the drawing at right. It's just as strong as the latter, and much simpler to mill for. You need only make a slot in the joining edges of the planks to receive the spline. You can make the slot with either a dado

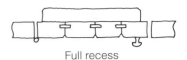

DOOR-FITTING STYLES

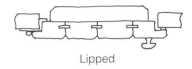

Full recess

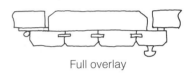

Lipped

Full overlay

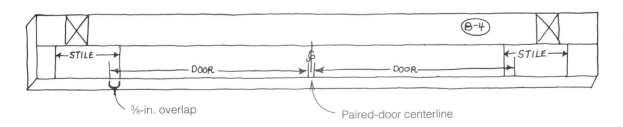

LIPPED-DOOR LAYOUT ON MODULE STORY STICK

STILE — DOOR — DOOR — STILE

⅜-in. overlap

Paired-door centerline

B-4

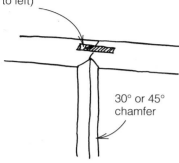

Spline (glued to
right-side plank
only — note gap
to left)

30° or 45°
chamfer

**Chamfered
tongue and groove**

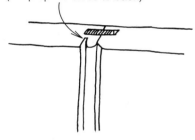

Potential weak area
(keep spline close to back)

**Beaded
tongue and groove**

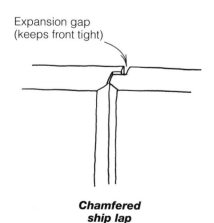

Expansion gap
(keeps front tight)

**Chamfered
ship lap**

blade on the table saw or a slotting cutter on a table-mounted router. To avoid a weak upper lip (a potential problem if you intend to run a bead along the edge), locate the bottom of the slot $\frac{3}{16}$ in. or less up from the back of the plank. Add the beveled edge using a 30° or a 45° chamfer router bit. Alternatively, you can use a special router bit to create a traditional bead.

As an alternative to the tongue-and-groove joint, make a ship-lap joint by running the stock by a rabbeting bit. Although you can hand-hold a router to cut rabbets, it's faster and safer to use a table-mounted setup. (My table-mounted setup is shown in the photo on p. 84.) Be sure to use hold-downs to keep the stock tight to the fence and table. Note in the bottom drawing at left that the overlapping rabbet is slightly wider than the underlying rabbet. This design ensures that the face of the joint stays closed when the door panel expands or contracts with changes in humidity. Adjust the width of the rabbet cuts by moving the router-table fence. Adjust the depth of the rabbet by moving the height of the bit. Make a series of sample cuts until the ship lap produces a flush face across the joining boards.

Assembling the planks and installing the braces

Gather together in bundles the planks required to make up each door and bring them up to the work table. Lay out the planks for a door. I lay out the width of the door so that the joints are equidistant from the side edges (see the drawing above).

Prepare for assembly by fixing two stopper strips at right angles to each other close to the edge of the work table. These strips help you orient the planks square and even to one another and provide a stop against

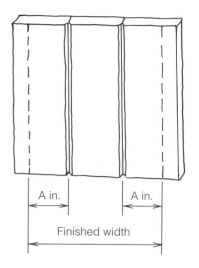

A in.

A in.

Finished width

*Lay out finished door
dimension on plank stock so
that joints are spaced equally
in from sides.*

which you can secure the door prior to attaching the bracing. In addition, I use blocks and wedges to hold the door planking in place (see the photo on the facing page).

Let-in braces If you intend to let in the top and bottom braces instead of using a diagonal brace, you must run a dado across the back of the boards (see the drawing on the facing page). To do this, first insert the splines into their grooves, gluing only one side to allow the planks to shrink and expand around the battens without splitting. Then wedge the planks against the stopper strips, outside face down. Remember to cut the edge planks to width so that the joints are evenly spaced from either edge and so that the overall width of the door is about $\frac{1}{4}$ in. oversize.

Next, set up a router (a plunge router is ideal for this job) with a $\frac{5}{8}$-in. straight-sided cutting bit with

With the planks for the door squared against two stopper strips, use blocks and wedges to hold the planks in place.

PLANK DOOR WITH LET-IN BRACE

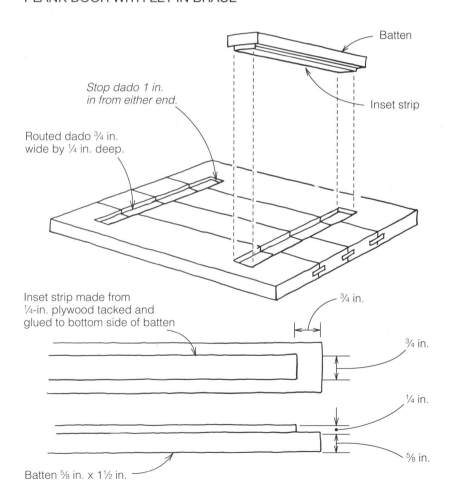

Batten

Inset strip

Stop dado 1 in. in from either end.

Routed dado ¾ in. wide by ¼ in. deep.

¾ in.

¾ in.

Inset strip made from ¼-in. plywood tacked and glued to bottom side of batten

¼ in.

⅝ in.

Batten ⅝ in. x 1½ in.

Rout the dadoes for the door battens (shown to the side of the door) using a shopmade guide.

a shank-mounted pilot bearing. Run the tool against a guide that you have set to the desired width of the dado and secured with screws square to the side stopper strip. Start and stop the router about 1 in. from either end — since the braces don't run to the edges of the door, you don't want the dado to either. Make the dado to the width and length of the ¼-in. plywood inset strip that is glued and screwed to the bottom of the batten (see the drawing on p. 81). This design allows the batten to shrink and expand without revealing the underlying dado.

Z-braces Installing a Z-brace is a little simpler. Lay out the planks and wedge them against the stoppers as described above. Then cut the top and bottom battens to length (again 2 in. shorter than the width of the door) and install them to their layout marks, spacing the ends in evenly from the edges. I use only one screw in the center of each plank, which allows the boards to change dimension without splitting.

Now lay out the end cuts for the diagonal brace by holding the brace in position (I keep the diagonal about 1 in. in from the ends of the batten) and marking the long points of the cut. Find the angle of the cut (which is the same top and bottom assuming the battens are installed parallel to each other) by holding a bevel gauge against the side of the diagonal and the edge of the installed batten, as shown in the photo at left.

Use a bevel gauge to determine the cut angle for the ends of the diagonal brace.

Cut the brace to the marks, apply glue to the ends and then fasten it in place to the cross battens with finish nails. Run in screws where the brace crosses the middle of a plank. Finally, install a chamfer bit in your hand-held router and run it around the edges of the Z-brace.

You can make a more sophisticated Z-brace by letting the ends of the diagonal batten extend into the cross battens, as shown in the photos at right. Make the joint by cutting the ends of the diagonal to the layout lines, then lay the brace on the cross battens to the marks. Trace the outline of the end cut. Remove the cross battens and cut the joint to the line with either a bandsaw or jigsaw. Use a chisel to trim the joints to fit the ends of the brace. Reinstall the top brace, set the diagonal in position and press the bottom brace firmly against it as you fasten this brace to the planks. Finally, fasten down the diagonal, again making sure to run screws only into the center area of the planks.

Trimming and shaping the edges

Before shaping the edges, you must cut the door to its final dimensions. First cut it to width following these steps: Plane one side edge flat and straight; set the rip fence of your table saw to the final width plus 1/64 in. and rip the door holding the jointed edge to the fence; then plane 1/64 in. off the ripped edge to reach the finished width. Now cut the door to height: Set the crosscut box on the table saw and crosscut one end of the door to ensure that it's square to the side edges (take off only the amount necessary to square the end); then slide the door over and crosscut it to final height.

If the door fully overlays the face frame or is fully recessed, I break the edges of the planks with a light chamfer. If the door must lap the frame, I make a rabbet around the door's perimeter with a straight bit

An alternative to using the standard Z-brace is to extend the ends of the diagonal brace into the cross battens, producing a shouldered Z-brace.

The shouldered Z-brace installed. Note the decorative effect of the buttons inserted into the countersunk screw holes.

fitted on the table-mounted router. (To prevent fitting and potential sticking problems should the door sag in the future, make the rabbet 1/8 in. wider than the specified overlap.) Normally, I would index the inside of the door to the router-table fence. In this way, if the door wobbled through the cut, the effect on the rabbet would be to make it shallower, not irreparably deeper. But in

Cut the rabbet for a lipped door on a table-mounted router, using a featherboard to keep the door tight to the fence.

The strength of the door, however, depends totally on your producing solid and durable joints between the frame components. For this reason, shy away from joints that possess inadequate glue surfaces, such as dowel or single spline-biscuit joints. As I show you in this section, I use either cope-and-stick joinery, or a variation of spline-biscuit joinery (doubling the biscuits at each joint). Of course, you may choose to use the classic mortise-and-tenon joint, though it's slow going producing it in the numbers necessary here. Although the mortise and tenon may be the strongest joint of all, I feel that the double spline joint comes close. A drawback of spline joinery, however, is that the rails must be at least 2¾ in. wide so that the slot doesn't protrude along an edge (see p. 70). These relatively wide rails can make for a rather heavy-looking door.

By choosing among a number of types and shapes of components, you can produce a wide variety of frame-and-panel doors. You can make the floating panel from a single plank (edge-joined from narrower boards if necessary) and shape the perimeter with either a flat rabbet or a raised profile; or from a row of tongue-and-groove planks (with either a beaded or a chamfered edge joint). You can also make a flat recessed panel from ¼-in. hardwood veneer plywood.

You can choose to join the frames with either a butt or a miter joint, and then give the frame's outside edge one of a wide variety of profiles. The inside edge of the frame may take the shape of the sticking (the male portion of the cope-and-stick joint), or you may chamfer or round it over, or add an applied molding. As I mentioned back in Chapter 1, each of these design elements helps to influence the period style of the cabinetry.

this case the braces get in the way — I have no choice but to run the door's outside face to the fence. To prevent problems, I install a featherboard made from scrap wood to keep the door face running tight to the fence (see the photo above).

FRAME-AND-PANEL DOORS

The most ubiquitous of all cabinet doors, traditional and otherwise, is the frame-and-panel door. This method of door construction, harking back to the Middle Ages, has more going for it than its strong aesthetic appeal — it produces a highly stable and strong structure. The secret is in the floating panel. Because the frame is nowhere attached to the panel, the latter may shrink or expand in response to environmental changes without affecting the overall size of the door. (Though the frame components are not immune to change, the amount of movement across their relatively small width has little effect on the door size.)

STYLE VARIATIONS IN FRAME-AND-PANEL DOORS

Panel styles and outside-edge profiles

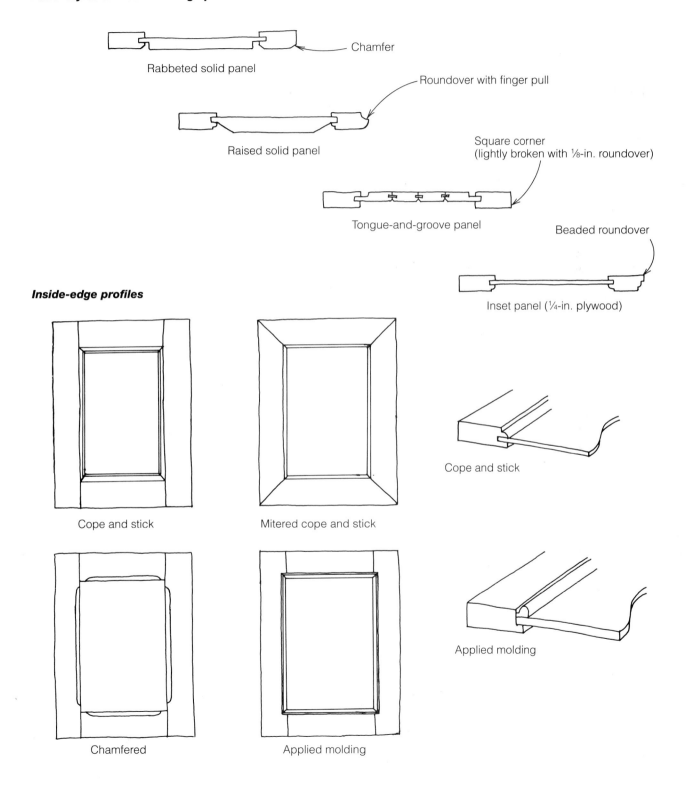

Rabbeted solid panel — Chamfer

Raised solid panel

Roundover with finger pull

Square corner
(lightly broken with ⅛-in. roundover)

Tongue-and-groove panel

Beaded roundover

Inset panel (¼-in. plywood)

Inside-edge profiles

Cope and stick

Mitered cope and stick

Cope and stick

Chamfered

Applied molding

Applied molding

Selecting and laying out the stock

After choosing the type of overlay (full, half, or full recess), lay out the overall height and width of the doors on the module story sticks (see the drawing below). While the length of the stiles is simply the height of the door, the length of the rails is found by laying out the width of the stiles – the rail length is the distance between the stiles (for splined butt joints). If the joints are cope and stick, be sure to add for the tongue at either end. Also use the story stick to lay out the overall size of the floating panel for each door; remember to leave an ⅛-in. gap between the panel edge and the bottom of the groove. Make up a master cutlist for these parts (see pp. 56-57).

When choosing stock from which to cut the door's rails and stiles, look first for boards with the straightest faces and grain. Reject stock with bowed or warped faces, suspicious grain patterns (definition: you don't know what the graining means, but you definitely don't want to find out when it's in a door), and severe coloration problems. If you have to ac-cept some curved boards, reserve them for the shortest components; lay these out with the concave side to the outside face of the door.

Also be rather fussy when selecting panel stock. In addition to avoiding obvious defects, bows and warps, try hard to match grain patterns for those panels that must be edge-joined. To ensure the best grain and color match possible, lay out the parts for a panel along the same length of stock. Be sure to add margins to the cutlist dimensions when setting down the rough layout of both the panel and the rail and stile stock. Refer back to pp. 62-63 for more hints on stock layout.

Edge-joining the floating panels

After cutting the panel stock to rough length, joint both edges straight and square to the face. I often make a final pass with a hand jointer plane (22 in. or 24 in.) to clean up any ridges left by nicked jointer knives or "snipes" made near the ends of the boards. The boards should join perfectly with just hand pressure.

LAYOUT OF DOOR COMPONENTS ON MODULE STORY STICK

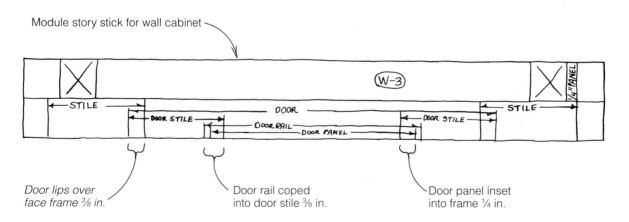

Module story stick for wall cabinet

W-3

STILE — DOOR — STILE
DOOR STILE — DOOR STILE
DOOR RAIL
DOOR PANEL
¼" PANEL

Door lips over face frame ⅜ in.

Door rail coped into door stile ⅜ in.

Door panel inset into frame ¼ in.

Gather the boards and lay out the panels, matching grain patterns as best as possible. When you're happy with the layout, mark across the joints with hatch marks and get ready to glue the boards together. Begin by setting the panel stock across two leveled plywood lifts and apply glue to each adjoining edge, as shown in the top photo at right. Roll or brush the glue out to an even film. I don't recommend using biscuits or dowels across the joint, because they add little to the strength of the panel (the ample glue surface of the butting edges provides more than enough strength) and, in my experience, contribute little to the alignment process.

Open up the clamp jaws enough to accept the panel. Because the pipes might stain the wood (especially oak) where the iron is wetted by the glue, hold the clamps away from the surface of the stock. Check to be sure the hatch marks are aligned before sliding the clamp jaws tight to the panel. Apply just enough clamping pressure to bring up a small, even bead of glue along the length of each joint. If you have to turn the crank hard to bring the wood together, something is wrong. Back off the clamps and check for a wood chip or other foreign object between the joints or a misjointed edge.

Most cabinet-door panels require only three clamps: two across the panel near the ends and a third placed between these under the boards between the lifts. Use a straightedge to check that the boards form a flat surface; if necessary, back off the clamps slightly and tap the boards with a rubber mallet to make it so. To ensure that the boards stay aligned at the ends of the panel, I often add cauls (hardwood 2x2s that

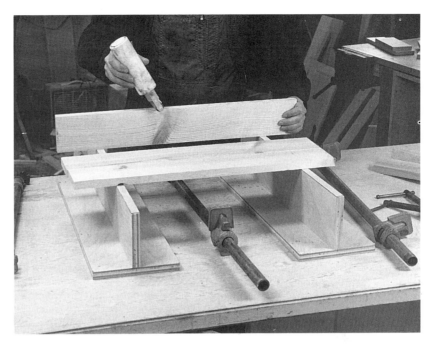

To glue up the boards for a door panel (top), first lay the stock across a pair of plywood lifts and apply glue to the adjoining edges. (Face the top edge of each lift with a strip of plastic laminate to avoid sticking problems.)

Next, clamp across the panel (above), applying just enough pressure to raise a small bead of glue along each joint. (Photos by Jim Tolpin)

Clamp cauls across the ends of the panel to keep the boards aligned. (Photo by Jim Tolpin)

inets, I prefer the first method; although it's perhaps the slowest, it produces the best-looking surface. The other two methods depend on flattening the wood through abrasion — no matter how fine the sanding, the surface will always be duller than that produced by slicing.

To surface a panel by planing and scraping, follow these steps: First, wedge the panel against a pair of stops fixed to the workbench. Next, plane at a 45° angle across the boards with a #4 or #4½ smooth plane, then turn the panel end for end and plane 45° in the opposite direction (see the drawing on the facing page). Now set the plane to take a fine cut and run it with the grain of the wood (note that the grain may change direction with each board in the panel). Use a straightedge to monitor your work.

When you have removed the angled plane marks and show a flat surface against the straightedge, switch to a well-sharpened cabinet scraper. Because the scraper is not affected by grain direction, you can pull it in one direction across the entire panel. When you've removed all plane marks, you're done. I usually final-sand the panel with 180-grit paper, followed by 220.

Surfacing with sanding machines mimics the planing processes in many respects. Begin with a 60- or 80-grit belt and run the machine at a 45° angle across the panel, working your way from one end to the other. Change to 100- or 120-grit and then run the machine lengthwise with the grain, moving gradually from one side of the panel to the other. Stop when the diagonal sanding marks have disappeared. Switch to a random orbit sander and work your way from 120- to 220-grit papers.

I've joined flat and true). To prevent the cauls from sticking to the panel permanently, I either apply plastic laminate to the working surface or add a strip of wax paper. Set the assembly aside to dry. Check the glue line occasionally, and scrape it off when it gets rubberlike.

Surfacing the panels

If you were careful to keep the panel boards even with one another during the clamping process (and especially if you took the trouble to use clamping cauls), you should have very little surfacing to do to bring the face of the joined panel perfectly flat. You have three methods of surfacing to choose from: hand planing followed by scraping; belt sanding followed by orbit sanding; or running the panels through a local cabinetshop's surface sander (followed by handing over some money). Unless I intend to paint the cab-

Shaping the panels

Having surfaced the panels flat and smooth, cut them to their finished width and height (see similar procedures on p. 83 for final-cutting plank doors). If the panel is to be installed into a door frame with an arched rail, the end of the panel must be cut to shape at this time (see instructions on milling an arched rail on pp. 95-96).

To form a rabbeted profile, run the panel through the table saw. (If the panel is arched, set up to rout the rabbet on the table-mounted router.) First cut the kerf into the face of the panel, using a scrap of stock the same thickness as the panel to gauge the proper width and depth of the cut. Then, after setting the fence and blade height to the test block, run the panel along its edge. (For safety and accuracy, install a high auxiliary fence to support the panel for this on-edge cut.) Be sure that the offcut goes to the side of the blade opposite the rip fence; otherwise it might bind between the blade and fence, shooting back at you as it is freed from the panel. Cut across the grain at either end of the panel first, then cut with the grain. This sequence prevents tearout at the corners of the rabbet. Check the fit of the tongue (created by the rabbet) in a sample of grooved frame stock.

To create a raised-panel profile, you have two choices: Either cut the raised bevel on the table saw, or run the panel by a shaping bit installed on a shaper or table-mounted router. The drawing on p. 90 shows the set-up and sequence of steps to follow on the table saw. The unique feature of a table-sawn raised panel is its size — few shaper bits can make such a large (and, as such, more traditional) profile. Make test cuts in scrap, and remember always to cut across the

PLANING AND SCRAPING A SURFACE

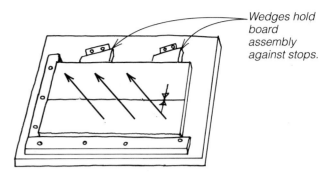

Wedges hold board assembly against stops.

1. Use a 9-in. to 12-in. smooth plane to plane 45° across grain.

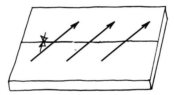

2. Turn board end for end and plane 45° across grain in opposite direction.

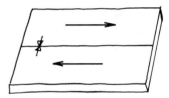

3. Use fine-set smooth plane to plane with grain (changes with board).

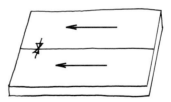

4. Use cabinet scraper to scrape off plane marks.

RAISED PANELS ON THE TABLE SAW

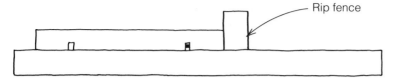

1. Set blade height and fence; cut shoulder cut (make cross-grain cuts first).

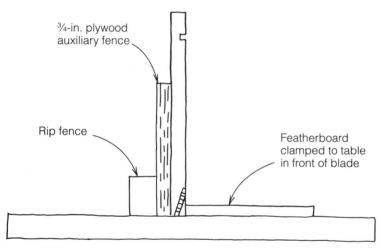

2. Attach auxiliary fence (shim if necessary between rip fence to make perpendicular to table); set angle and height of blade, placement of fence from blade; cut raised bevel.

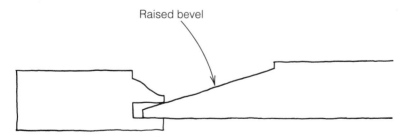

Ideal fit: Raised bevel touches front edge of groove when panel edge is 1/16 in. from groove bottom. Repeat Step 2 on scrap until this is achieved.

grain first, then with the grain. Check the fit of the panel in a length of frame stock.

If you choose to shape the raised panel on a table-mounted router, install the cutter on at least a 2½-hp router (with its thrust bearings in good shape). Do not attempt to remove all the profile in one pass. Instead, set the first cut to remove only about a third of the waste. Make two more passes to the finished size — the tongue should fit freely, but not loosely, into the grooved door frame. Test-fit sample blocks. Again, follow the cross-grain-first, with-the-grain-second cutting sequence to prevent tearout of the profile at the corners.

After cutting the profile on either the table saw, router or shaper clean it up with sandpaper fixed to a block shaped to the form of the profile. Use either rubber blocks that adapt to the shape, or carve a softwood block to the mirror image of the profile. Attach the sandpaper with spray adhesive or double-stick tape. Because a panel is designed to float freely when installed in its frame, the place where the panel touches the inside of the rails or stiles can shift seasonally. For this reason, stain and seal the panels prior to assembling the door.

Milling the rails and stiles

If you intend to use either splined-butt or cope-and-stick joints to join the corners of the frame, cut the rails to their finished length but leave the stiles long (they will be cut to length when the assembled door is sized to its final dimensions). If the joints are to be mitered, leave both the stiles and rails about 3/16 in. overlong. In all cases, leave the components at least 1/8 in. oversized in width.

Lay out the stock for each door on the work table, orienting the concave faces of any curved components toward the outside face of the door. Use your aesthetic sense to help orient the grain. Notice in the top drawing at right how changing the grain directions of the frame and the panel affects the sense of balance in a door. If a pair of doors has adjoining stiles, lay out both doors and match the grain. Mark the components with the pyramid orientation system (see pp. 66-67) and the module symbol. You are now ready to mill the joints and inside edges of the frame.

Double spline-biscuit joinery
To create a double spline joint, begin by following the procedures outlined in Chapter 6 for face-frame biscuit joinery (pp. 70-72), but with one exception. Rather than making the first slot with the base of the biscuit joiner held to the work table, add a ³⁄₁₆-in. shim in between. (This spacing works with my Porter-Cable joiner; determine the proper shim spacing for your tool by making up a sample.) Holding the tool to the centerline mark, run in the cutter. Next, turn the stock over, transfer the centerline mark to the new face, and run the cutter in a second time (see the bottom drawing at right). Follow the same glue-up and assembly process for single-biscuit joinery, except for the obvious need to add a second wafer at each joint.

Set up a router with a chamfer or roundover bit and shape the inside edge of the rails and stiles. Be sure to stop the cuts on the stiles. I like to end a decorative edging about ³⁄₄ in. from the butt joint. On the rails, you can either stop the edging or let it run full length to butt against the stiles.

To form a groove to receive the panel along the inside edges of the frame, I use a ¹⁄₄-in. slotting cutter in-

ORIENTATION OF GRAINING IN DOOR COMPONENTS

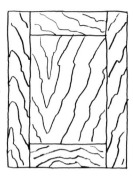
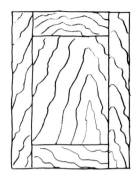

Aesthetically unstable grain pattern

- *Graining in panel suggests upside-down triangle.*

- *Graining in stiles makes them appear to lean outward.*

- *Graining in rails leads eye away from center of door.*

Balanced, stable graining

- *Panel stabilized.*

- *Graining in frame leads eye into door.*

SLOTTING FOR DOUBLE-BISCUIT JOINT

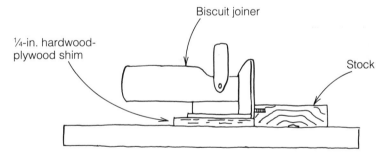

Biscuit joiner

¹⁄₄-in. hardwood-plywood shim

Stock

1. Support tool on plywood shim and make first slot.

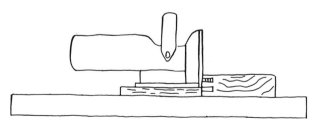

2. Turn stock over on opposite face and make second slot directly over first.

To cut stopped slots on a stile, begin by holding the end of the stile against the first stop block. Swing the board into the spinning slotting bit, and then run it by until the leading end hits the second stop block. Then swing the board away from the bit.

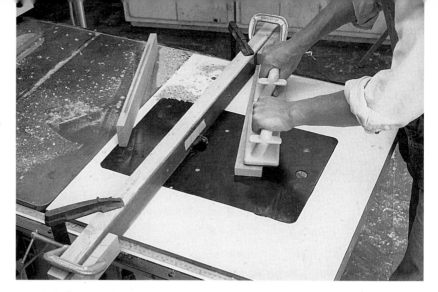

stalled on a table-mounted router. (I go down to a $^{15}/_{64}$-in. cutter if the panel is to be made up from hardwood-veneer plywood, which is invariably slightly undersized.) If the frames are to be miter-joined, however, I use a sticking joint, which provides both an inside decorative edge shape and a panel groove.

Using hand-pressure hold-downs to keep the stock tight to the fence and table, run the rails by the slotting bit after checking the position and depth of the slot on scrap stock. Then run the stiles, with blocks clamped on the fence to start and stop the groove before they reach the ends (as shown in the photos on the facing page). To help align the blocks, make marks to indicate the location of the groove in the adjoining rails, and run the grooves in the stiles just clear of this point.

Cope-and-stick joinery You'll need either a table-mounted router or a shaper to cut cope-and-stick profiles along the edges of the frame stock. I use a matching set of cutters: one to cut the groove and decorative profile (the sticking) along the edge of the stiles, and another to cut the tongue and mirror image of the profile (the cope) into the ends of the rails. I install the cutters on a 3-hp plunge router attached to the side extension table of my table saw. These bits are available in a variety of profiles, but all are designed to create a shallow mortise-and-tenon joint as a portion of the cope-and-stick profile.

Familiarize yourself with your cutter set by making a series of cope-and-stick joints in scraps of door stock. First cut the cope into the ends of the wood. The height adjustment is somewhat arbitrary—adjust it so that

COPE-AND-STICK JOINTS

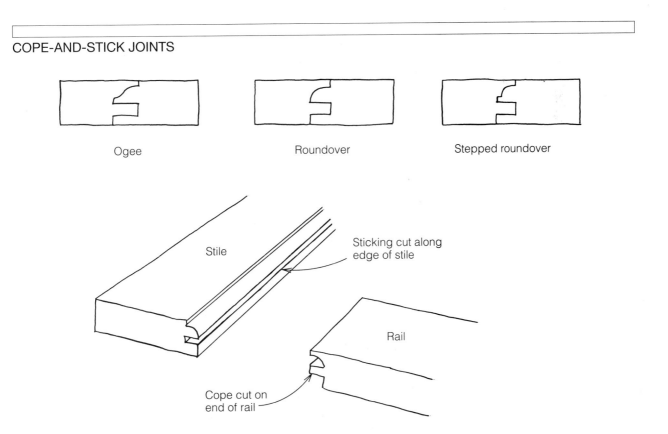

Ogee

Roundover

Stepped roundover

Stile

Sticking cut along edge of stile

Rail

Cope cut on end of rail

To make the cope cuts at the ends of each rail, use a shopmade carriage to guide the stock past the coping cutter.

the first step of the decorative profile is at least $\frac{1}{16}$ in. deep. Don't overdo it, however, or you'll bring the tongue too close to the back of the frame, making a weak underside lip in the sticking. Next cut sticking to match the coped ends, adjusting the height of the sticking cutter until the meshed joint produces a perfectly flush face. Don't hog out too much wood with these cutters — always take the cuts in at least three stages to avoid overloading the router or overheating the bit.

When you feel comfortable with the process, go through the marked and bundled door components and separate out all the rails and stiles (unless the corner joints are to be mitered, in which case you need only cut the grooved sticking along the inside edge of both rails and stiles). Set up the coping cutter, adjusting the height so a sample joint meshes perfectly with a sample of the sticking cut. Then cut across the ends of all the rails (and any mid-stiles). Use a shopmade carriage to guide the stock through the cut (as shown in the photo at top). Double-check to see that you have made all the required cope cuts, and then switch to the sticking cutter.

Cut scraps until the cope cuts on the rail ends fit the sticking perfectly and then run the inside edge of all the rail and stile stock by the bit. Use hold-downs to keep the boards tight to the fence and to the table, and remember to take a series of successively deeper cuts. When finished, check to be sure all the frame parts

Run the inside edges of the rail and stile stock by the sticking cutter to cut the groove and decorative profile along the edges of the frame stock.

To create an arched upper rail for a cabinet door, first trace the outline of the template pattern onto the rail. Cut the rail close to the line, then rout the final shape with the template attached to the rail.

have been shaped — don't forget that mid-stiles must receive sticking on both edges. Finally, recollate all the components back into their respective door sets.

Milling an arched rail If you wish to create an arched upper rail for the cabinet doors, the first thing you have to do is draw the design for the arch to full scale and make a pattern (unless you intend to use commercially made preformed router templates). Design the arch so that the same pattern will work for doors of varying widths (aim for about a 2-in. range).

Use draftsman's ship's-curve templates or a flexible batten to draw the arch on a sheet of vellum. Work at getting a pleasing curve. When you're satisfied, trace the design onto a thick sheet of transparent Mylar (available at office-supply stores) with a photographic marker pen. Be sure to extend out the design an extra 2 in. to 3 in. Cut the Mylar to the line, and you now have a pattern from which you can lay out a routing and cutting template. Make this template from a knot-free, straight-grained piece of ½-in. to ¾-in. thick solid wood or void-free plywood. Trace the outline of the Mylar onto the face of the stock, cut to the line with a bandsaw or jigsaw, and then smooth the arched shape with rasps, files and a cabinet scraper. Be careful to keep the edge square to the face.

Set the template aside for a moment and get out all the rail stock to be cut to an arch. Crosscut the rails to their exact length and then mill the joints, making either a coped cut or a pair of slots for biscuits. Now center the template on the rail and trace the pattern, as shown in the top photo on p. 95. Using a bandsaw or jigsaw, cut the rail close to, but not on, the line — within ⅛ in. is fine (middle photo, p. 95). To make an exact duplicate of the template, set up a router with a shank-bearing, flush-cutting trimmer bit. Use double-stick tape — I use the heavy-duty "poster tape" (3M Cat. #109) — to attach the template to the rail and then run the router along the arched edge (bottom photo, p. 95). Be sure to keep the shank bearing tight to the template as the cutter mimics the shape in the rail below.

With the true shape of the arch cut into the rail, the next step is to run either a groove or a sticking profile along the curved edge. Do not, how-ever, attempt to run the rail edge freehand by the router bit! Instead, set up a wood or Plexiglas bushing on the router fence to guide the template (see the drawing below). This strategy not only ensures that the sticking conforms exactly to the shape of the arched rail, but it makes a potentially hazardous operation quite safe. Note that the bushing per-forms the same function as the shank bearing on a flush-trimming bit.

To shape a solid panel into an arch, follow the procedure outlined above for the rail. You will, however, first need a new template. You can use the Mylar pattern already taken from your full-scale drawing if you modi-fy it by cutting the arch back to the depth of the rail's groove (less ⅛ in. for clearance). For example, if the sticking groove is ⅜ in. deep, mark a line ¼ in. in along the arched edge of the Mylar. The pattern now repre-sents the outside of the panel's arch. Make a cutting and routing template by tracing this new arch along the length of a board. Then proceed as outlined above.

Assembling the frames and panels

With the panels cut to size, stained and sealed, and with all the milling completed on the rail and stile com-ponents, it's time to put the pieces together to create a door. Begin by collating the frame stock and pan-els into door sets. Dry-fit the frame around the panel and check that the joints align properly and that the panel fits the groove. Check to see that the height of the door to the outside edge of the rails — and the width to the outside of the stiles — is about ¼ in. oversize. When you're satisfied with the fit, set up a pair of lifts on your work table.

Begin assembly by applying glue to both sides of each of the frame joints

SETUP FOR CUTTING STICKING IN ARCHED STOCK

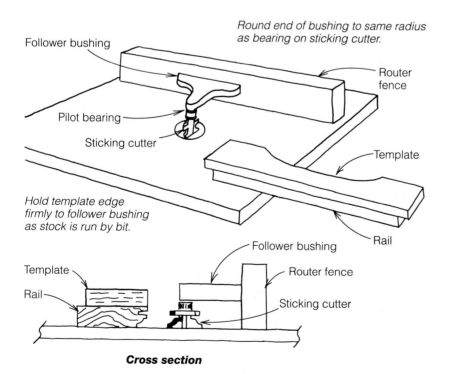

Follower bushing

Round end of bushing to same radius as bearing on sticking cutter.

Router fence

Pilot bearing

Sticking cutter

Template

Hold template edge firmly to follower bushing as stock is run by bit.

Follower bushing

Rail

Template

Rail

Router fence

Sticking cutter

Cross section

(and, of course, into the slots for biscuits). Don't overdo the glue, but spread just enough to obtain a thin, even film on the adjoining surfaces. Keep the glue away from the inside corners of the frame joint, and to be doubly sure that the panel won't become attached to the frame rub some wax on the corners of the panel. Using your hands and a rubber mallet, press the frame together around the panel. Center the panel in the frame. If the panel is too loose and rattles, you can pin it to the frame with a pair of ⅛-in. dowels. Locate these pins at the top and bottom center of the panel where the panel's edge inserts into the frame groove. Drill the pilot hole from the back of the door, being very careful not to drill through the face of the door. Finally, wipe off any excess glue, and set the assembly across the pair of lifts.

With a butt- or cope-joined frame, position the clamps parallel to the rails and exert just enough clamping pressure to close the joints completely. Be sure to check the underside face. For a mitered frame, use a pair of clamps across the width and length of the frame.

After using a straightedge to assure yourself that the face of the door is resting flat, pull diagonal measurements (from the inside corners of the frame) to check for square. If necessary, loosen the clamps a bit and tap the frame into alignment. Write the time of clamping in chalk on the door and set it aside to dry. At temperatures above 65°F, leave the clamps on for at least one hour (assuming you're using carpenter's aliphatic yellow glue). After removing the door from the clamps, surface the frame joints in a similar fashion to the way you surfaced the face frames (see pp. 76-77). Be careful not to mar the raised panels.

After gluing the frame joints and pressing the frame together around the panel, set the assembly across a pair of lifts and apply the clamps.

Shaping the outside edge

Begin the final outside shaping of the frame by cutting the door to its final specified size. Joint one side, then set the rip fence of the table saw to width plus 1/64 in. Make the rip cut, then trim off the 1/64 in. on the jointer. Place the crosscut box on the saw table, trim one end of the door (cutting off only the amount necessary to square this end to the side) and then cut the door to exact height.

If the door is to be half-inset, run a rabbet around the edge in a similar fashion to that used to rabbet a panel (see pp. 83-84). Alternatively, you can make the rabbet with a router-mounted rabbeting bit. Create other edge shapes by installing the appropriate bit on the table-mounted router. To avoid tearout at the corners, remember to cut first across the grain (the ends of the door) and then along the grain. Use hold-downs and cut the profile in at least two passes (unless you are creating only a light roundover or chamfer).

PULL-HARDWARE DRILLING JIG

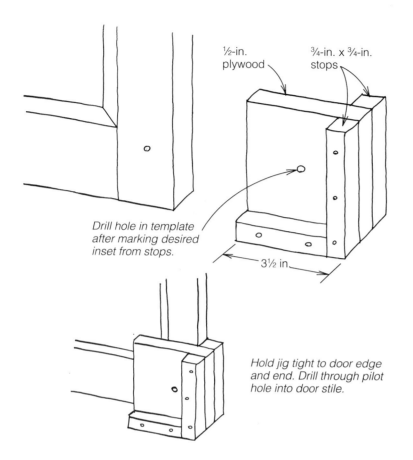

½-in. plywood

¾-in. x ¾-in. stops

Drill hole in template after marking desired inset from stops.

3½ in.

Hold jig tight to door edge and end. Drill through pilot hole into door stile.

PREDRILLING FOR HARDWARE

I find it much easier to predrill for knobs or pulls while the door is flat on the work table than to wait until the doors are hung on the cabinets. To locate the pilot holes for the hardware quickly and accurately, make up a simple drilling jig as shown in the drawing at left. If possible, use a drill press to make the jig's guide hole (which will ensure that the hole is square to the face of the jig). To use the fixture, index the stops on the jig to the end and edge of the door and drill away. But be careful here: You must be sure that you are drilling in the correct corner of the door. Double-check the module cards to be sure you have the correct door in hand and to see to which side the hinges go.

If you intend to hang the doors with cup hinges (see pp. 144-146), predrill the 35mm cup holes for these now too. For an accurate and efficient job, use a commercially made hand-held drilling jig and guide (available from Veritas Tools, see the Sources of Supply on pp. 194-196), or set up a drill press with a back fence and a pair of end stops to index the hole to the edge and end of the door (see the photo at left). Test your setup by drilling sample holes in a scrap length of stile. Check the overlay after temporarily installing a pair of hinges to this test stile. Before drilling the real thing, be sure to lock down the depth stop on the drilling jig or drill-press quill — it's not much fun to drill a 35mm hole through the outside face of an assembled door.

One way to drill holes for cup hinges is to set up a drill press with a fence and pair of end stops.

BUTT-HINGE MORTISING TEMPLATE

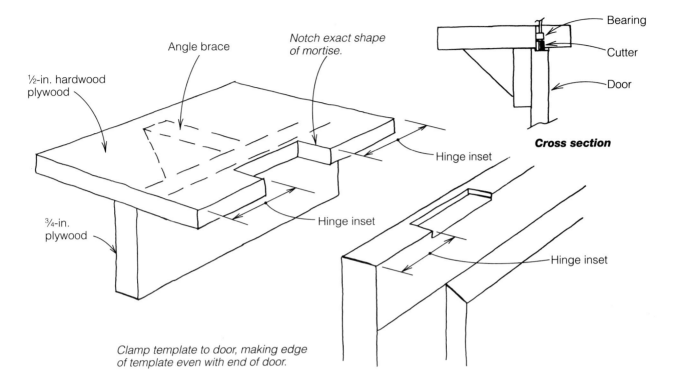

Angle brace

Notch exact shape of mortise.

½-in. hardwood plywood

¾-in. plywood

Hinge inset

Hinge inset

Hinge inset

Bearing

Cutter

Door

Cross section

Clamp template to door, making edge of template even with end of door.

To prepare full-recess doors to receive butt hinges, I use a router with a shopmade cutting template to make the mortise. A special mortise bit, equipped with a shank bearing to ride against a template, cuts the mortise into the door edge. I make the mortise almost deep enough to contain both leaves of the hinge. In this way I don't have to make a mortise in the edge of the face frame. I set the depth of the cut to allow $1/32$ in. of the hinge leaf to show, which defines the gap between the edge of the door and the face frame. Since the corners of the mortise are rounded, I use a chisel to trim them square.

Predrill for standard formed hinges by holding them in position on the back face of the door. I use a combi-nation square set to the inset I desire to index the position of the hinge. Install a Vix bit (a self-centering pilot-hole drilling bit) to your drill motor and predrill all three attachment holes.

At this point, you might choose to finish the doors, though you can wait until you've assembled the drawers. Although this procedure violates my general rule of grouping all similar processes together (since the cases and certain other components will be finished later), applying the finish now serves to protect the doors from handling stains and breaks up a potentially overwhelming process into manageable segments. For information on finishes and finishing technique, see Chapter 10.

8

DRAWER CONSTRUCTION

After the cabinet doors, the next most important element of any kitchen is the drawers. The combination of a well-made face front and an appropriate choice of hardware contributes greatly to the look and feel of a kitchen. Indeed, for most cooks, the more drawers the better — beyond styling, drawers organize and bring stored items within easy reach.

Although a kitchen drawer is essentially nothing more than a box within a box, much is demanded of it. According to industry standards, a typical "medium duty" drawer must support a surprising amount of weight: 100 lb. of static load exerted on the face end of the drawer when fully extended (you'll understand the need for this if you picture a ten-year-old turning a bank of drawers

into a ladder to get to a cookie jar); and 75 lb. of dynamic load (the drawer must be able to run smoothly in and out at least 100,000 times carrying this amount of weight). Not only must the drawer support these weight loads without complaint, it must also be easy to adjust for smooth running and for proper alignment of the face front.

Other desirable features are kitchen drawers that self-close when held within a few inches of the cabinet face. The drawers should extend well out of the cabinets — either fully or within 4 in. to 6 in. of the back. And, of course, there should be a positive stop to prevent the drawers from coming all the way out, but the stop must not make it difficult to remove the drawer from the cabinet for cleaning.

To meet these tough standards, I build kitchen-cabinet drawers almost exclusively out of hardwood plywood or solid stock and join the corners of the box with either slot biscuits, a lock rabbet or router-made dovetails. I place the four-sided drawer box on high-quality metal runners and bolt (rather than screw) a "false" face front to it with fittings that allow a full range of adjustment. In this way, I'm assured of having trouble-free drawers for the life of the cabinets.

MATERIALS
Before describing the materials with which I make drawers for traditional-style cabinetry, I think it might be instructive to tell you of some materials that I don't use. I never, for example, use fir plywood or melamine-

covered fiberboard for the boxes. Although these sheet stocks are in common use in production cabinet-work, I feel that their appearance cheapens the quality of the cabinets. I also avoid unidirectional plywood. Though popular because all the veneers run with the length of the panel (meaning that no end grain shows along the top edge of the drawer box), there are a couple of drawbacks: The material produces relatively weak joints (unless dove-tailed); and it is commonly available only in lauan "mahogany," a wood that I feel does not blend well with most traditional American cabinet designs. Aesthetics also steers me away from using either formed plastic or metal combination slide and side components. Although these newly available fixtures make fast work of drawer construction — and meet all the demanding functional requirements — I feel they look quite out of place.

What I do use to build drawer boxes is ½-in. thick oak-, ash-, or maple-veneered plywood (I edge-band the exposed top edge), or ⅝-in. to ¾-in. solid wood. For the bottom panel, I almost invariable use ¼-in. maple plywood. For runners, I choose from a variety of European-made bottom-corner-mounted metal slides with nylon roller bearings. These slides are available in three duty ratings, slide out to full or three-quarter extension, and are self-closing and easy to install. If I need full-extension heavy-duty slides (100 lb. or more static load), I use a side-mounted slide (see p. 38).

LAYOUT AND DIMENSIONING

Before going to the module story sticks to work up the sizes of the drawer components, you must first decide on three things: the style of

This set of graduated drawers features fully inset face fronts and hand-turned cherry knobs. Adjustable drawer-face attachment fittings have allowed the installer to set the faces to an even margin with the surrounding cock beading.

The author likes to build kitchen-cabinet drawers out of solid stock or hardwood plywood, joining the corners with a lock rabbet and using European-type corner-mount slides.

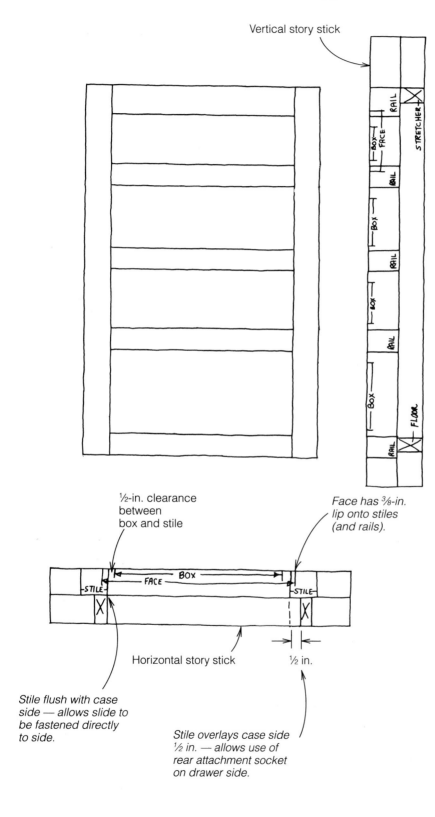

STORY-STICK LAYOUT OF DRAWER BOX AND FACE

Vertical story stick

RAIL
STRETCHER
BOX
FACE
RAIL
BOX
RAIL
BOX
RAIL
BOX
FLOOR.
RAIL

½-in. clearance
between
box and stile

Face has ⅜-in.
lip onto stiles
(and rails).

STILE
FACE
BOX
STILE

Horizontal story stick

½ in.

*Stile flush with case
side — allows slide to
be fastened directly
to side.*

*Stile overlays case side
½ in. — allows use of
rear attachment socket
on drawer side.*

overlay or recess; the type of runner hardware; and the kind of joint you'll use to make the box. All three factors affect the dimensions of the drawer box.

Determining face-front and drawer-box dimensions

Begin the drawer layout by dimensioning the drawer face. On the module's story stick, lay out the face in relationship to the face frame both horizontally and vertically (see the drawing at left). Account for the overlap of full or partial overlays, and for the gap between the face and frame if the drawer is full recess. Measure and record the size of the face on the module card.

Now go on to determine the overall width, depth and height of the drawer box. If you are using standard European-type bottom-corner-mounted runners, allow ½-in. clearance to either side of the box, and make the box at least ⅝ in. lower in height than the frame opening. Check the clearance specifications supplied by the manufacturer for other types of slide hardware.

To determine drawer depth, measure the distance between the outside face of the face frame and the inside of the cabinet's back panel. Subtract the amount of recess (⅜ in. for lipped recess; ¾ in. for full) and an additional ¾ in. to allow clearance for the rear runner socket. Note that where partitions or sides come flush to the side edge of a stile, rear sockets are not necessary because the guide rails attach directly to the case side. But still subtract ¾ in. from the depth — you may someday wish to snake a wire through the back of a cabinet. Record the box dimensions on the module card.

Cutlists and stock layout

Having determined the overall dimensions of the drawer box and face fronts, the next step is to develop a cutlist of components. The faces are easy: Go through the module cards and list the lengths under columns specifying stock widths (see p. 56). The drawer-box parts, however, require a little more development.

To determine the lengths of box sides and ends (as well as the size of the bottom panel), you must first decide what thickness of stock and which joints you intend to use. I employ the fail-safe method of drawing a sample box to full scale and then measuring the resulting dimensions of the components (you can build a sample box if you prefer). My drawing provides me with subtraction factors. I need only subtract these factors from the overall size of the boxes listed on the module cards to come up with component dimensions (see the drawing at right). I compile the results in a cutlist, again listing lengths under columns specifying stock widths.

Lay out the drawer components on the stock following the techniques described in Chapter 5. If you intend to apply edging to plywood box components, remember to subtract from the overall height of the sides to account for the edging. Also remember always to lay out the sheet stock with the widest runs first. Any waste areas may then be used to make up narrower components. When puzzling out the bottom panels, try to arrange the layout so that the grain runs consistently from front to back in the drawers. Feel free, however, to override this strictly aesthetic concern to make the most efficient use of your stock.

SUBTRACTION FACTORS FOR SIZING COMPONENTS

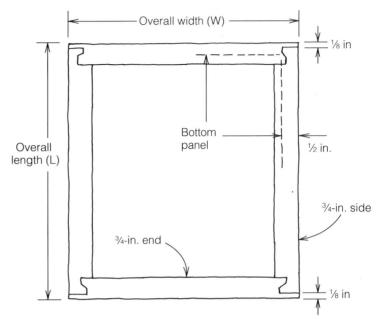

Top view of drawer box with lock-rabbet joint

Factors

Length of side = overall length (L) − ⅛ in. − ⅛ in. = L − ¼ in.

Length of end = overall width (W)

Bottom panel:

Width = W − ½ in. − ½ in. − ⅛ in. (clearance) = W − 1⅛ in.

Length = L − ½ in. − ½ in. − ⅛ in. = L − 1⅛ in.

Another aesthetic concern (assuming the cabinets are stained, figured wood rather than painted) dictates how I lay out the drawer fronts for adjoining drawers and for a bank of drawers. In the former case, I'm careful to lay out the fronts so that they adjoin on the same board. Before cutting, I mark them on the back side with a pyramid surrounding the module symbol and with arrows pointed toward one another.

FACE LAYOUT FOR BANK OF DRAWERS

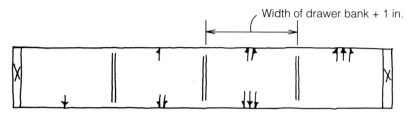

Width of drawer bank + 1 in.

Lay out sections of board to drawer-face width.

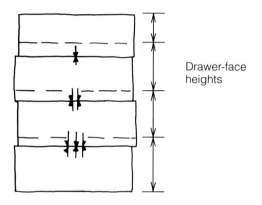

Drawer-face heights

Edge-join sections, then rip and join to drawer-face heights.

FLUSH-TRIM SETUP TO SURFACE EDGINGS

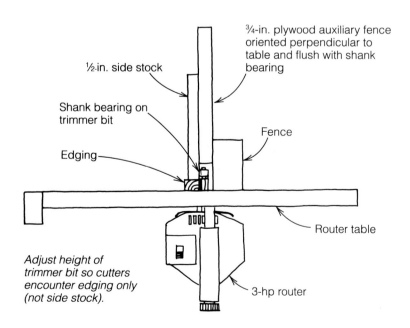

¾-in. plywood auxiliary fence oriented perpendicular to table and flush with shank bearing

½-in. side stock

Shank bearing on trimmer bit

Edging

Fence

Router table

3-hp router

Adjust height of trimmer bit so cutters encounter edging only (not side stock).

In a bank of drawers, I feel that the fronts look best if the grain patterns blend smoothly together from the edge of one front to the edge of another. To achieve this effect, I work with one length of board, sectioning it up to the rough length of the faces and then edge-joining the pieces together (see the top drawing at left). I make sure the resulting width will accommodate all the faces in the bank plus cutting and joining margins. When the assembly is dry, I lay out the individual drawer faces, mark the back faces for orientation and relationship to one another, and then cut them to width.

Sizing the components

To cut out the components to their final dimensions, refer back to the techniques presented in Chapter 5. If you are using edge-banded plywood, apply the edging before cutting the runs to length. You can use either solid-wood strips or a wood-tape veneer for this edging. If you choose the former, apply the strips and then set up a flush-trimming bit on the router table (as shown in the bottom drawing at left), which significantly speeds up the process of surfacing the strip edges to the plywood. When using tape applied with a hot iron, I trim the tape to the edge using a block plane or a specialized edging plane.

After cutting out the box parts, collate them into sides and ends — not into drawer sets. For the sake of efficiency, it's best to make all the side joints first and then retool to make all the end joints (see below). Check for missing parts by taking a total count of sides and ends: The sum should be four times the number of drawers.

Once you've cut the drawer faces to size, shape the edges as you did the doors (see pp. 83-84). If you are mak-

Drill the back of the drawer faces for the attachment fittings.

ing a lipped edge, make the rabbet at least 1/8 in. wider than the specified overlap to give yourself clearance when fitting the face to the drawer box. To ensure crisp corners, remember to make the cuts across the grain first, then with the grain along the sides. After shaping and sanding the resulting profile, set up a drill press to predrill the back of the face front for a pair of attachment fittings. (Do this now only if the faces are to be fully recessed; otherwise wait to cut these holes until after the boxes are assembled, as explained on p. 113.) I use the drawer-front adjusters from Blum (see the Sources of Supply on pp. 194-196), which require a 20mm hole drilled 7/16 in. deep. Space the holes about 3 in. in from either end. Finally, sand and finish the faces. (See Chapter 10 for information on finishing.)

DRAWER-BOX JOINERY

I use one of three methods to join the drawer sides to the ends: a spline-biscuit butt joint, a lock rab-

bet or a machine-cut dovetail. The last is impressive in appearance and has exceptional strength, but it takes the most time to lay out, cut and assemble. The first two joints are much simpler to cut and are thus faster to produce. They are adequate in strength for most drawer applications. Because I like the appearance of the lock rabbet at the top of the corner joint (which you see more often than the side), I lean toward using this joint.

Lock-rabbet joint

For use in a drawer box, a lock rabbet is a great improvement over a simple flat rabbet. In the latter joint, there is no physical meshing of the side and end parts — the only things resisting the tension and compression loads exerted on the drawer box are a few finish nails and the glue line. The lock rabbet, in contrast, forms a strong mechanical link between the parts.

To make this joint, you can use a lock-rabbet bit in a table-mounted router and a pair of shopmade car-

LOCK-RABBET SETUP

Depth of rabbet into side is half side thickness.

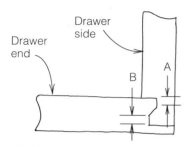

Flat B must be adjusted to equal fixed length of flat A.

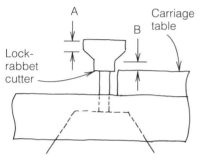

Adjust B to equal A by changing height of cutter.

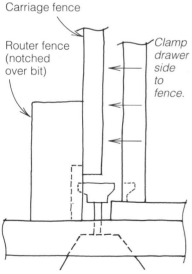

Adjust depth of cut by sliding fence away from (or toward) cutter.

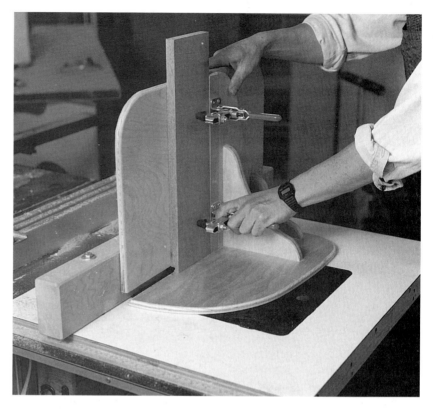

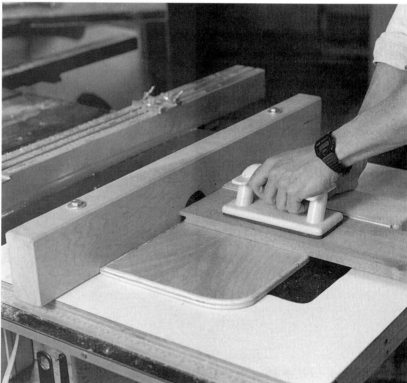

Using a pair of shopmade carriages, cut lock rabbets in the drawer side (top) and end pieces (above).

riages. Set the bit height so that the upper cutting flat A equals the exposed portion of flat B above the carriage table (as shown in the drawing on the facing page). Bolt or clamp a fence of 1½-in. stock to the router table and slide it over to the side of the bit. (Check to be sure that the face of this fence sits perpendicular to the table.) Mark and then cut a notch in the fence just to clear the height and length of the bit; spin the bit by hand (the router should still be unplugged) to check that it turns freely through the notch. Adjust the 1½-in. fence sideways until the cutter extends out from the carriage's sliding fence one-half the thickness of the drawer stock.

Using a scrap the same thickness as the drawer stock, clamp the board to the sliding carriage (inside face to the fence) and run it by the bit, as shown in the top photo on the facing page. Now, without changing the router setting, run a second piece of scrap—this time on the second carriage with the face to the table (see the bottom photo on the facing page). Note that the base plates of both carriages must be of equal thickness. If the cutting flats A and B are exactly equal in size, the joint will mesh perfectly. If not, adjust the height of the bit slightly, trim off the previous cuts on the scraps, and again run the boards by the bit. Keep fine-tuning the height adjustment until you get a perfectly meshed joint.

Now run all the drawer-side stock through the bit, making sure to cut the rabbet in both ends. If the bit is causing tearout at the shoulder of the joint (a common problem with veneered plywood or dull bits), run the pieces backwards by the bit. (This cut with the direction of rotation is called a "climb cut.") Hold on tightly to the carriage because the

bit tends to pull the stock through for you. You may feel more comfortable making the climb cut in two stages. To do this, attach another fence to the 1½-in. fence—this one need be only ⅛-in. or 3/16-in. thick plywood. Notch the plywood to fit over the bit, clamp or screw it temporarily to the fixed fence, and then run the carriage against it. Remove the temporary fence to make the full depth of cut.

To make the cuts in the drawer-box end pieces, again run scrap stock face down through the cutter on the carriage. Increase the depth of the cut by moving the fence back from the bit. Keep cutting and adjusting until the end cut is deep enough to allow the outside lip of the rabbet to come flush with the outside edge of the drawer side. When you're satisfied with the fit, run all the end boards through the cutter.

Now remove the lock-rabbet bit and install a slotting cutter in the table-mounted router. Choose a width that allows the drawer-bottom plywood to fit snugly—most hardwood plywood requires a 15/64-in. groove. Adjust the height and depth of the slot using scrap stock. The groove should be at least ¼ in. up from the bottom of the drawer sides to allow room for glue blocks, and it should cut no more than halfway into the thickness of the stock. Run both side and end boards by the bit. Be sure to orient the joint side (the inside face) of the pieces to the fence. Finally, collate the boards into drawer units, adding the bottom panel.

Spline-biscuit joint
Spline-biscuits create a strong, mortise-and-tenon-like joint that is relatively fast to produce with a hand-held biscuit joiner (slower than the lock-rabbet joint but decidedly faster than making dovetails).

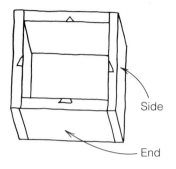

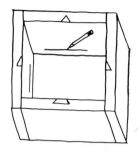

Side

End

1. Dry-assemble and mark top edge with pyramid sections.

2. Mark a chalk line on inside of each board to indicate position of groove for drawer bottom.

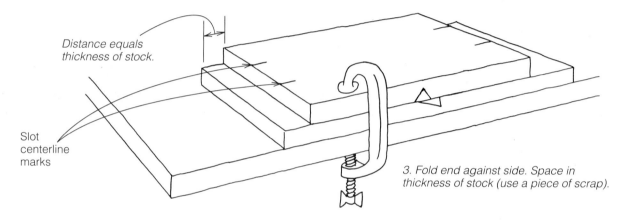

Distance equals thickness of stock.

Slot centerline marks

3. Fold end against side. Space in thickness of stock (use a piece of scrap).

Begin by laying out the four parts of the drawer box. Mark the top edges with the pyramid symbol as shown in the drawing above. Then, holding the box together temporarily, mark a light chalk line to indicate the approximate location of the groove for the bottom panel. The presence of this line and the pyramid symbols will help you keep the boards oriented, and will later help you locate and orient the boards to be grooved for the bottom panel.

Make the slots at one corner by following this sequence of steps: First, fold an end board against a side, keeping the end's edge in a distance equal to the thickness of the drawer stock (see the top photo on the fac-

ing page). Clamp the two pieces securely together and to the work table. Be sure the edges are flush and that the end is located precisely to a scrap piece of stock. Now, mark the centerline of the slots on the exposed face. Center one slot on drawers up to 5 in. deep; deeper drawers can receive two or more biscuits. Be sure to space the centerlines at least 1½ in. in from the edges.

Finally, set the joiner to cut for #20 biscuits and run the tool first into the end of the top board (the drawer-box end) and then, standing the tool on edge, into the face of the lower board. Note in the bottom photos on the facing page that I use the scrap of drawer stock to help support the joiner.

To set up for cutting spline biscuits in the drawer stock, use a scrap of drawer stock to position an end board the thickness of the stock in from the end of a side board.

With the joiner supported by a scrap of drawer stock, cut the slots into the end of the upper board (the box end).

Stand the joiner on edge to slot the face of the lower board (the box side).

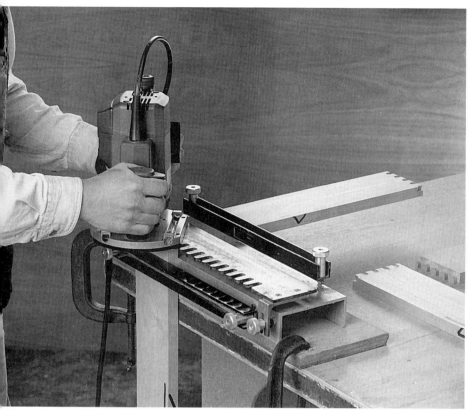

A commercially made router template and bit setup speeds up the task of cutting dovetails for drawer boxes.

Unclamp the pair of boards and make up another set. Pay attention to your pyramid symbols to keep the parts correctly oriented to one another. Repeat the slotting procedure at the remaining corners of the box. Cut the groove for the bottom panel as described on p. 107.

Machine-cut dovetails

There is little question that most people regard the presence of dovetailed drawers in a set of kitchen cabinets as a sign of high quality. Whether this feature is strictly traditional is another matter entirely, since period kitchen cabinetry (as opposed to the furniture of that era) did not necessarily have dovetailed drawers. The question for the cabinetmaker, however, is this: How badly do you want to see dovetails in the kitchen drawers? If you are set on them, I recommend that you purchase a commercially made router

template and bit setup. You could, of course, make all the dovetails by hand — I just hope you have another place to prepare food for the next few months!

Because all templates work a little differently, follow the specific procedures described in the manual that comes with your machine. Here I will give instructions common to all router dovetail methods.

Unless your machine allows you to change the spacing of the dovetails, you must first size the width of the drawers so that the pins either end on a half or a whole pin, not in between. Then cut the parts to the lengths specified in your manual. For my Sears model, the front and back boards are cut to the overall width of the drawer box while the sides are cut to the overall depth minus the thickness of the stock. Be sure your stock is free of warp — just one board can transmit its warp to the entire box. Gather the parts into drawer sets and then lay out the boards, marking the top edges with the pyramid symbols. I also mark the inside faces of the boards with a line representing the groove for the bottom panel. These orienting marks help me keep the parts in order and facing correctly as I set up each corner for routing.

Install the dovetail cutter and template guide bushing into the router and set the depth according to the instructions in your manual. Set up the template base and fingers. You may also be instructed to install stops (registration pins) in certain locations on the jig. Now insert scrap sized to the drawer stock (most templates cut a side and an end at the same time) and make a test cut. On my jig, the sides are vertical and the ends lie horizontal. Your manual will tell you how to adjust the depth of the cutter (which determines the tightness of the joint) and the position of the template fingers (which controls the depth of the sockets). To ensure a precision fit, be sure you are holding the router base flat to the template and the bushing tight to the fingers. Also check to see that the stock is tight to the registration pins. Blow away any accumulated sawdust.

Run the router first with a climb cut (from right to left) to cut the shoulder. Then cut from left to right, letting the router bushing follow the template fingers. Repeat this pass to be sure you've removed all the waste.

When you are happy with the fit (which should be snug, but not so tight there is no room for a film of glue), you can begin cutting the real thing. Set up one set of parts just ahead of the jig on the workbench and begin with one corner. Work your way around the box in a consistent fashion — I always go clockwise. On most templates, after cutting one corner, you remove only one component and fit the new piece against the remaining one, then replace that with the second new piece. To keep confusion down, watch the orientation of the pyramid symbols and the bottom-panel groove mark.

Once you've dovetailed all the pieces, set up a router slotting cutter or a dado bit on the table saw to cut the groove for the bottom panel. Lay out and cut the groove so it runs through the sockets on an end board, which allows a pin from the side board to cover its exit.

Once you are comfortable with the process, you'll find that cutting the dovetails goes surprisingly quickly and predictably. Just make sure that all the settings on both the router and the template are firmly locked in

place. To avoid cutting the wrong end of a board, pay close attention to your orientation marks. And one final word of advice: Always make up extra drawer stock in case of any errors in cutting the dovetails.

ASSEMBLING THE BOX

I struggled with a lot of drawers before realizing that it would be much easier to sand the inside faces of the sides and ends and bottom panel prior to assembly. I suggest sanding the stock to 180 grit and then lightly wetting the surface with a damp rag to raise the grain. Final-sand with 220 grit. (See Chapter 10 for more information on sanding technique.)

With the inside sanding taken care of, dry-fit the box pieces — leave out the bottom panel for now — and check to make sure that the joints fit snugly with the parts forming a perfect square. Measure corner to corner for equal dimensions. Make any adjustments by lightly paring any problem joints with a chisel. Now try the box around the bottom panel — the joints should still be snug and the box square. If not, trim the edge of the panel with a block plane and try again.

When satisfied with the dry fit, disassemble the pieces, apply glue to the joint surfaces and reassemble the box around the panel. Add clamps if necessary to draw the joints tight and to hold them while the glue dries. You'll notice in the photo on p. 112 that I'm using clamping cauls with the clamps. The cauls help distribute the clamp pressure and protect the sides from being marred by the clamp heads.

Before setting the box aside, turn the box upside-down, check it for square and straight, and then add

glue blocks as shown in the photo. I sometimes use hot-melt glue, which gives the blocks instant grab, dispensing with the need to clamp or tack the blocks in place.

With a lock-rabbet or spline-biscuit joint, you have the option of driving a few finish nails across the joint, which allows you to unclamp the assembly and move on to the next box. While you could feasibly nail across a dovetailed joint, the nail heads might split the tails. Even if they didn't, the nail heads would look out of place and unsightly. After the glue has set, remove the clamps and use a router to round or chamfer the top edge of the box. Finally, sand the outside of the drawer to 220 grit with a random orbit sander. When all the boxes are assembled and sanded out, I suggest that you apply finish to them before storing them away. (See Chapter 10 for details on finishing techniques.)

With the drawer assembled and clamped, add glue blocks to support the bottom panel and hold the box square.

DRAWER-FACE ALIGNMENT JIG

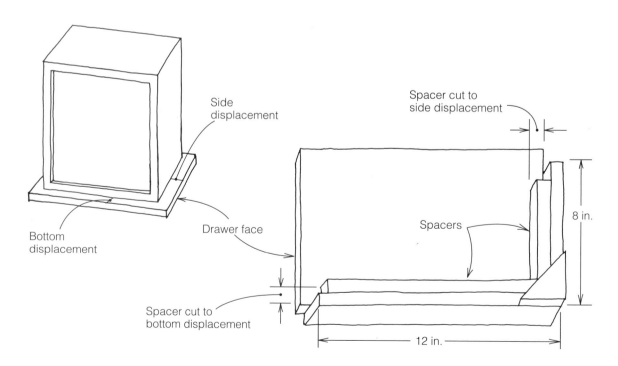

ATTACHING THE FACE FRONT TO THE BOX

If the drawer face is to be fully recessed into the face frame, I wait until the cases are assembled and the drawer boxes installed before attaching the face (see pp. 151-152). With lipped or full-overlay faces, I attach them now.

Begin by drilling a pair of $^{11}/_{64}$-in. dia. shank holes (for the drawer-front adjusters' #8-32 machine screws) in the front end of the drawer box. Space them about 2 in. in from the sides and centered in the box. To locate where to drill the 20mm hole for the adjuster fittings on the back of the drawer face, hold the drawer box against the back of the face and then mark the center of the hole by running an awl through the shank holes. The trick, of course, is to know where to hold the drawer to the face. To do this quickly and accurately, use the alignment jig shown in the drawing on the facing page.

To build the jig, first refer to the horizontal module story stick and find and note the distance between the end of the face front and the drawer side. Then determine the distance between the bottom edge of the drawer and the bottom edge of the face. Find this distance by making a mock-up to see how much the runners hold the drawer up from the mid-rail upon which the runners rest and then adding this figure to the amount of overlay. Now cut out two strips of wood, one sized for side displacement and the other for bottom-edge displacement. Attach these spacer strips to two lengths of wood joined at a corner (see the drawing).

In use, hold the jig tight to the bottom and side edges of the drawer face. Then bring the drawer box

tightly to the spacers and mark the hole centers with the awl. Remove the box, take the drawer face to the drill press and drill the pair of 20mm holes $^7/_{16}$ in. deep (a soft cloth placed between the face front and the drill table will protect the finish from damage). Bring the face back to the work table and tap in the drawer-front adjusters. Be sure the ridges around the rim of the fitting are facing up so that they won't pull out.

Before installing the face to the box, drill for the pull or knob hardware. To locate the centerpoint of a drawer face to drill the shank hole for a knob, lightly draw diagonals from each corner. The intersection is the exact middle of the face. To locate a pair of holes for a pull, find the centerpoint and then extend a line to either side with a pencil and a combination square. Make up a miniature story stick as shown in the drawing at right to mark the holes.

Now screw the drawer face to the box with machine screws through the box and into the adjusters. Leave the face a little loose — you'll adjust the fit later and tighten the screws down when you install the boxes into the cases. Once the faces are snug to the boxes, you can drill through the hardware holes into the drawer-box end. When the pulls or knobs are installed, the bolts further secure the faces to the boxes. No amount of drawer slamming should loosen them up.

With the face frames, doors and drawers completed, the time has come to put together the cases. And soon after that, the moment of truth: attaching the face frames and installing the doors and drawers. If you have heeded well the story that your story poles have told you, everything should fit together perfectly.

LAYING OUT FOR KNOBS OR PULLS

Knob

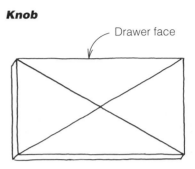

Draw diagonals from corner to corner. Intersection is centerpoint of drawer face. Mark with an awl and drill for knob.

Pulls

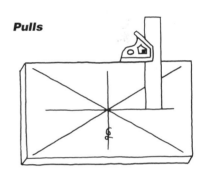

1. Draw diagonals; draw square line from edge through intersection.

2. Set blade of combination square to intersection and draw horizontal centerline.

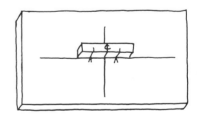

3. Make up story stick showing centerline and position of pull-attachment holes.

4. Hold stick to horizontal centerline and mark.

9

CASE
CONSTRUCTION

Cabinetmakers can choose from a wide variety of methods for putting together the case panels. But to ease the layout and cutting processes, I opt for methods that do not require parts to be rabbeted or dadoed together. Relatively recent innovations in the methods of case joinery — for example, spline biscuits and RTA (ready-to-assemble) fasteners — give immense strength to the most basic butt joint. These are the joinery systems I will show you how to use in this chapter.

I wait to build the cases until after the other major components of the cabinets — doors, drawers and face frames — are built and finished. In this way, my small shop stays free of space-eating plywood cubes for as long as possible. And once I do put the cases together, I can slip in the doors, drawers and other fittings and bring the nearly completed cabinets to the kitchen site, where they are out of my hair and safe from dings and scratches — a condition my old woodshop instructor diagnosed as "shop rash."

PREPARING THE PANELS FOR ASSEMBLY

To begin this stage of production, go to the stacks of sized panels that you've stored against a wall, read the labels on their edges showing their module affiliation and function (see pp. 61-62), and collate the stock into component groupings: floors (and ceilings, if wall cabinets), sides, partitions and stretchers. Next, gather the tools and jigs on the work table that you'll need for the following processes: marking and drilling bolt holes in the base-unit floors for attaching the adjustable leg sockets; marking and slotting for biscuits (or marking and drilling for RTA fasteners); and drilling shelf-support holes in sides and partitions.

Predrilling for adjustable legs

Make up a jig to help you locate the bolt holes for the adjustable legs relative to the front edge of the floor panel (see the drawing on the facing page). I set the jig's guide hole to create a toe-kick depth of 3 in. once the face frame and toe board are installed; if you want more toe space, set the hole farther back. If you wish to inset the head of the bolt into the floor, which is a good idea to keep items from catching on the cover

This cross-sectional view shows three commonly used case joints: spline biscuit (top), ready-to-assemble fastener (middle) and dado (bottom).

JIG FOR LOCATING ADJUSTABLE LEGS

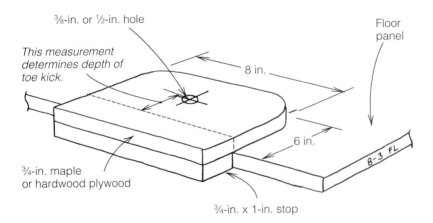

⅜-in. or ½-in. hole

Floor panel

This measurement determines depth of toe kick.

8 in.

6 in.

8-3 FL

¾-in. maple or hardwood plywood

¾-in. x 1-in. stop

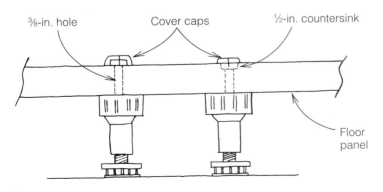

⅜-in. hole

Cover caps

½-in. countersink

Floor panel

Cover-cap options

cap, make the guide hole in the jig ½ in. in diameter. Otherwise make it the bolt-shank size of ⅜ in.

To drill the hole, install a ½-in. brad-point bit into your drill (I use Stanley's "Speedbore" bit, available at any building-supply store). Clamp the jig in place on the inside face of the floor panel, and then drill the countersink hole. Make the hole just deep enough to accommodate the head of the leg bolt (use a stop collar to prevent you from going too deep). Repeat this step at all leg locations, and then switch to a ⅜-in. bit to drill out the shank hole. You will find that a brad-point bit has less tendency to tear out the veneers, which is especially important if you're not countersinking the hole. To locate a hole at a corner, align the edge of the guide to the end edge of the floor.

Slotting for spline biscuits

While the floor panels are still up on the work table, you can prepare to make the slots for the spline-biscuit wafers. Speed the layout process by using either a marked stick or a clamp guide (a clampable straight-edge tool) to locate the centerlines of the slots. On the stick (or a piece of tape applied to the clamp guide) lay out the wafers evenly across the floor components. You should use at least five wafers for 24-in. deep base units and three for 12-in. wall units. Now lay a floor panel (underside face up) on the work table and mark the centerlines of the slots along each end edge.

If a partition joins the floor, find its position from the module story stick. Flip the floor panel right side up and mark the location of the partition along the front edge. Use a square to draw out the partition line across the floor. To reduce errors when going

Using a marked stick speeds up the process of laying out the slots for the spline biscuits on the floor panel.

Use a piece of scrap case material to set the position of the floor panel on the side panel for slotting.

on to slot the end of the partition, always draw the line on the left side of the partition wall as you face the cabinet. Make an X to the right side of the line to indicate the location of the partition.

Now set aside all the floor components but one. Bring up the sides and stretchers (or ceiling) for this module and set up the biscuit joiner. Adjust the joiner to make #20 slots, and check to be sure that the runners are clear of sawdust (otherwise it may not make a full-depth cut). Also bring a scrap of case plywood stock to the work table — anything over 1½ in. wide and as long as the depth of the floor components will do.

To begin making the slots, lay one of the side panels down on the table inside face up and place the floor upside-down over it. Use the piece of scrap to position the floor on the side panel (as shown in the photo at

right on the facing page). The floor should rest the thickness of the case stock in from the bottom edge of the side. Clamp the two components together and to the work surface.

Lay the scrap down to help support the base of the joiner (see the photo at left below) and center the base on the slot centerline layout mark to the far right. (Sawdust is expelled to the right on these tools — the area to the left stays free of debris.) Turn on the tool and make a slot. Slide the machine to the next layout mark to the left and repeat.

With the floor slots completed, stand the tool on its face and align the base to the centerline mark of the last slot made in the floor panel. Now run the machine into the side panel. Continue to make the matching slots, this time moving the machine to your right. Now unclamp the components, reset the floor over

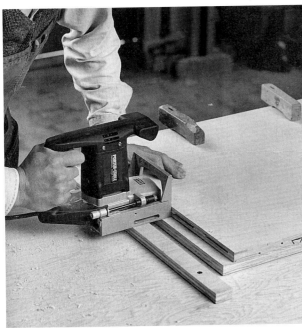

With the spline-biscuit joiner centered on the layout marks on the edge of the floor panel, cut the slots from right to left. Note the scrap of case plywood used to support the base of the tool.

Stand the joiner on its face to make matching slots in the side panel.

SETTING UP A PARTITION PANEL FOR END SLOTTING

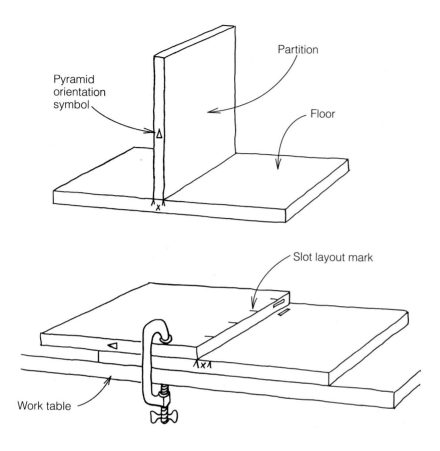

Pyramid orientation symbol

Partition

Floor

Slot layout mark

Work table

screw in between the slots and between the last slot and the edge of the panel. To locate the pilot holes, draw a line through the center of the slots and then eyeball the spacing between. Run the pilot bit from the inside of the panels.

Predrilling for RTA fasteners

To prepare the panels for lag-bolt-type RTA fasteners (I use Häfele's "Confirmats," see the Sources of Supply on pp. 194-196), you must predrill shank and countersink holes. I use a commercially made jig (available where the Confirmats are sold) to guide a special stepped drill bit through the side panel into the floor. You can get by without this rather expensive jig if you have a good eye and a steady hand. Be sure to predrill a small pilot hole at each layout mark if you opt for the freehand route (see the photo on p. 124).

Temporarily clamp the floor and stretchers (or ceiling) to the side panels before drilling the holes. Take diagonal measurements to be sure the case is square before running in the drill. Keep your eye on the depth of the countersink portion of the hole. It should be just deep enough to allow the head of the RTA fastener to bury itself flush with the surface of the panel. (You adjust the depth of cut by changing the position of the stop collar/roller bearing fixed with Allen screws to the drill-bit shaft.)

To drill for a partition, first fix the partition temporarily in place from below the floor panel with $1\frac{5}{8}$-in. self-tapping drywall screws. Be sure the partition sits square to the floor and then run in the stepped countersink drill. I always use the bit without the drill guide for this process.

Preparing for shelf supports

One of the more tedious jobs in cabinetmaking is drilling holes in side

the other side panel, and repeat the process. In a similar fashion, set the stretchers (or ceiling) on the side panels and make biscuit slots in these components.

To slot for a partition, lay the partition panel down on the floor panel so that its bottom edge aligns with the left-side layout mark on the floor. Clamp it securely in place (making sure the pyramid orientation symbols are correct) and proceed with the slotting process outlined above.

If you wish to screw the panels together, eliminating the need to clamp the box together while the glue dries, predrill for the $1\frac{5}{8}$-in. self-tapping drywall screws now. I run a

Using a commercial jig and a specialized self-centering bit allows you to drill parallel rows of holes for shelf clips.

panels to receive hole-mounted shelf clips. In larger cabinets needing more than two shelves (pantry units, for example), I sometimes opt instead for shelf standards. Though I don't like the appearance of the tracks, they install quickly and painlessly. To make the tracks somewhat less obtrusive, I recess them into a dado, which I form with a router guided along a straightedge.

To drill rows of holes for shelf clips, I use a commercially made jig (see Sources of Supply on pp. 194-196) that features two parallel bars machined with guide holes every 32mm (1¼ in.). In conjunction with the jig, I use a 5mm self-centering bit (supplied with the jig) in a hand-held power drill. Other models of drilling jigs are available. Some have only a single bar, and others feature a variety of bushings to accommodate different hole sizes.

You can, however, get by with a piece of ¼-in. tempered Masonite pegboard instead of the commercial jig. It won't last long — its accuracy as a drilling jig may suffer after only a few uses — but it is inexpensive and easily renewable. To use the pegboard as a guide for drilling the shelf-clip holes, cut a piece to the size of a base-unit side panel (make a second board for the wall unit) and mark which holes correspond to the location of the ¼-in. shelf-clip holes. To prevent misdrilled holes, tape over the unused holes on both sides of the board (see the drawing at right). Also be sure to mark the front and top reference edges on both sides of the board.

PEGBOARD SHELF-HOLE DRILLING JIG

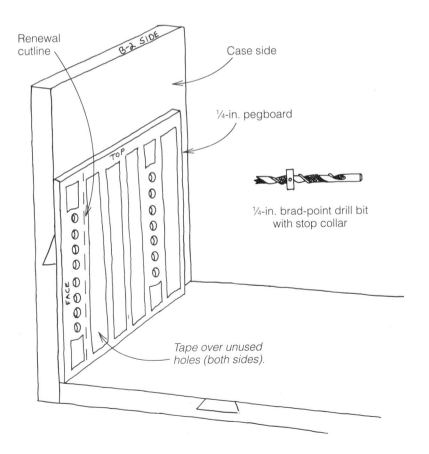

Renewal cutline

B-2 SIDE

Case side

¼-in. pegboard

TOP

FACE

¼-in. brad-point drill bit with stop collar

Tape over unused holes (both sides).

Clamp the pegboard to the inside face of a side panel and drill through the two rows of untaped ¼-in. peg holes. Use a stop collar to prevent drilling all the way through the panel component. When the holes in the pegboard are worn out, mark and untape a new set of holes parallel to the old. Rip a strip off the front edge of the pegboard so you can continue to use this edge to align the jig to the front edge of the side panel (as shown in the drawing on p. 119).

ADDITIONAL PANEL CUTS

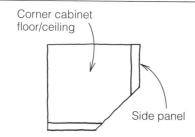

Notch partition panel around nailer.

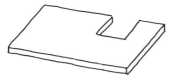

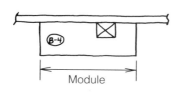

Notch floors around posts and other protrusions.

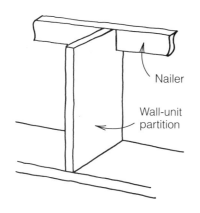

Cut edge of sides to 45°; cut off 45° corner in floors and ceilings.

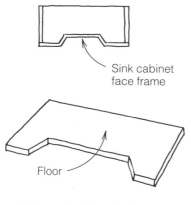

Cut inset into floor for knee space.

Additional cutting of case components

Although at this point the case components are cut to size, you may still need to make some additional cuts (see the drawing at left). Wall-unit partitions must be notched to go around the nailers. Other notches in side or floor panels may be necessary if the cabinets must be fit around posts or other wall protrusions (the dimensions should be defined on your site story poles). The face edge of corner-cabinet side panels must be cut to a 45° angle; the floor panel receives an angled cut also. And the floor of the sink cabinet must be cut back if the design calls for the doors to be set back.

Finish application

Though it's not imperative, I strongly recommend finishing the panel components before assembling them into cases. I have two reasons for working this way: First, finishing is generally easier to do, and thus likely to be of higher quality, when you can lay out individual pieces flat across a pair of sawhorses or lifts. Second, to reiterate a point made earlier, I don't like my shop to be filled any longer than necessary with a bunch of cumbersome cubes. If the case components are prefinished, the time between assembly of the case, through installation of face frames, doors and drawers, to the cabinet leaving the shop is shortened considerably. Refer ahead to Chapter 10 for information about finishing case components.

ASSEMBLING THE CASES

With the prep work on all the panel components behind you, the relatively easy task of fastening the pieces to one another awaits. Begin by clearing the work table of all tools and materials — you're going to con-

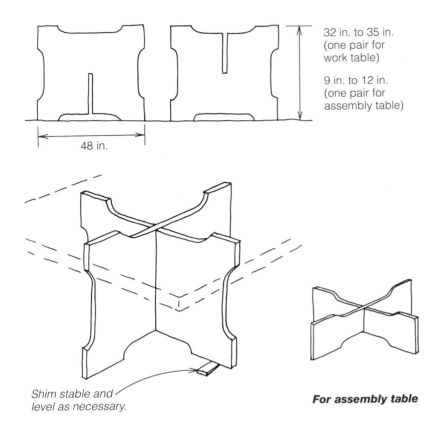

32 in. to 35 in.
(one pair for
work table)

9 in. to 12 in.
(one pair for
assembly table)

48 in.

Shim stable and
level as necessary.

For work table

For assembly table

vert this surface into an assembly platform. To do so, build a second pair of interlocking plywood supports to hold the table about 12 in. off the shop floor (see the drawing above). Take the time to level and flatten the table surface, adding shims where necessary between the supports and the shop floor. I make circular cutouts in the supports (see the photo on p. 134) to lighten them for storage.

Now go through the stacks of case components, this time collating the panels into modules. A base unit consists of two sides, partitions (if specified), a floor, two stretchers and a back panel of ¼-in. sheet stock. A wall unit is comprised of two sides, any partitions, a floor and a ceiling, a nailer and a back panel.

Spline-biscuit assembly

Begin the assembly process by gathering the following tools and materials onto the assembly platform: the module story sticks; #20 biscuits; a glue bottle with a slotted tip (to get the glue deep into the wafer slots); 1-in. and 1⅝-in. drywall screws; at least four pipe clamps long enough to span the width of the cabinet; two drills (a Phillips-headed driver drill and a drill fitted with a drywall-screw pilot bit); a tape measure; and a light (13 oz.) hammer.

Stand the floor panel and side panel against a pair of stops to set up the first case corner. The wedge holds the floor panel temporarily in place against the side.

Once the first corner is assembled, clamp the second side panel to the floor.

Now bring one module's panel components to the platform. Then go to your stack of face frames and dig out the module's face frame, which you'll attach after assembling the case (see pp. 124-127). The first step in the assembly process is to erect one corner of the cabinet by joining the floor to one side. To help hold the panels upright and together initially, make up a wedged-stop system. Install a pair of stops square to each other near the left front edge of the platform and then screw down a third stop at an angle. Make a wedge to fit between this stop and a floor panel.

To set up the first case corner, run glue into the slots of both panels, insert the wafers into the floor panel, and then put the two components together against the stops. (Check to be sure the pyramid marks on the edges of the panels are visible and oriented correctly.) Now drive the wedge snugly in place, as shown in the photo at left above. The corner should support itself upright and

square. Secure the joint by driving drywall screws across the butt joint at each of the predrilled pilot holes. Leaving the case corner wedged to the stops, insert the wafers and use pipe clamps to hold the second side panel to the floor. Then clamp the stretchers (or ceiling) in place, check the assembly for square, and run in the screws. If there is a partition, install it in the same fashion.

To set the partitions to the stretchers, stand the case right side up on the platform. Now tack the module story stick for this cabinet to the case sides just below the front stretcher, orienting the case-side layout lines on the stick to the real thing. Move the partition to meet its layout marks and then lightly tack the stick to the face edge of the partition. Tack any additional partitions to the stick. Secure the partition(s) to the stretcher by driving a drywall screw down through the front stretcher into the top of the partition(s). Then remove the story stick and tack it to the back edge of the case, being careful not

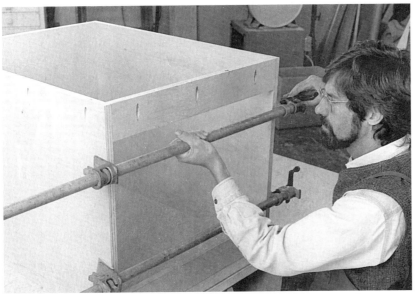

Finish the case assembly by clamping the stretchers between the two side panels.

SETTING PARTITIONS

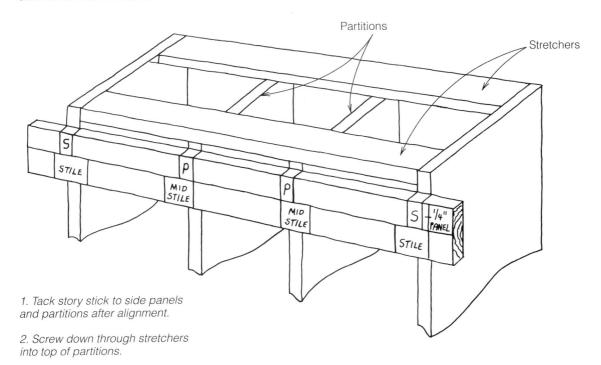

Partitions

Stretchers

S
STILE

P
MID STILE

P
MID STILE

S — 1/4" PANEL
STILE

1. Tack story stick to side panels and partitions after alignment.

2. Screw down through stretchers into top of partitions.

3. Repeat at back of cabinet.

With the side panels clamped to the floor and stretchers, drill pilot holes for the RTA fasteners and then run in the fasteners.

RTA assembly

To assemble the case with lag-bolt-type fasteners, follow the same basic procedure outlined above for spline-biscuit joinery. Set up the first corner in the wedged stops, and run in the fasteners. Repeat the process at each corner of the case after clamping the side to the floor and to the stretchers (see the photo at left).

INSTALLING THE FACE FRAME

With the case now assembled, it's time to install the face frame. There are three ways to do this: nailing the frame to the front edges of the case; screwing through the face frame into the case edges; or pocket-screwing through the case into the back of the frame. The first method is quick but dirty, because all the nail holes must be filled with putty. Unfortunately, even the best color match still looks like holes filled with putty.

The second method — screwing instead of nailing — takes more time but makes a stronger attachment and a better-looking job. You'll find that the wood plugs covering the screw heads blend better than nail holes and are not offensive even when they do show. The last method of attaching the face with pocket screws produces an exceptionally strong and entirely invisible connection, although it is perhaps a little slower to do than face-screwing.

Face-nailing or face-screwing the face frame

Use the module story stick to lay out where the case sides attach to the face frame (see the drawing on the facing page). You will first need to use a square to transfer the case-side panel positions to the opposite side of the module story stick. Make the marks along the top and bottom edge of the face frame. Note that the

to turn the stick end for end. Again orient the partition(s) to their layout marks, tack them to the stick and then drive a screw down through the back stretcher into the partition. Add two more screws to each stretcher and then remove the stick.

To prepare to attach the back panel, lay the case down on the platform, front edge down. Use diagonal measurements to check the back panel for square. If it's off, correct it by recutting or planing the edge. Now set the back (good side facing in) on the case and shift the case square to meet the edges of the panel. When you're happy with the alignment, tack all four corners of the back to the case. Then drill pilot holes and install 1-in. drywall screws every 8 in. or so around the perimeter of the back. Mark a line indicating the center of the partition(s) and screw here as well.

frame often overhangs the sides to account for applied panels or for scribing the stile to a wall.

Now stand the case up on its floor, apply a light film of glue to the case edges, and then secure the frame to the case with pipe clamps. (A helpful hint: Press the frame against the glue, remove it and let things sit for a few minutes. The glue gets quite tacky, keeping the frame from slipping around too much during the clamping process.) While clamping, be careful to keep the layout marks on the frame aligned to the case sides. Also, position the clamp heads to the back of the case. This setup allows you next to tilt the case onto its back, using blocking to lift it clear of the clamp heads (see the bottom photo on p. 127).

Set up a drill with either a pilot bit for nails or a countersink and shank-hole bit for screws. Drill through the face frame (with holes spaced about 8 in. apart) and then hammer in the nails or drive in $1\frac{5}{8}$-in. drywall screws. Remove the clamps and fill in the holes with either putty over the nail heads or with wood plugs over the screw heads.

I make wood plugs on a drill press with a plug cutter (see the top photo on p. 126). To ensure a good color and grain match between the plugs and the face frame, try to use scraps of the same stock from which the frames were cut. Free the plugs from the scrap board with the tip of a screwdriver. Lightly coat the countersunk hole with glue, then tap in the plug, being careful to orient the grain of the plug parallel to the frame. Cut the plugs close to the sur-

ORIENTING FACE FRAME TO CASE

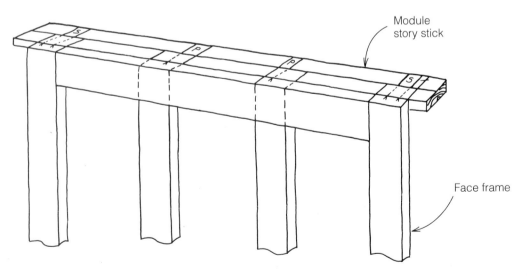

Module story stick

Face frame

1. Square side position marks to opposite side of pole.

2. Mark top edge of face frame from stick.

Use a plug cutter on a drill press to make plugs to cover screw heads.

face with a fine saw, and then chisel them flush to the frame (see the photo below). Finish up with a cabinet scraper followed by a fine sanding.

Pocket-screwing the face frame

The procedure for installing a face frame with pocket screws is the same as for nail or screw installations, except that you must predrill pocket-screw countersink holes around the outside perimeter of the case. Predrilling the holes, which you can do either before or after the case is assembled, requires the use of a jig. I use a commercial model made by Kreg, as shown in the top photo on the facing page. To attach a partition to the frame, drill the pocket holes on a side of the partition that won't be seen — toward a bank of drawers or a blind corner, for example. If

Chisel the plug flush to the surface after cutting it to within about ⅛ in. of the surface.

both sides are easily visible, there is little choice but to use face nails or screws. One caveat: Because the pocket screws tend to shift the face frame as they draw it tight to the case, you have to use more clamps to hold the frame in position. I take the time to move a clamp directly next to a pocket hole before cinching down the screw.

With the face frames installed, the cases are nearly completed. Once the doors and drawers are finished (the subject of the next chapter), the steps remaining are to install door and drawer hardware (and other storage hardware fittings such as lazy Susan brackets) and then the doors and drawers themselves.

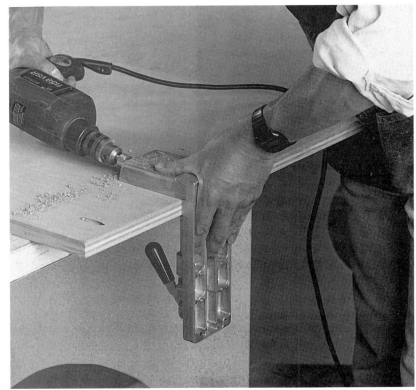

Use a jig to predrill holes for pocket screws around the outside perimeter of the case.

To install a face frame with pocket screws, clamp the frame to the case and run in the screws through the predrilled holes.

10

FINISHING

Once I've made the doors, drawers and face frames and milled the case panel components, I apply one of a variety of finishes (either a surface or a penetrating type). While some people prefer to wait and finish at the end, I like to do it now, before the cases are assembled. In this way, when I assemble the cases and install their various components, I can get the cabinets out of my shop — they're ready to become part of the new kitchen.

Although the choice of finishes confronting modern cabinetmakers is seemingly endless, I have chosen to include here only those that work well without a lot of specialized tools or skills — in other words, those that have worked successfully for me. Thus I won't be showing you

how to apply polyesters, catalyzed lacquers or catalyzed varnishes, which are unquestionably the most durable finishes available for wood. I leave these toxic and tricky-to-apply chemicals to the professionals. But that does not leave you without good choices. The finishes I do suggest using can give years of very good protection and, in some cases, a much more attractive finish.

The best finish materials and techniques are only as good as the surface you put them on. Preparation is not half the battle, it's more like four-fifths the battle. And proper prep work means more than just sanding the wood smooth. It means making sure the environment of your shop (temperature, humidity, dust) is under control. It means sanding the wood with the right materials and in

the proper sequence, including raising and then knocking down the grain of the wood. And finally, it means taking the time to apply the finish (especially a stain or paint) to wood samples to satisfy yourself of the color and texture of the results — and of your application skills.

SELECTING A FINISH

Choosing the type of finish for your cabinets is a critical step. Your decision whether to let the natural color and grain of the wood show, to change its color through staining, or perhaps to hide the wood (though not necessarily its texture) under coats of paint is fundamental to the statement you are making about the style of your kitchen. The correct choice of finish can transform a mundane kitchen of generic styling into a dramatic expression of a certain period of American history.

Another consideration is performance — you may have to compromise aesthetics to get greater durability. For example, a hand-rubbed penetrating-oil finish enriches wood with a deep, in-the-wood, lustrous beauty. But it is a finish whose application is never entirely done, because it requires regular renewal to repair scratches and maintain the sheen. A tough, on-the-surface finish such as polyurethane varnish, on the other hand, requires almost no attention beyond an occasional cleaning, but the grain and texture of the wood are lost behind a dense layer of plastic. And unlike penetrating oils, which acquire a rich patina over time, some of these hard plastic finishes tend to develop an unsightly yellowish tinge.

You must also consider how much time and skill you need to apply certain finishes successfully. Whereas penetrating oils require only the simplest of techniques and basic environmental controls to achieve superb results, on-the-surface finishes are far more finicky. More than likely you'll have to spend some time developing your brushing skills to avoid creating runs, sags or thin spots. In addition, you must keep your shop dust-free, warm and dry throughout the application and drying cycles (far more so than with oil finishes).

Toxicity may be a concern for you as well. Many of the oils and varnishes use solvents and driers that cause ill effects in many people, and few respirators work efficiently enough to prevent the chemicals from affecting you over the course of a day. This factor alone may push you in the direction of water-based or citrus-oil-based finishes.

Cabinetmakers can choose from an enormous variety of finishes. Shown here are some of the author's favorites.

In the chart on pp. 130-131, I list the finishes that I have found work well for kitchen cabinetry. All produce a reasonably durable finish, and none requires difficult application techniques to achieve smooth, consistent results.

In my own work, I am willing to do more maintenance in exchange for beauty, so I choose to use penetrating oils on all exposed wood surfaces (I now use citrus-oil-based varieties for health reasons). If I want a painted surface on my early American or Shaker cabinetry, I make up my own milk paint (see pp. 141-143). On the interior plywood surfaces of the cabinets, however, I apply clear, hard, on-the-surface type finishes. Here I am looking more for speed of application, durability and ease of maintenance over beauty.

FINISH MATERIALS

Type		Typical generic names	Toxicity	Application tool	Drying time
Penetrating oils	**Petroleum-oil based**	antique oil, Danish oil	moderate	cotton rag	4-6 hr.
	Citrus-oil based	plant oil, citrus-based oil	low	cotton rag, brush	24 hr.
Varnishes	**Oil/varnish mix**	N/A	moderate	cotton rag	4-6 hr.
	Gelled	gel finish	moderate	cotton rag	1-2 hr.
	Oil-based (alkyd, polyurethane)	liquid plastic	moderate	brush, spray	2-6 hr.
	Water-based (acrylic, polyurethane)	water-borne finish	low	brush, spray	½-1 hr.
Shellac	**Clear and orange**	clear, amber, orange, white	low	brush, spray	½ hr.
Paints	**Oil-based**	oil paint, enamel	moderate	brush	6-8 hr.
	Water-based	latex, latex enamel	low	brush	2-4 hr.
	Casein-based	milk paint	low	brush	2-4 hr.

Moisture resistance	Stain resistance	Abrasion resistance	Fade resistance	Ease of repair	Solvent for cleanup
low	low	low (but scratches tend not to show)	moderate (dulls)	easy (requires only reapplication)	mineral spirits
moderate to high	low	low (but scratches tend not to show)	moderate (dulls)	easy (requires only reapplication)	citrus oil
moderate	moderate	moderate	moderate to high	easy (requires only reapplication)	mineral spirits
low	moderate	high	high	easy (requires only reapplication)	mineral spirits
high	moderate	high	high	hard	mineral spirits
moderate	moderate	high (polyurethane very high)	high	hard	water
low (dewaxed moderate)	high (except to alcohol)	high	high	easy (redissolves with reapplication)	denatured alcohol
high	moderate to high	moderate to high	high	easy (requires only reapplication)	mineral spirits
high	moderate	low to moderate	moderate (dulls)	easy (requires only reapplication)	water
high	high	high	high (already dull)	easy (requires only reapplication)	water

PREPARING THE STOCK FOR FINISHING

It's a frustrating experience to lay down a beautiful finish over a large panel and then discover some previously unnoticed penciled hieroglyphics leaping out at you — too late to do anything about them. The only solution is to inspect each board or panel carefully before applying the finish. Erase pencil layout marks or notations, and rub off any oily handprints with a rag dampened with mineral spirits. Remove ripple-like milling marks left by planer blades or router shaping bits (which indicate that you were probably pushing the stock too fast) with a sharp hand scraper.

If you are adept with a belt sander, you can use this tool armed with a 100- to 120-grit belt to get rid of the mill marks. Unfortunately, while a belt sander works quickly, in inexperienced hands it can easily remove too much material. The results are uneven, wavy surfaces or ruined edge profiles. Another drawback is that the heavily abraded wood can never develop the depth of sheen it might otherwise gain from an oiled or varnished finish.

While the components have been waiting for finishing, they sometimes suffer dents and dings in the faces or along the edges. Unless the defect is more of a gouge than a depression, you may be able to raise the wood back to the surface by steaming. Lay a damp cotton rag (avoid synthetics) over the dent, than apply heat from either a flat-tipped solder iron or small fabric iron. In seconds, the steam should swell the fibers and the depression will likely become a bump. Don't sand the bump flush to the surface until the wood has dried thoroughly

(wait at least 12 hours). If you rush it, you could end up with a dent again.

Sanding

Sanding is the step that separates a good finish job from a superb one. While it is possible to skip sanding altogether and hand-plane all the surfaces smooth, this technique demands an inordinate amount of time and skill. There may be little choice but to go through the time-consuming, and sometimes downright tedious, process of sanding.

Unless the milling process has imparted deep ripples or grooves in the wood's surfaces, you should be able to start off with 100-grit aluminum oxide "production" paper. Don't use garnet or flint papers, which often scratch as much as they smooth. You can also use grey or gold-colored stearate papers designed primarily for sanding hard finishes. These papers are self-lubricating abrasives that keep cutting longer than other types of paper because they don't clog as fast. Always use a good dust mask when creating fine sawdust (I use 3M's #8560 double-strap mask). If you can afford one, buy a full-face mask that blows filtered air across your face.

Assuming you aren't blessed with an inordinate amount of elbow grease (or the desire to use it), you'll likely use a power tool to rub the paper against the wood. In recent years I've moved away from the classic half-sheet and quarter-sheet orbital sanders and now use palm-size random orbit sanders almost exclusively for this task (see the photo on the facing page). They produce results more quickly and with even fewer swirl marks than the standard orbitals. Unfortunately, my random orbit sanders all have round pads, so I have to go back to a quarter-sheet sander to get into the corners. Resist

A random orbit sander produces a better finish in less time than the standard quarter-sheet orbital.

the temptation to move these power tools quickly. They need time to do their job well — 1 in. per second is not an unreasonable pace.

After going over the surface with 100-grit paper, vacuum off the dust and sand again with 120 grit. If the wood is to be painted, the surface is now probably smooth enough (soft woods may need to go another grit). Interior case surfaces also need only be sanded to 120. For clear finishes on solid wood, continue up the grits, from 120, to 150 or 180, to 220. Don't go farther, since you'll only burnish the wood, which interferes with the adhesion or absorption of many finishes. And don't skip from 120 to 220. If you do, many sanding scratches will be left behind. You won't see or feel them until you lay down the first coat of finish or stain.

Raising the grain

If you're working with a water-based finish, it's important to raise the grain before you apply the first coat of finish. As soon as the wood fibers near the surface come into contact with moisture of any sort, they tend to stand up. Rather than waiting for the harder-to-sand finish to initiate this phenomenon, wipe a water-dampened cotton rag over the wood after the 180-grit sanding sequence. After the wood has dried thoroughly (wait overnight), final-sand with 220. Vacuum off the dust and the stock is ready to accept the first coat of finish. If you're used to applying finish without first raising the grain, you'll be surprised at how smooth this first coat will feel.

PREPARING THE SHOP FOR FINISHING

If a final finish is only as good as the surface it is applied to, one could say that the surface is only as good as the environment in which you make it good. Or in other words, a piece of wood ready to receive its finish gets that way — and stays that way — only if you make your shop clean, warm and dry from the beginning to the end of the finishing process.

After all the sanding has been done, and preferably a day before the finish work is to start, vacuum the shop from top to bottom. Start with exposed rafters and other dust catchers, then work your way down the walls to the floor. Clean the filter in the shop vacuum regularly to prevent fine dust from re-entering the atmosphere. Don't use a torn filter for the same reason. To settle the fine dust that inevitably finds its way into the shop air anyway, use a water-misting bottle (available from any garden shop). Add just enough moisture in the air to settle out the particles. The air will become noticeably cleaner with just a little misting.

Setting up the finishing area

Most finishes produce their best results when applied at room temperature (65°F to 80°F). Note that both the wood and the finish should be in this temperature range, not just the ambient air. When applying penetrating oils and oil-based varnishes, air humidity generally does not present much of a problem; 60% or less

Setting up a clean, warm and well-lit finishing area is an important part of any finish job. Note also the finisher's protective equipment: respirator, neoprene gloves and full-length apron.

is acceptable. If you are using water-based products, however, you have to keep a closer eye on humidity. If the level rises to more than 90%, the finish may dry slowly and never harden properly.

After clearing the area where you'll apply the finish, lay down some kind of drop cloth to protect the floor and to prevent it from getting slick and unsafe to walk on. Plastic obviously won't work since it's already slick. Painter's cotton drop clothes are unsafe if you are using oil-based products, since a saturated cloth can ignite spontaneously. My answer is to lay down large sheets of scrap cardboard, which I can often get from my plywood supplier. The drips are largely absorbed by the cardboard, and when the finish hardens, I take the cardboard sheets to the dump.

Prepare yourself for applying the finish by wearing overalls or a full-coverage apron and a suitable respirator. Since I don't like the smell of even water-based finishes — though they are thought to be non-toxic — I wear a carbon filtration mask when applying them. To keep the finish from being absorbed into my body through my skin, I always wear stripping gloves made of neoprene.

Other safety items to have on hand include a fire extinguisher (rated "ABC" for extinguishing paper, oil and grease fires), a metal pail with an airtight lid for wet rags, and replacement filters for your respirator (change them when you start smelling the finish). You should also make sure that you work with adequate ventilation, provided either by a fan drawing fresh air to where you are working or a vacuum hose pulling fumes away.

PENETRATING-OIL AND OIL/VARNISH FINISHES

To bring out the beauty in my cherry, oak and other figured hardwood cabinetry, I apply a hand-rubbed oil or oil/varnish finish to the exposed wood surfaces. Although I know I'll have to maintain the finish with an occasional wipe down of furniture polish or perhaps a few additional coats of oil, the look and feel of this incomparably rich finish is well worth the effort. But an oil or varnish finish may not be appropriate for all cabinets or all surfaces.

Only once did I use this type of finish on the plywood interiors — and I regretted it. Not only was the finish expensive and time-consuming to apply, but the surface did not stand up well to the abuse of having leaky soap boxes and rusty cans sitting on it over long periods of time. Also, the solvents in oils and varnishes outgas for a long time. It was nearly a year before I could open a cabinet door without smelling the finish.

Changing the color of the wood

Before applying a clear oil or varnish, you must first decide whether you are going to stain the wood. It's imperative that you stain and then top-coat finish some wood samples to determine the final color of your proposed stain. Don't rely on the color chips offered by the stain manufacturer, since they can't possibly represent your exact variety of wood or the hue change imparted by your particular top-coat finish.

When choosing a stain, make sure it's compatible with the oils or varnishes you'll use in the top coats. Most makers of penetrating oils offer pigmented oils to use as staining undercoats. Note that successive

To capture the popular 'country look,' apply a white gel-type wiping stain. Spread a generous coat on the door with a rag, then immediately wipe away the excess, leaving behind a buildup of white stain in the crevices and corners of the door frame.

top coats of clear oil tend to deepen the color, though not so much as continuing to apply the pigmented oil. Some woods — maple, pine and cherry in particular — tend to blotch when stained with oil-based products. Most suppliers can offer you a conditioner that reduces this problem, or you can use a thinned wash of clear (dewaxed) shellac prior to applying the first coat of stain. Don't bother brushing on the shellac; instead, wipe it on with a clean wad of cotton cheesecloth. Quickly wipe off the excess with a lint-free cotton rag.

For a less messy staining job, use gel-type stains (see the photo above). These stains apply evenly without running or dripping and produce a very uniform change of color. Because they don't penetrate the wood as deeply as more fluid stains, the wood rarely needs to be conditioned to prevent blotching. You must overcoat a gel stain with a compatible top coat — some gels are oil based, while others are water based. I suggest using the gel varnish supplied by the maker of the gel stain.

Creating "pumpkin pine"

If you are building a Colonial-era pine kitchen, you can vastly improve the look of the cabinets by hurrying the patina that pine acquires over many years — a hue known to New Englanders as "pumpkin pine." To make the stain, add ¼ oz. of raw-sienna oil pigment to 1 qt. of mineral spirits. Wipe the mixture onto the pine evenly and then wipe off the excess after letting it sit several minutes. If overlapping areas look darker, rub them out with a rag dampened with mineral spirits. Let the stain dry overnight and then apply two or three top coats of orange shellac, rubbing out the top coat to a soft sheen (see below for details on rubbing out finishes).

Applying penetrating-oil finishes

With the wood sanded out smooth and vacuumed off, wipe away any remaining dust with a tack rag. You can purchase these sticky cheesecloths at a paint store, or you can make your own by soaking a clean piece of linen or cheesecloth in mineral spirits and then, after wringing it out, sprinkling in a few drops of varnish. Work the varnish through the cloth until the rag feels sticky rather than damp. Store cloths in resealable plastic bags or a tightly sealed glass jar.

Always plan to finish both sides of any solid-wood surface; otherwise, you are inviting the wood to warp as changes in moisture content shrink or expand only the unfinished face of the board. The shopmade nail board and drying rack shown in the drawing on the facing page allows

SHOP-BUILT DRYING RACK

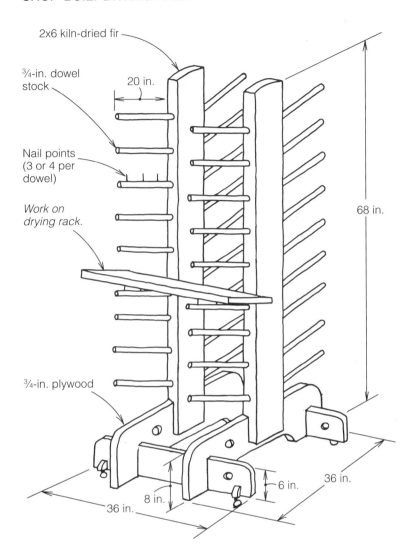

2x6 kiln-dried fir

¾-in. dowel stock

20 in.

Nail points (3 or 4 per dowel)

Work on drying rack.

¾-in. plywood

68 in.

6 in.

36 in.

8 in.

36 in.

you to set wet panels aside good side up. The nails prevent the wet finish from sticking to the dowel supports.

Begin by applying a generous first coat of penetrating oil, working the finish into the pores by rubbing the wet surface with 320-grit wet-and-dry silicon-carbide paper. This action creates a slurry of oil and wood dust that quickly fills the open pores. Within 15 minutes, wipe off any un-

absorbed oil with a clean rag. Check the finish every few hours and wipe off the excess oil that inevitably gathers at larger pore openings. If left to harden, the excess will form tiny nodules that must be sanded off. Wait overnight to apply the second coat of oil; if you don't you'll only re-dissolve the first coat, wasting much of the second coat when you wipe off the excess.

Prepare the first coat to receive the second by sanding the surface with 400-grit wet-and-dry paper. Naphtha makes a good lubricant, or, alternatively, you can use self-lubricating stearated papers. To sand outside curves on profiles and rounded corners, soften the paper by crumpling it into a ball, which will take the shape of the curve. On inside curves, use shaped sanding blocks (available from mail-order sources). Again wait overnight and apply the third and final coat. If there are any small defects that need to be filled, use a colored soft putty prior to the final coat. After the finish has dried for two to three days, you have the option of applying a paste wax containing a fine rubbing compound. The wax adds a bit more water and abrasion resistance to the finish and allows you to obtain an absolutely smooth surface with a deep sheen.

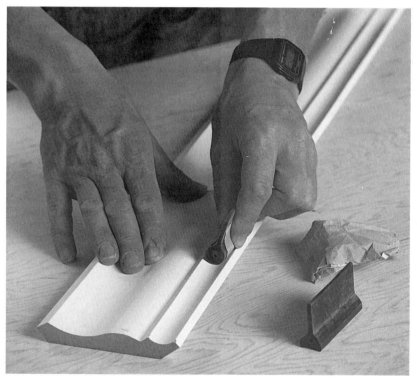

Sand inside profiles with shaped sanding blocks. On outside curves, use crumpled sandpaper.

Making your own oil/varnish finish

To achieve the look of an in-the-wood finish while gaining a large degree of the protection offered by hard surface finishes, you can mix up your own hybrid finish of oil and varnish. This mix builds quickly and produces a deep luster with a little elbow grease. To concoct the finish, mix equal parts of polymerized tung oil and alkyd varnish. Thin the first coat with mineral spirits (about half and half) to drive the mix deep into the wood. Apply subsequent coats as you would a regular penetrating oil.

A finish similar in look and ease of application is available commercially in the form of varnish gels. Like the oil/varnish home-brew, these gels build very quickly and allow you to create a rich hand-rubbed luster.

CLEAR SURFACE FINISHES

When I'm looking for an easy-to-apply but highly durable clear finish and I'm not overly concerned with highlighting the grain and texture of the wood, I opt for one of a variety of on-the-surface finishes. Most often, I use a water-based polyurethane. I like the non-toxic fumes and the results: a very hard, clear film that is highly resistant to abrasion, moderately resistant to moisture and easy to clean. Almost exclusively, I coat cabinet interiors with the gloss version of this product.

I also use polyurethane varnish on the exterior solid-wood surfaces, though I switch to a satin finish on the last coat to reduce the rather artificial glasslike sheen. I've also had good results with shellac (it gets bad press, but holds up surprisingly well in areas not subjected to standing water or spilled alcohol), and mixed results with brushable lacquers.

Applying surface finishes

Applying a surface finish requires much more care and refinement of technique than applying a penetrating oil finish. For best results, follow these precautions: Never shake a can of varnish or shellac to mix it. Always stir clear finish gently in a figure-eight motion with a clean stick (some manufacturers recommend you not even stir their gloss clear finishes). The idea is to reduce bubbles, and the effort needed to sand down a finish full of them. To avoid blemishes caused by semi-hardened particles, never use the finish directly out of the can. Always transfer it first into a clean jar or bucket through a filter.

Use high-quality, soft, flexible china-bristle brushes to lay down oil-based varnishes or shellacs. (I've also had good results with foam brushes.) Because natural bristles tend to lose their shape in water, use synthetic fiber (nylon is softer and thus better than polyesters) for water-based clear finishes. Before dipping the brush in the finish, wet the brush thoroughly with the finish solvent and then shake and wipe it dry. Wetting the brush with the solvent helps keep the finish from sticking up in the heel of the brush and allows the material to flow more smoothly from the brush onto the wood. To avoid infesting the brush with bubbles, never wipe the bristles against the side of the container to remove excess material. Instead, tap the brush against the side of the jar or bucket.

After sanding and tack-ragging the surfaces, thin the finish half and half with its solvent and apply the first wash coat. Brush across as well as with the grain. When this coat is dry, knock down the raised grain and dust particles with 180-grit stearate paper. Continue with the top coats, applying each layer undiluted. Set

HANDLING TECHNIQUES FOR CLEAR FINISHES

Stir (never shake) finish in figure-8 pattern.

Always transfer finish to clean bucket through a filter.

Don't remove excess by rubbing brush against bucket.

Instead, tap brush from side to side.

When the last top coat has dried thoroughly (3 to 4 days for varnish, 12 hours for shellac), knock down any dust particles with 500-grit wet-and-dry paper and then apply a paste wax with rubbing compound. The harder you rub, the more lustrous the sheen and silkier the feel.

PAINTING THE CABINETS

Any latex-enamel paint designed for interior trim work is a good choice for painting your cabinets. For a slicker and perhaps slightly more durable finish, you could go with oil-based enamels. Your paint store can mix up any color you can imagine.

If you are looking for a pickled (also called a "limed") finish, you can apply gelled white stain to the wood then wipe it off, leaving behind a whitish residue clinging to crevices and porous wood grain. To preserve the look, coat with a gel varnish. To get that bleached, stone-white look, apply — you guessed it — bleach to the wood. And if you want to reproduce the look of a real, honest-to-goodness Colonial or Shaker painted cabinet, mix up a batch of environmentally friendly (and incredibly durable) milk paint.

Applying paint to wood

Assuming the wood has been well smoothed to at least 120 grit, vacuum and then tack off any remaining dust. Fill any dings or natural defects with a hardening wood putty such as Durham's "Rock Hard." Sand the putty flush when it's dry. To seal the wood to help the paint cover evenly — and to stop bleed-through of sap on resinous wood such as pine — apply a primer coat of white shellac. Sand out the subsequent raised grain with 180-grit stearate paper.

Setting up a light at a low angle makes it easy to detect dust, heavy brush strokes or missed spots in the finish.

up a light on a stand to shine at a low angle across the wetted surface (see the photo above). Dust, brush marks and "holidays" (uncoated areas) will leap out at you. Sand between coats with 280-grit stearate or 320-grit wet-and-dry paper held to a soft sanding block. Vacuum and tack-rag up the dust.

Let the finish flow off the brush — don't sweep vigorously across the surface to spread the material as you would paint. Work the strokes from the dry areas back to the wet to prevent the buildup of overlaps. If runs or sags should develop, unload the brush and use it like a sponge to absorb the extra material. When applying shellac, prepare to move quickly because it dries in minutes.

Handle paint with much the same care you would give varnish: Stir, don't shake it; and always filter it into a clean container. Because paint is thicker than varnish, however, use a stiffer natural-bristle brush or a polyester synthetic. Dip the brush only about a third of the way into the paint, tap off any excess, and then spread the paint onto the surface. Work the material across the wood, and then with the grain. Always apply new strokes of paint to dry areas, drawing them back to the wet. Use an unloaded brush to absorb drips and sags. Lift off a stray bristle caught in the paint by pushing against it with the end of the brush.

Apply at least two moderately thick coats of paint over the shellac primer, sanding between each with 220-grit stearate paper held to a soft sanding block. View the surface in a strong side light to detect runs, streaks, dust or holidays. When the final coat has dried (wait at least overnight), buff out dust and brush marks with 400- or 500-grit wet-and-dry paper lubricated with water or naphtha.

Varnishing over paint
Standard house paints have been improved to the point where the once common technique of varnishing over paint to increase durability has become virtually unknown. But the side effect — a rich luster and deepening of color — makes the practice well worth reviving for painting traditional kitchen cabinetry.

Once the paint is well dried, scuff the surface with 320-grit wet-and-dry paper to help the varnish adhere. Tack-rag off the dust and apply a coat of alkyd or traditional spar varnish (avoid polyurethane, which doesn't stick well to the flatting agents used in most satin or semi-gloss paints). Sand and then apply a final top coat. When this has dried for at least three to four days (longer if you're using spar varnish), buff out the finish with polishing compounds.

WORKING WITH MILK PAINT

Coatings made from the dried milk curd of dairy animals have been used for nearly every conceivable paint application — from a whitewash for houses and barns to a primer undercoat for the finest oil paintings of the Renaissance masters. In early America, milk paints were commonly used to protect and give color to a wide variety of furniture, from Windsor chairs to Shaker cupboards. If you've ever tried to strip some dull, coarse-looking paint from an antique with little success, you've already experienced one remarkable attribute of milk paint — its excellent resistance to solvents. (In fact, it takes a highly caustic stripping agent developed for automobile enamels to get the stuff off.)

Although solvent resistance is one good reason milk paint would make an excellent choice for kitchen cabinets, other attributes clinch the deal. Milk paint adheres extremely well to wood, offers high abrasion resistance and is nearly impervious to water (calcium caseinate, the bonding agent of milk paint, is essentially a near-waterproof glue). Yet while the paint is wet the brushes clean easily in water. Its only serious drawback is that the earth-pigmented colors of milk paint are notoriously dull and coarse in texture. But there are, as you'll see below, some things that can be done to remedy this. Finally, milk paint is environmentally "soft": It's non-toxic in application and in use, and it uses no petroleum products. Only strict vegetarians need have reservations about its political correctness.

A formula for milk paint

While it is possible to buy ready-mixed milk paint in powdered form (see the Sources of Supply on pp. 194-196), the volume you'll need for a full kitchen makes the price rather daunting. To make your own, go to a local dairy or store for skim milk, to the garden shop for slaked lime, and to a paint store for boiled linseed oil, whiting (calcium carbonate) and earth pigments. (If you have no luck getting the last two ingredients, refer to the Sources of Supply.) You can also use alkyd pigments, which make for a finished surface that is less coarse.

Then follow this traditional formula to make ½ gal., which is enough to apply the first coat on an average-size kitchen: Put 6 oz. of lime in a gallon bucket and then add ½ gal. of skim milk. Stir the lime into the milk, then stir in 4 oz. of linseed oil. Now sprinkle the whiting into the bucket, stirring constantly. Use 3 lb. of whiting — the mix should become cream-like. Test for proper consistency by dipping in a brush and then lifting it out — a thread of paint should run off the brush. If a sheet forms, it's too thin and you need to add whiting. If the paint sticks to the brush, it's too thick and you need to add milk.

Color the paint by stirring in earth pigment (or alkyds). First, however, do a sample ½ pint and keep careful track of the amount of pigment added. Test the color after letting the paint dry on a sample board; the hue lightens considerably when dry.

To make the paint glossier and more water resistant, add 2 oz. more lime and 4 oz. more linseed oil to the brew. Alternatively, you can varnish over milk paint with a water-based or polyurethane varnish. Because milk paint has a short shelf life, plan to use each batch within two to three days. You'll know it's gone bad if it emits a strong ammonia smell (which means the casein is breaking down).

Applying milk paint

While milk paint handles much like any other paint, it does have some idiosyncrasies. For example, bristle brushes are not recommended — use synthetic-fiber or foam brushes. Also, don't seal or prime the wood because milk paint adheres best to raw wood. Apply at least two coats (preferably three) to ensure even coverage, sanding as usual between each. If you don't like the final color when the paint dries thoroughly, there is no need to fret. You can change the hue of milk paints by wiping water-based gelled stains over the top coat.

Antiquing a milk-paint finish

If you're not willing to wait for natural wear and tear to "age" the painted surfaces (meaning your children are grown up and out of the nest), you can hurry the process in several ways: distressing the wood underlying the paint (you should really do this before applying the paint); crackling the top coat; and sanding through the top coat to reveal different-colored undercoats.

Distressing is an art form. Too much, or applied to the wrong places, and it looks faked. Too little, and it sticks out like a sore thumb. If you have access to authentic, well-used antiques, study where and how they have worn. In general, you'll find that areas around door handles, outside corners, and knee- and foot-height moldings suffer the most wear. Duplicate these wear patterns by sanding, banging and scratching the wood.

Use an old belt-sander belt to distress the area around the door knob before applying the paint.

To crackle the finish, giving it an un-mistakable sign of age, apply a gel formulated for this purpose (see the Sources of Supply on pp. 194-196) between the second and last coats. For the best results, carefully follow the manufacturer's suggestions.

Perhaps the most effective tech-nique for giving your cabinets a feel-ing of age born with honor is to sand through the top coats in the areas that you distressed earlier. If you ap-plied a red first coat — typical of early American painting practices — this dull red peeking through the top coats in the worn areas says "antique" to most people without their even knowing why. Again don't overdo it; you don't want your kitchen to look as though it's been through an auto-matic car wash.

Rub through the finish with fine sandpaper to produce an antiqued effect.

11

INSTALLING DOORS, DRAWERS AND OTHER COMPONENTS

After assembling a case from its panel and face-frame components, the next step is to install the hardware for the doors, drawers, shelves and any storage fixtures. Door and drawer hardware goes in quickly and effortlessly with the use of certain jigs. These aids locate and hold the fittings in position while you drill for, and then run in, the attachment screws. After installing the doors and drawers, you orient them to the face frame and get them to function smoothly by adjusting the hardware.

Now is also a good time to install shop-built or commercially made storage fixtures such as lazy Susans, slide-out produce bins, waste receptacles and tilt-out sink trays. Though you could wait to mount these fix-tures until after the cabinets are in-stalled, you'll find it easier to manip-ulate the cabinet to a comfortable working position on a raised assem-bly platform than to crawl about in-side a fixed, dark cabinet.

INSTALLING THE DOORS

Assuming that you've already pre-drilled the holes for the hinge hard-ware (see pp. 98-99), installing the doors to the cases involves these few steps: attaching the hinges to the doors (and hinge plates to the face frames or case sides if you are using European-style hinges); putting on pull or knob hardware; installing the doors to the case; and fine-tuning the hinges so that the doors operate smoothly while sitting square and flat to the case. The procedure for in-stalling the doors differs slightly de-pending on the hinge style used.

Installing doors with European cup hinges

To install a door with European cup hinges, begin by laying the door down on a clean blanket spread on the work table. Place the hinge cups into the pair of 35mm holes drilled in the back of the stile and screw them in place, using a straight stick to align the hinges to the edge of the door stile (as shown in the photo on the facing page). If you are using more than one type of cup hinge in the cabinets (mixing varieties that provide different opening angles, for example), double-check the module card to be sure you are installing the correct pair on each door. Next, at-tach the pull or knob hardware into the predrilled holes. Finally, apply

Install the cup hinges to the back of the door, using a straight stick to help align the cup-hinge mounting wing plates to the edge of the door stile. (Photo by Jim Tolpin)

stick-on bumpers to the top and bottom corners.

Now install the hinge plates to the cases. If you are using cup hinges designed for use with face-frame cabinets, attach the plates to the inside edge of the face-frame stiles. If the doors are fully recessed, install the cup-hinge plates either directly to the case side (if the side is flush to the edge of the face-frame stile) or to a spacer (which brings the side flush). I use a simple jig to locate the hinge plates quickly and precisely (see the drawing below).

HINGE-PLATE LOCATING JIG

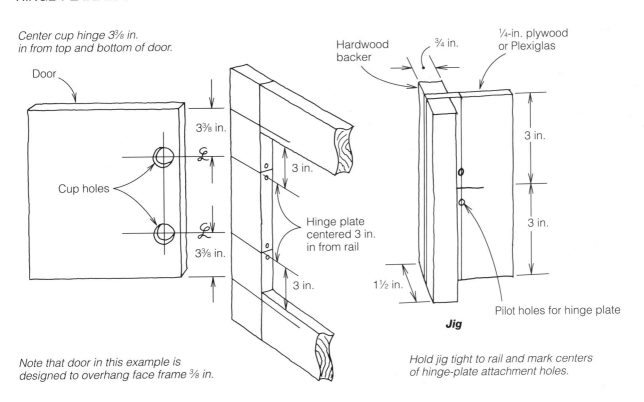

Center cup hinge 3⅜ in. in from top and bottom of door.

Door

Cup holes

3⅜ in.

3⅜ in.

3⅜ in.

3 in.

3 in.

Hinge plate centered 3 in. in from rail

Note that door in this example is designed to overhang face frame ⅜ in.

Hardwood backer

¾ in.

¼-in. plywood or Plexiglas

3 in.

3 in.

1½ in.

Pilot holes for hinge plate

Jig

Hold jig tight to rail and mark centers of hinge-plate attachment holes.

Install the door to the case by sliding the cup-hinge arms on the door into the hinge plates on the case. Since the layout of the hinge-plate locating jig is referenced to the cup's position on the doors, the parts should mesh together without a whimper. Note that some types of Euro-hinges clip on to the plates, while others require you to screw the arm in place.

The wonderful thing about cup hinges is their range of adjustment. You can adjust the up-and-down position of the door by sliding the hinge plates up and down on their attachment screws (the holes are slotted). Adjust the door side to side by loosening the adjustment screw on the hinge arm (the adjustment is somewhat different on cup hinges designed for cabinets without face frames). To make a recessed door sit

flush to the frame, reposition the arm where it attaches to the plate.

Installing doors with formed or surface hinges

To install a door with formed or surface hinges, begin as usual by installing a pair of hinges and the pull or knob to the predrilled holes in the door (to the face of the stile if you're using surface hinges and to the back if using formed hinges). Now lay the case on its back and set the door in position, using a straight length of wood to reference it to the bottom edge of the face-frame rail (as shown in the top photo on the facing page). Check the side-to-side overlay by measurement, making a light pencil mark on the frame. If the hinge is self-closing, be sure to press against the spring of the hinge while aligning the door; otherwise the door will be thrown off position when you screw the hinge down. When everything looks good, drill through the hinge plate holes with a Vix bit and then run in a pair of screws.

Some types of formed hinges have elongated holes on the plate that attaches to the stile, allowing side-to-side or up-and-down adjustments (rarely both). It's possible, however, to adjust formed hinges even without this feature. To change the position of the door, open it at least enough to clear the inset rabbet and gently press up (or pull down — it depends which way you want to move the door) on the side of the door opposite the hinges. The hinges warp slightly from the strain, changing the hang of the door. It may not be too high tech, but it does seem to work nine times out of ten.

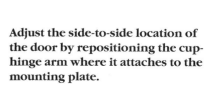

Adjust the side-to-side location of the door by repositioning the cup-hinge arm where it attaches to the mounting plate.

To help keep the doors aligned to each other and to the face frame, clamp a straight length of wood to the frame before you screw the formed or surface hinges down.

If a lipped door binds when closing but is otherwise perfectly aligned, plane the rabbet wider to clear where it interferes with the face frame. A rabbet plane is the tool of choice for this task, though a long-handled chisel would do.

If a door is warped, its stile opposite the hinges may close unevenly against the face frame. If this door is one of a pair, the warp announces itself loudly at the meeting line. To adjust for this condition, insert thin shims — I like to use scraps of sand-paper — between one of the hinge attachment plates and the back of the

Use a rabbet plane to widen a door rabbet. Remove the door if you need to trim the full length of the rabbet.

FITTING A FULL-RECESS, BUTT-HINGED DOOR

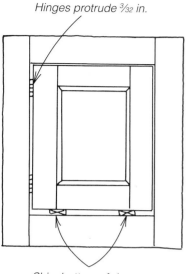

Hinges protrude ³⁄₃₂ in.

Shim bottom of door with ³⁄₃₂-in. shims.

Plane top and side edge of door to even margin.

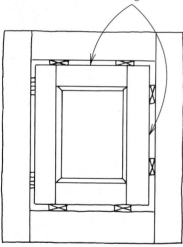

Use ³⁄₃₂-in. shims as feeler gauges to test gap for even margin.

Note: gaps exaggerated for clarity.

door. Shimming behind the top hinge plate, for example, draws in the door at the opposite corner.

Installing doors with butt hinges

To install a full-recess door with butt hinges, begin by attaching the hinges to the pair of mortises you made in the door edge earlier (see p. 99). Also install the knob or pull as well as the magnetic catches. Keeping the case upright on the assembly platform, slip the door into the opening. Insert shims ripped to the desired size of the gap between the bottom of the door and the face-frame rail (I like a ³⁄₃₂-in. gap, as shown in the drawing at left). This gap must be the same amount as the protrusion of the hinge leaves along the side of the door. Assuming the door and the opening of the frame are square, you should be rewarded with a consistent margin line along the top and opening side edge.

Check the top and opposite side of the door. If the gap margin is not similar and even, make it so by planing the door edges until a shim "feeler gauge" just slides in between. Now mark the location of the hinge leaves on the face-frame stile, using a knife rather than a pencil for precision. Break apart the hinge (to protect your sanity, always use loose-pin butt hinges) and install the leaves to the marks. There's no need to make a mortise for the plates, since you've already mortised for both leaves on the door. Mark the center of the screw holes with an awl, then use a Vix bit through the holes in the leaf plate to drill the pilot holes. Screw the plates to the edge of the face frame and then install the door to the case by meshing the hinges back together and slipping in the pin.

Butt hinges are difficult, but not impossible, to adjust. You can change

the side-to-side position of the door by either deepening the mortise of the top or bottom hinge or by shimming it out. Sandpaper works well for shimming — the finer the grit, the less shimming effect. Raise or lower the door, or move it in or out, by filling and then redrilling the holes for the frame-mounted hinge leaf. Then redrill and reinstall the hinge to a new, adjusted position.

Because the face frame may distort slightly during the installation of the cabinets, wait to make final door adjustments until after the installation is complete (especially if the doors are fully recessed).

INSTALLING THE DRAWERS

Bring all the drawer boxes up onto the work table, and then break open the packs of drawer slides. Separate the slide components into two piles: drawer-box runners and case-side guide rails. Then collate these into left- and right-hand components. Set the guide rails aside for the moment, and then proceed to install the runners to the lower side corners of each box. Snug the front of the runners to the back of the drawer-front face (because fully recessed drawer fronts are not yet installed, flush the runners to the front of the box). Avoid splitouts by predrilling pilot holes for the attachment screws. Finally, stick on the adhesive-backed bumpers to the upper inside corners of the face front. The drawers are now ready to go into the cases.

Prepare the cases to receive the drawers by installing the guide rails. The front of the guide sits on a face-frame rail about ¹⁄₁₆ in. in from the frame's face and attaches to the side edge of the stile. If the stile overhangs the partition or side wall by at least ¹⁄₂ in., you can secure the back

Separate the drawer runners into right- and left-hand pieces, placing them to the appropriate side of the assembly area, then install them flush to the front of each drawer box.

of the guide rail to a plastic socket accessory attached to the back wall of the cabinet. The socket is advantageous because it allows you to make side-to-side and up-and-down adjustments. Unfortunately, full-extension slides are not designed to be used with sockets — instead, you must attach them directly to the case sides (see below).

In the photo at right, I'm using a commercially made jig (generally available from the manufacturer or supplier of the slide hardware) to hold the guide rail in position while I attach both the front and back. If you can't use the socket (either because there's not enough overhang clearance from the face-frame stile, or because you're using full-extension slides), add a vertical spacer strip — cut in thickness to the width of the overhang — toward the back of the case side. Using the jig, attach the guide to the face frame and to the spacer. If the case side is flush to

Using a jig to hold a drawer guide rail in position makes it easy to attach the guide at the front and back of the cabinet.

DRILLING JIG FOR DRAWERS WITH FULL-RECESS FACES

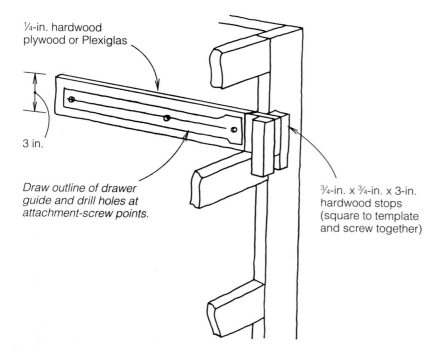

¼-in. hardwood
plywood or Plexiglas

3 in.

Draw outline of drawer
guide and drill holes at
attachment-screw points.

¾-in. x ¾-in. x 3-in.
hardwood stops
(square to template
and screw together)

the frame, a spacer is not necessary and you can attach the hardware directly to the side panel.

If the drawer front is fully recessed into the face frame, the front of the case guide rail must not come out to the front edge of the face frame. Instead, locate it ¹⁄₁₆ in. in from the back of the face frame. Because the factory-made jig won't work in this situation, make up your own drilling guide from a scrap of thin plywood or Plexiglas (see the drawing above). Use a drawer guide as a template to help you locate the attachment holes along the jig.

Installing and adjusting the drawer box to the case

Slide the box into the case, meshing the drawer runner into the case guide rails as you gently lift the box over the stops embossed on the rails.

Check to see that the drawer face sits flat to the face frame. If not, either the box is out of square or warped or one or both guides are not perpendicular to the face of the cabinet. Usually you need only adjust the "capture" rail — the case guide that lips over the nylon roller on the box runner (on Blum slides, this is the one to the right). Slide the rear socket to one side or another (or shim between the guide and the spacer strip or face frame) until the face squares with the frame. Move the opposite-side guide rail if more adjustment is necessary.

It often happens, especially with out-of-square boxes, that you cannot get the face to sit flat without binding the drawer to the guides. To fix this problem, remove the drawer, take off the runners and, using a table saw or table-mounted router, rabbet the area where one of the runners sit. Going ⅛ in. deep is usually sufficient to get you the necessary clearance. If you need more clearance, rabbet both sides. Be sure to set any corner-joint finish nails out of the path of the sawblade or router bit.

Finally, check the drawer box for rocking. Even though the drawer may shut smoothly and flat to the face, it can still rock on the guides. This problem is usually caused either by a warped box or by the guides not being level with one another. In either case, make the necessary adjustments by moving the back of one of the case guides up or down.

Now with the drawer shut, loosen the face-attachment fitting's fastening bolts and adjust the face front until it sits centered and level. If the rabbet on a lipped drawer face hits the frame no matter how you adjust the attachment fitting, enlarge the rabbet with a rabbet plane.

Installing full-recess drawer face fronts

As you may remember, the face fronts were left off drawers going into full-recess-type cabinets (see p. 113). Now is the time to install them. You'll need a pair of steel centering pins designed to fit into the holes (20mm for Blum fittings) you drilled for the drawer-face adjusters. These pins, which are available from the supplier of the fittings, will tell you where to drill the shank holes for the attachment bolts.

To attach the faces, slide the drawer box into the case, set the centering pins in the adjuster holes, and then hold the face to the front of the box. When the gap margin between the face front and the face frame is equal on all four sides (I use wood shims as reference stops), press the pins into the box end board. Drill the shank

To install a full-recess drawer face front, first insert centering pins into the holes for the drawer-face adjusters.

Use wood shims to hold the face evenly in the opening and a screw installed temporarily at the knob location to help manipulate the piece. Press the face into the drawer box behind.

Remove the face and drill shank holes at the marks left behind by the centering pins.

holes at the pin impressions, tap the adjusters into the 20mm holes, and then install the face to the drawer box. Fine-tune the fit before cinching the bolts down.

Now install the knobs or pulls to the drawer face. First, locate the centerline and mark the holes (see the drawing on p. 113), then drill the holes through the face and through the drawer-box end. Use long machine screws to attach the hardware (the screws provided with the knobs may not be long enough).

Installing "false" drawer fronts

If you wish to fix the drawer front of a sink cabinet permanently in place (though you may want to hinge it to provide access to a sink tray, see pp. 153-154), you can still use the adjusters as attachment fittings. In this way, you can easily fine-tune the position of the front.

Prepare for the false front by fastening a pair of nailers across the opening in the face frame. Now the installation process is similar to that outlined above: Place the centering pins in the adjuster holes, hold the front in position and press the pins into the nailers. Then drill the shank holes. Finally, tap in the adjusters and bolt the front in place.

Attach the face by inserting screws through the pilot holes into the fittings.

INSTALLING SHELVING

To install the shelves (which you may wish to remove before transporting the cabinets to the site), insert sets of pins into the holes, or clip sets of shelf hangers onto the standards. Set the shelves in place and test the fit. There should be a little side play to allow easy removal — 1/8 in. is about right. Trim the shelving if necessary.

There should not, however, be any rocking motion. If there is, either the holes are off or the shelf is warped. Test for the latter first by removing the board and sighting it — your eyes are very good at seeing even a slight amount of distortion. If you do spot some warp, all may not be lost. You may be able to eliminate the rocking simply by flipping the board over or by turning the back edge to the front.

If more than one shelf rocks, the rows of holes (or shelf standards) are probably out of level with one another. While it's possible to move and reposition the offending standard, there is little you can do about a misdrilled row of holes. Fortunately, there is something you can do about the shelf-support clips: Add bits of fine-grit sandpaper to them until the shelf ceases to rock. Trim the sandpaper to the shape of the support and glue the paper in place. Repeat the process for all the other shelves using this misdrilled row of holes. To prevent these customized clips from coming out during subsequent handling of the cabinet, tape them temporarily in place with packing tape.

Tilt-out sink trays attached to the back of hinged false drawer fronts make good use of the space between the sink and the face frame. (Photo courtesy Rev-A-Shelf)

INSTALLING COMMERCIAL STORAGE FIXTURES

In recent years, aftermarket fixtures that expand the storage capacity and utility of stock kitchen cabinetry have become widely available. Most of these fixtures are easy to install, requiring little, if any, modification to the cabinet cases. Because of their usefulness and relatively low cost, I install almost all the items discussed here in every kitchen that I build.

Tilt-out sink trays

Sink trays, mounted to the back of the false drawer front, are useful for holding soap bars, wash pads and sponges right where you need them. Made of either plastic or stainless steel, they are designed to make the most of the otherwise wasted space between the bowls of the sink and the cabinet face frame. Most sink trays come with a pair of hinges for mounting the face front to the frame; check the enclosed directions for specific instructions about mounting and adjusting them.

Generally, you install the mounting hinges first to the inside edges of the frame stiles, then to the back of the face front. Because the holes on the attachment plate are elongated to allow for up-and-down adjustment, center the screw in the oval-shaped hole. Be sure to keep the bottom of the attachment plate at least 3/16 in. off the frame rail to allow room for downward adjustment.

Make installation of the hinges to the front easy by clamping the face front in position before drilling the pilot holes for the hinge screws. Again, center the screws in the elongated adjustment holes. Once the hinges are in place, test the closing action and the alignment of the front to the frame. Make any necessary adjustments and then install the tray to the back of the face.

Slide-out bins

Slide-out bins come in a wide variety of shapes and sizes. Some are mounted to slides attached to their bottoms, while others slide along side-mounted hardware, similar to a drawer (see the top photo on the facing page). To ensure a trouble-free installation, carefully follow the instructions that come with the fixture. You should also receive drilling templates and instructions on how to adjust the hardware for smooth operation. Before purchasing these fixtures check to be sure that your door openings are wide enough to accommodate them. If the fixture mounts on slides between two walls, the spacing is critical. Check the specifications before building the case, or figure on adding spacers to existing partition walls.

Slide-out towel bars

I usually mount slide-out towel bars either to the inside of the sink cabinet along one wall, or within a separate, narrow cabinet joined to one side of the sink unit. There are two basic mounting types: side mounted and top mounted. In both cases, you install the bars by extending out the tongs and running screws through the exposed mounting holes in the base plate. Take advantage of the fact that the cabinets are not yet installed by tilting the cabinet on its side or roof — the force of gravity helps hold the fixture in position (see the bottom photo on the facing page).

Attach the mounting hinge for the sink tray to the inside of the cabinet and the back of the drawer face front. Here, the installer is using a scrap block the same thickness as the full-inset face front to help orient the hinge plate.

Slide-out utility bins (right) make good use of the space under the kitchen sink. The fixture at left is a slide-out waste basket.

With the cabinet on its side, install the slide-out towel bar to the inside of the cabinet.

LOCATING LAZY SUSAN PIVOT POINTS

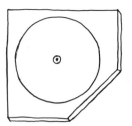

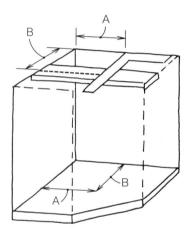

1. Set shelf on floor, check clearance around perimeter, then mark centerpoint through hole.

2. Measure to centerpoint, squaring out from back of cabinet. Find point at top of cabinet ceiling or nailer) and drill small hole to transfer mark to underside.

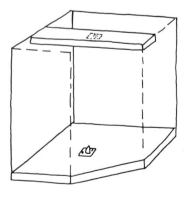

3. Install pivots, orienting pins over centerpoints.

Lazy Susans

One way to make good use of blind corner cabinets, which are notorious for poor accessibility, is to install a lazy Susan. The hardware for most lazy Susans is straightforward: two pivot points and a two-piece telescoping pole to which the circular shelf trays are bolted.

Locate the floor pivot by laying one of the shelf trays on the floor of the cabinet. After checking the clearance around its circumference, mark the outline of the hole through which the pole passes. Then remove the shelf and eyeball the center of the outline. Laying out the roof pivot is a little trickier. First, of course, there must be a piece of wood to lay out to: Unless the cabinet has a ceiling (it will if it is a wall cabinet), install a 4-in. wide plywood nailer brace across the cabinet so it passes over the approximate center of the fixture. Using a framing square, measure out square from each wall, noting the distance to the centerpoint on the floor. Again using the square, establish this point at the top of the cabinet. Transfer the top centerpoint to the underside of the brace or ceiling by drilling a small hole at the centerpoint.

Attach the pivots to the floor and brace, centering them over the marked centerpoints. Now slide the pole through the shelf trays, set the bottom of the pole on the floor pivot, and telescope the inside pole until it captures the ceiling pivot. Secure the poles together with the setscrew, slide the trays up the post to the desired spacing and the lazy Susan is ready to roll.

Half-moon swing-out shelves

Another way to make good use of a blind corner cabinet is to install half-moon-shaped shelves that swing out of the opening. An optional, though

Half-moon swing-out shelves equipped with slides can extend well out of the cabinet opening, making good use of a blind corner cabinet. (Photo by Bruce Greenlaw)

more expensive, feature is the addition of slides that allow the shelves to come farther out of the cabinet, which is a quality appreciated by people with impaired mobility.

Since there are several varieties of these fixtures and ways in which they are mounted to the cabinets, follow the manufacturer's instructions carefully, with one exception: Some manufacturers recommend attaching the pivot points directly to the back of a face-frame stile. I have found that the weight of the shelves when loaded can distort the frame. To create a stronger attachment point, I glue and screw a second piece of wood — a ³/₄-in. by 1¹/₂-in. square length of hardwood — to the

back of the stile. I also screw it to the floor and to the top stretcher.

Once again, be sure that the cabinet opening will accommodate the fixture, and note that the addition of slide-out hardware increases the clearance requirement.

Tray dividers

While it is certainly possible to build your own dividers of ¹/₄-in. plywood, sliding them into floor and ceiling-panel grooves, you can't beat the time savings of installing coated metal tray dividers (see the photo on p. 158). These fixtures have the added advantage of allowing side access to the trays, which means no more losing small trays forever to the dark recesses of an enclosed cubby hole.

Tray dividers mount to clips screwed to the floor and back wall of the cabinet (viewed from above).

The divider bar mounts to clips installed to the floor and back wall of the case. I mount the clips to the bar and then lay out their positions with a framing square. After predrilling pilot holes, I screw the clips in place.

Slide-out cutting boards

To create a cutting board that slides fully out of a cabinet yet provides a firm work surface without having to be removed and set on the counter, use a heavy-duty, full-extension slide designed specifically for this purpose. Accuride's model 340-176 supports up to 100 lb. fully extended and is designed for use with 1½-in. butcher block (see the Sources of Supply on pp. 194-196).

Mount this type of slide directly to the case sides (or to spacers that bring the sides flush to the edge of the face frames). With the Accuride slide, attachment clips mount to the ends of the cutting board. These clips allow the board to be easily removed from the body of the slide — a welcome feature for cleaning or for using the board in another location.

INSTALLING SHOP-BUILT STORAGE FIXTURES

You can, of course, also build your own storage fixtures. Although this can be time-consuming work, there are several advantages. First, you have the ability to custom-size the fixtures to your cabinets, making the most of your space. Second, instead of settling for metal or plastic components, you can make these fixtures almost entirely from wood. And finally, some of the stand-alone projects — the plate rack (pp. 162-163) and tamboured-door appliance garage (pp. 164-166) in particular — add a good measure of traditional charm. Although I do introduce you to some new techniques in building

some of these projects, most draw on the cabinetmaking procedures already covered in this book.

Slide-out shelves

Although any shelf can be made to slide out of a cabinet by adding drawer guides, the result is not that practical. To keep items from sliding off a moving shelf, it is necessary to add edging strips to the back and sides (a front strip is optional). I make the edge strips in different heights, placing the largest to the rear edge, and shape and round the strips before assembly.

Use the module story stick to determine the layout of the shelf components (as shown in the top drawing

Slide-out shelves greatly improve the accessibility of kitchen cabinets. The shelves shown are installed on full-extension, corner-mount slides.

at right). Remember that most slide hardware requires ½-in. clearance to either side. To keep the layout and joining processes as simple as possible, I avoid rabbeting the edging strips around the shelf panel. Instead, I use splines or spline biscuits to make the joint, adding screws to draw the edgings tight to the panel. Where the screws would show along the front edge, I drill countersink holes and cover the heads with wood plugs.

Slide-out sink shelf One of the most often used cabinets in a kitchen is the unit that supports the kitchen sink. Unfortunately, because of the plumbing fittings, it is also one of the most difficult cabinets to access or make efficient use of. A slide-out shelf unit helps solve both these problems. A light pull on either cabinet door brings the contents of the sink cabinet out into full view while providing easy access from either side. If you wish, you can add waste basket(s) to the unit; feeding and dumping the trash then become quick and easy.

Note in the drawing at right that I've secured the pair of doors to the front of the shelf assembly, and used heavy-duty, side-mounted, full-extension slides to support the unit. To ensure strength and longevity, use ¾-in. plywood (finished with a polyurethane varnish) for the sides as well as the bottom. Run a bead of waterproof silicone caulk along the seam between the shelf base and sides. In this way, spills are confined to the shelf unit, where you can see and clean them up, instead of working their way into the joint and eventually through to the cabinet floor.

Revolving recycling bins
You can now buy lazy Susan-type recycling bins, but similar fixtures are fairly easy to build yourself. My de-

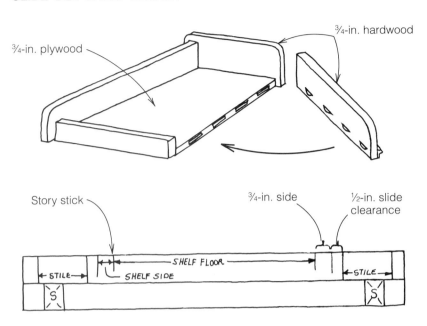

SLIDE-OUT SHELF DESIGN

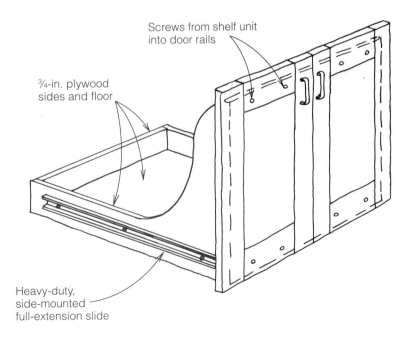

SINK-CABINET SLIDE-OUT SHELF UNIT

MULTI-BIN RECYCLING FIXTURE

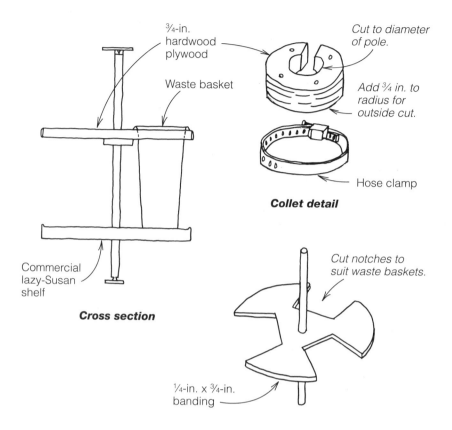

¾-in. hardwood plywood

Waste basket

Cut to diameter of pole.

Add ¾ in. to radius for outside cut.

Hose clamp

Collet detail

Commercial lazy-Susan shelf

Cross section

Cut notches to suit waste baskets.

¼-in. x ¾-in. banding

sign uses the pivots, pole and lower shelf from a standard, commercial lazy Susan. The only thing you'll need to make is the upper disc to support the plastic garbage pails.

Make this disc from ¾-in. hardwood plywood, cutting out notches to contain the bins. Be sure to purchase your bins ahead of time — choose different colors to help distinguish the recyclables — then lay out the cuts to fit. For a first-class job, add a wood banding to the circumference and notch cuts of the disc, making sure to account for their presence when laying out the notches. Secure the disc to the pole with the collet and hose clamp arrangement shown in the drawing above. Set the height of the disc so that most of the weight of the bins is supported by the lower shelf.

Door-hung mini-pantries

To make better use of every inch of pantry space, you can install shelves to the back of the doors. There are a number of drawbacks, however: To prevent items from falling off the shelves as the door opens and shuts, a stop must be installed across each shelf. In addition, the adjustable shelves must somehow be locked in place. And finally, the shelves must be kept narrow to reduce their capacity and thus discourage overloading (which would stress the doors).

In the design in the drawing on the facing page, I made the shelves just wide enough to hold typical canned goods (including quart-size canning jars). I also made the stops do double duty: they not only keep stored items in place, but also act to hold the

A door-hung 'mini-pantry' brings stored items within easy reach of the user. This design has fixed shelves, but you can also make the shelves adjustable, as shown in the drawing below. (Photo by Brian Vanden Brink)

PANTRY-DOOR SHELVING

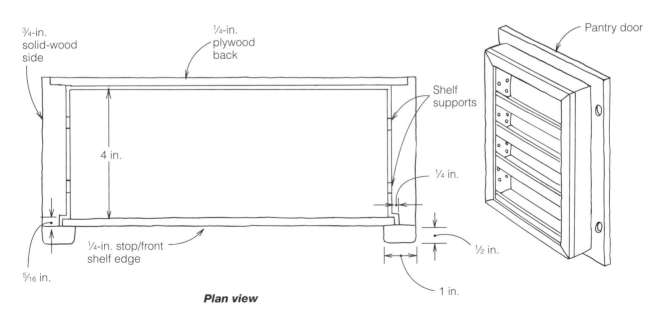

¾-in. solid-wood side

¼-in. plywood back

Shelf supports

Pantry door

4 in.

¼ in.

¼-in. stop/front shelf edge

⁵⁄₁₆ in.

½ in.

1 in.

Plan view

shelves in place. I made a ⁵⁄₁₆-in. wide by ½-in. deep rabbet along the edges to form a groove in which the shelf stop can slide. The shelves adjust on pins set into holes, or, alternatively, on clips installed to standards.

Plate racks

There is probably no storage item that speaks more strongly of the traditional country look than a plate rack. You can install the rack between any wall units, though hung over a sink the fixture becomes fully functional, allowing you to put your dishes away without bothering to wipe them dry.

At first glance my plate rack, complete with arched apron and filigree, may appear complicated and difficult to build (see the drawing on the facing page). In reality, it is not. The plate dividers are nothing more than dowels inserted through holes in the base rail and glued into matching holes in the ceiling. (Clamp these two pieces together and drill them at the same time on the drill press to ensure precise alignment. Be careful not to drill all the way through the ceiling piece.) Lay out the arched apron by marking the centerline height of the arch and the two end points. To draw the curve, bend a ¼-in. square strip of clear wood — make it about 12 in. longer than the arch — until it touches all three points. Attach the ends of the strip to extension boards (see the photo on the facing page) and draw a line along the edge of the strip. Cut to the curve with a bandsaw or jigsaw.

To create the filigree, first make a template of the cut-out shape in posterboard. Trace the filigree on the apron and then cut to the line using either a jigsaw, scrollsaw or coping saw. Drill a starting hole large enough to insert the blade and additional holes at sharp bends to help the blade make the turn. Clean up the cut with files and then round over the edge with a router fitted with an ⅛-in. roundover bit (I use CMT #838-190, see the Sources of Supply on pp. 194-196).

A wall-hung plate rack is a distinctive feature of traditional kitchens. (Photo by Kevin Ireton)

PLATE RACK

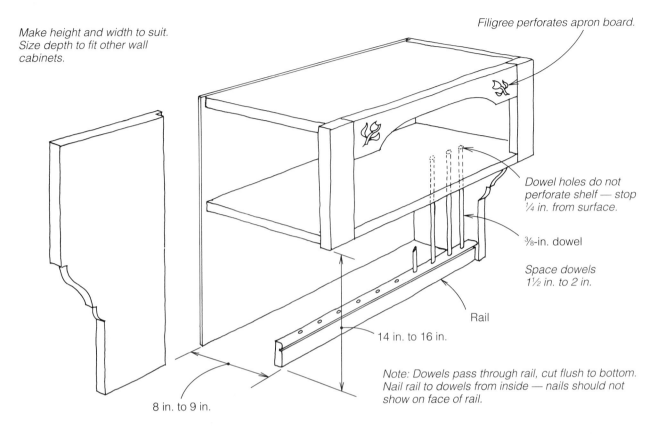

Make height and width to suit. Size depth to fit other wall cabinets.

Filigree perforates apron board.

Dowel holes do not perforate shelf — stop ¼ in. from surface.

⅜-in. dowel

Space dowels 1½ in. to 2 in.

Rail

14 in. to 16 in.

8 in. to 9 in.

Note: Dowels pass through rail, cut flush to bottom. Nail rail to dowels from inside — nails should not show on face of rail.

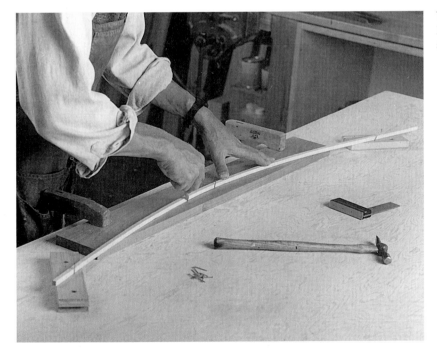

Use a square strip of clear stock to lay out the curve for an arched apron.

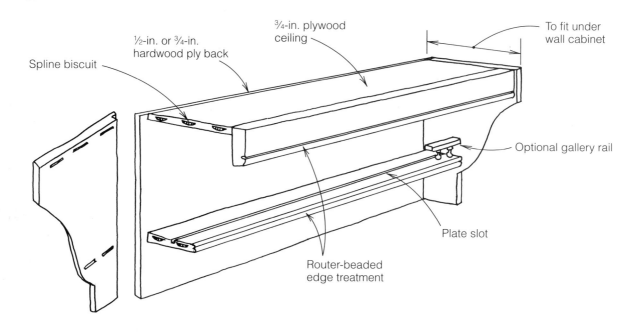

Spline biscuit

½-in. or ¾-in.
hardwood ply back

¾-in. plywood
ceiling

To fit under
wall cabinet

Optional gallery rail

Plate slot

Router-beaded
edge treatment

**An appliance garage with a
rollaway door can conceal
toasters, blenders and other
small countertop appliances.
(Photo by Bruce Greenlaw)**

Under-cabinet display racks

Like the plate rack shown on p. 163, the under-cabinet display rack may look a bit complicated, but it's really quite simple to build. Develop a pleasing shape for the side boards on a full-scale drawing, then trace the drawing onto the wood using a pounce wheel. The toothed disc of the tool perforates the paper, leaving a dotted line on the wood. (Alternatively, make the drawing on posterboard to create a cutting template.) To make the shaped sides identical, hold the boards together with double-stick tape and cut them out at the same time.

Using a table-mounted router, cut rabbets along the inside back edge of the side boards to receive the plywood back board. Also use the router fitted with a beading bit to make decorative profiles along the front edge of the plate shelf and the lower edge of the top rail. I like to biscuit-join the ceiling and shelf to the side boards. If I also use screws to join

the sides to these components, I countersink the screws and cover the heads with decorative buttons.

If you wish to add a gallery rail to the front edge of the shelf, you can purchase the parts from a building-supply center or through mail order. Install the rack by screwing through the back into the wall studs.

Appliance garages

To maintain a traditional and uncluttered look throughout the kitchen, you may wish to hide your modern chrome and plastic counter appliances. But to keep them readily accessible, you want to keep them on the countertop and plugged in. The answer to this dilemma is to provide the appliances with a garage, complete with a rollaway door (see the photo at left). Tambour works well for the door and goes with most traditional styles, though I would have reservations about using it in a strictly Colonial-era setting.

TAMBOUR-SLAT MILLING PROCEDURE

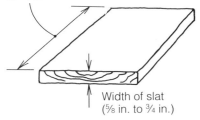

Length of
tambour + ½ in.

Width of slat
(⅝ in. to ¾ in.)

1. Thickness-plane stock to width of slats and joint edges.

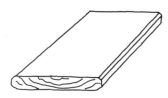

2. Shape edges.

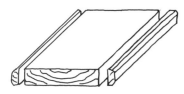

3. Rip off slats and repeat process.

1 in. to
1¼ in.

Note: Make starting slide wider to allow room for finger notch.

To make your own tambour, set the slats face down against squaring stops and glue a piece of light canvas to the back side.

You can buy ready-made tambour in a variety of woods, as well as the slide hardware. It's not difficult, however, to make your own (see the drawing at left). First, cut and shape the slats from a board following this sequence of steps: Surface both faces (the thickness of the stock will be the width of the slats) and joint both edges. Then round or chamfer the edges with a router bit. On the table saw, rip off the slats from each edge of the board — I make the tambour ¼ in. thick — and repeat the steps until the board is used up. Cut the slats about ½ in. overlength. I make the starting slat a bit wider than the others to allow me to work in a finger slot or attach a knob.

To create the tambour door, lay out the slats face down on a smooth flat surface using stops to hold the ends even and square to the first slat (see the photo above). Cut out a piece of light canvas (10 oz. or less) about 1 in. narrower than the finished length of the slats, and a bit longer

ROUTING TAMBOUR-GUIDE GROOVE

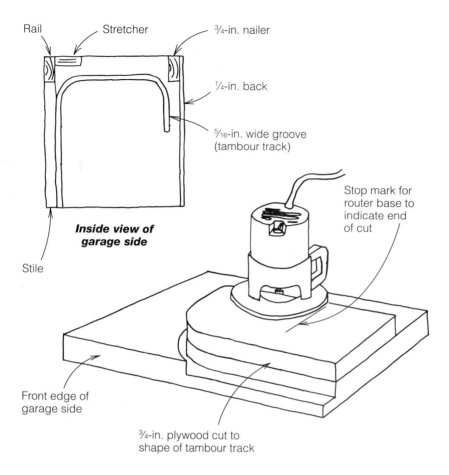

Rail

Stretcher

¾-in. nailer

¼-in. back

⁵⁄₁₆-in. wide groove
(tambour track)

**Inside view of
garage side**

Stile

Stop mark for
router base to
indicate end
of cut

Front edge of
garage side

¾-in. plywood cut to
shape of tambour track

than the total height of the tambour. Spread white glue on the back of the slats and on one side of the canvas. Apply the canvas carefully, centering it between the ends and smoothing out the wrinkles and air pockets as the material absorbs the glue. Don't move the assembly until the glue has thoroughly set. Then cut the tambour to its final width, using the crosscut jig on the table saw to ensure that you cut it square.

Make the track for the tambour by routing a groove along the inside face of the side boards (see the drawing above). First, make up a template in ¾-in. plywood to mimic the path

of the track. Temporarily screw it in place on the inside face of the garage side. Install a ⁵⁄₁₆-in. cutter with a top-bearing pilot (CMT #811-081B) into the router and make the cut, holding the bit tight to the template. Stop at the mark indicating the end of the cut. After fastening the sides of the garage to the top rail, stretcher and back, test the action of the tambour in the track. Sand the back of the slats if necessary to reduce their width and ease binding. A coating of wax from a candle stub helps the tambour run smoothly.

Mobile work islands

Creating a work island that stores out of the way under the existing counter area is an excellent way to add work space to a small kitchen. You can design your mobile island to serve a variety of functions. The two designs shown in the drawing on the facing page represent a mini-baking center and a food-preparation area. For the former, I've specified marble for the countertop (the best material on which to roll out dough), slide-out shelves for bowls and a swing-up shelf for the electric mixer. The second island, featuring a butcher-block counter, knife drawer and slide-out waste or compost bin, is ideal for chopping up vegetables and meats.

Build the island following essentially the same construction techniques for building standard base units. Instead of installing a ¼-in. back panel, however, I recommend using ¾-in. plywood, which gives the island needed stability. In the drawing, note how a false door (and optional drawer front) serve to hide the island when it's stored away. Finally, for smooth handling in motion and security in use, install full-swivel, locking casters (available from The Woodworkers' Store, #67165).

MOBILE WORK ISLANDS

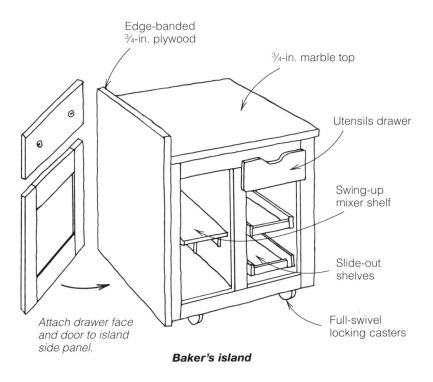

Edge-banded ¾-in. plywood

¾-in. marble top

Utensils drawer

Swing-up mixer shelf

Slide-out shelves

Full-swivel locking casters

Attach drawer face and door to island side panel.

Baker's island

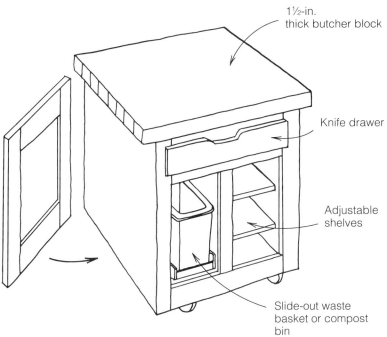

1½-in. thick butcher block

Knife drawer

Adjustable shelves

Slide-out waste basket or compost bin

Food-prep island

This mobile work island features slide-out shelves and a sliding two-tier cutlery tray.

12

CABINET INSTALLATION

With the cases assembled and finished and doors and drawers built and installed, the time has come to install the cabinets in your kitchen. Unless you are fortunate enough to be building the cabinets in an attached garage, however, you must first deal with getting them safely to the site. As you'll see below, there are certain techniques you can use to prepare and load the cabinetry that will help minimize "road rash."

Once on site, installation of the cabinet modules should go quickly and smoothly if you first establish level reference lines around the perimeter of the kitchen. With the cabinets fixed in place, you'll install the applied end panels, fit the running moldings, and then reinstall and adjust fixtures, shelves, doors and drawers.

TRANSPORTING THE CABINETS

Begin the preparation of the cabinets for shipping by removing any loose components: primarily adjustable shelves and loosely fitting sliding or revolving fixtures (most lazy Susans can be safely left in place). If you feel it necessary to reduce the weight of the cabinets, remove the drawers and doors and transport them separately. In either case, consider removing the pull hardware. If left in place, drawer and door pulls are likely to inflict damage as well as suffer it themselves.

Wrap the faces of the cabinets with sheets of cardboard (you can find large pieces at your local appliance or bicycle store), securing them in place with staples to the cabinet

backs. Be careful to staple only to the outside edges, avoiding the thin plywood back panel. Besides protecting the wood, the cardboard keeps the doors and drawers tightly shut. Because the back will never be seen, you needn't bother protecting this face.

Loading techniques

Living in the Pacific Northwest, I'd never consider delivering cabinets in an open pickup truck or trailer — it's a sure way to make it rain (and this climate needs little coaxing). That's unfortunate because an open vehicle is much easier to load and allows you to stack the cabinets much higher than is possible in most closed vehicles.

Whether loading in an open or closed space, follow these basic procedures: Load the biggest and heaviest cabinets first, then place blanket-wrapped smaller cabinets, shelving, applied end panels and fixtures inside them. As you continue to load, juggle with the orientation of the cabinets to produce the snuggest fit possible — in my experience, most damage results from cabinets shifting during the ride.

As you stack a second layer of cabinets over the first, screw them together wherever possible. I turn the second-layer cabinets upside-down and screw the stretchers together. Tie down the cabinets securely to the trailer or truck side walls. Final-ly, gather the running moldings together into taped bundles, orienting the profiled faces inward.

SITE PREPARATION

In Chapter 4, I showed you how to record site measurements and develop case dimensions with a set of story poles (see pp. 49-55). Use the vertical pole from this set to create the reference lines to which you can set the base and wall units. At 4-ft. to 6-ft. intervals around the perimeter of the kitchen, mark the height of the top of the base sides and the lower edge of the wall-unit sides as shown on the story pole. Be careful to keep

To prepare the cabinets for shipping, wrap the faces and sides with sheets of cardboard.

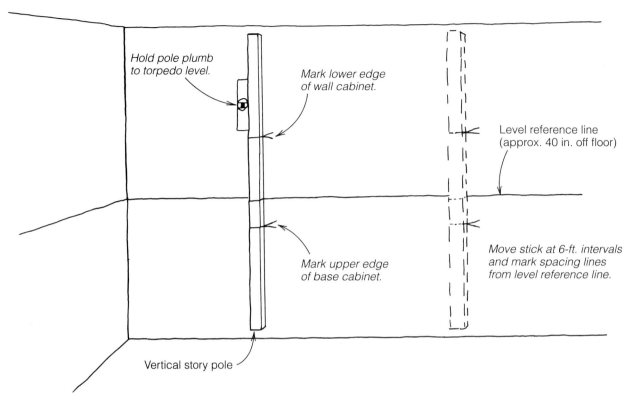

Hold pole plumb
to torpedo level.

Mark lower edge
of wall cabinet.

Level reference line
(approx. 40 in. off floor)

Mark upper edge
of base cabinet.

Move stick at 6-ft. intervals
and mark spacing lines
from level reference line.

Vertical story pole

the pole plumb (I tape a torpedo level to one edge) and aligned to the 40-in. height level reference line. Join the marks with a straightedge and you have your setting lines.

Unless you intend to use adjustable leg levelers, the next task is to build the support frame for the base units. Working with kiln-dried 2x4s (be finicky about using only straight stock), cut and assemble the frame to the design dimensions. Screw the sections together, being sure to keep their top edges flush, and then set the assemblies in place on the floor. Screw the frame to the high point of the floor and then work out from there, leveling the frame with dry cedar or pine shims (see the top photo on the facing page). Take diagonal measurements to ensure that the frames sit square before securing them permanently to the floor. Trim

the shims flush. Now cut 3½-in. strips of ¼-in. hardwood plywood and apply them to the exposed faces of the base frame (see the bottom photo on the facing page). Miter the outside corners and use glue and ¾-in. brads to secure the strips in place. Don't worry about any gaps between the veneer and the floor, since they will be covered later by shoe molding.

Although you considered site access during the early layout stages of the cabinets (see p. 27), it wouldn't hurt to make a final check before bringing in the cabinets. If necessary, take passage doors off their hinges, move furniture out of the way and roll back carpeting (or cover it with cardboard). Don't attempt to move the larger units without either a helper or a swivel-wheel dolly.

Screw the base frame to the floor, using shims where necessary to keep the frame level.

INSTALLING THE BASE UNITS

Begin the installation with a corner unit. Set the cabinet in place on the frame (or install the leg levelers into their sockets) and check that the top edge is even to the reference line. Make fine adjustments to base-frame-supported units by backing off the floor-attachment screws and adjusting the leveling shims; leg levelers require only turning the leg into or out of its socket.

If the face frame butts to a wall, you must scribe the stile's overhanging "ear" to the wall surface. With the cabinet set in place and leveled, the

Apply strips of ¼-in. plywood veneer to the exposed faces of the base frame.

untrimmed ear will hold the cabinet slightly away from its final position. To establish this position, first set the compass scribe to the distance between the end of the cabinet and its layout mark on the back wall (see the drawing below). Now, holding the compass level, draw a line mimicking the wall surface down along the face of the face-frame stile; be sure to keep the compass leg tight to the wall surface and level with the pencil point. If you allow the compass to deviate from level, the line will not accurately represent the wall surface. Cut to the line with a jigsaw, and then plane in a slight underbevel. Press the edge into the wall surface. The end of the cabinet should now sit precisely to the layout mark.

Don't yet secure the corner unit to the wall or base, however. Instead, continue to set the other base units to one or both sides of the corner unit, adjusting their heights to the level line and their face frames flush to one another. Clamp across the frames, drawing them tight and flush before running in the connecting screws (see the top photo on the facing page). If you've designed pilaster moldings to go between the units, screw these in place as you go along. If you have face frames designed to bridge over two or more units, install these now too.

After setting a run of base cabinets, hold a long straightedge across their faces and shift their alignment true to the tool. Then secure them to the base frame with 1⅝-in. drywall

SCRIBING FACE-FRAME EAR TO UNEVEN WALL SURFACE

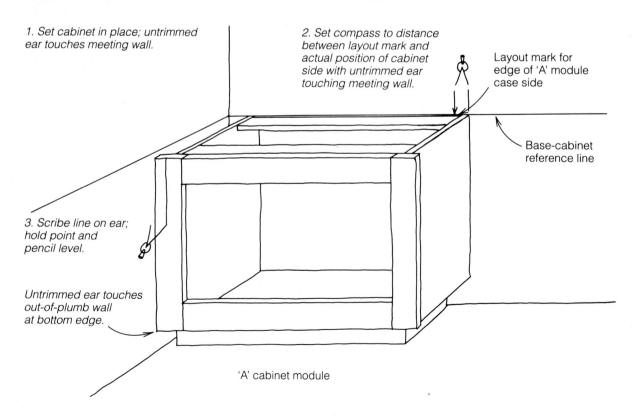

1. Set cabinet in place; untrimmed ear touches meeting wall.

2. Set compass to distance between layout mark and actual position of cabinet side with untrimmed ear touching meeting wall.

Layout mark for edge of 'A' module case side

Base-cabinet reference line

3. Scribe line on ear; hold point and pencil level.

Untrimmed ear touches out-of-plumb wall at bottom edge.

'A' cabinet module

screws driven through the cabinet floor. Either countersink and plug the screws, or leave the heads on the surface and cap them with plastic press-on covers. Also fix the cabinets to the wall studs with 2½-in. or 3-in. drywall screws run at an angle through the back stretcher, as shown in the photo below. Use shims to fill any gaps between the cabinet backs and wall surface at these attachment points.

If you're installing a peninsula or island unit on adjustable leg levelers, it's a good idea to screw blocks made up from pairs of 2x4s to the floor under the cabinet. Then you can screw or bolt the cabinets to these blocks to ensure a wobble-free installation. Use shims to fill in the gap between the blocks and the leveled cabinet floor.

To connect adjacent cabinets, clamp them flush together across the face frames and run in screws from the side.

Use long drywall screws through the back stretcher into the wall studs to secure a base cabinet to the wall.

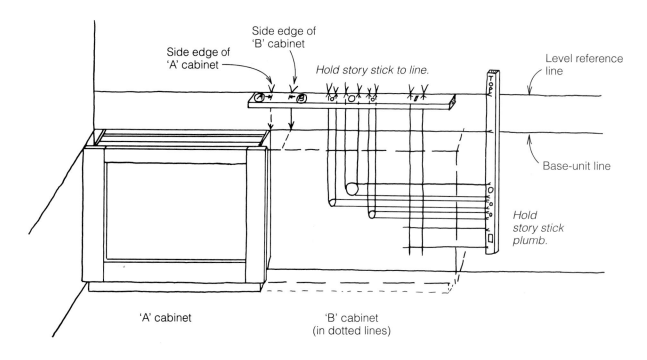

Side edge of 'A' cabinet

Side edge of 'B' cabinet

Hold story stick to line.

Level reference line

Base-unit line

Hold story stick plumb.

'A' cabinet

'B' cabinet (in dotted lines)

Laying out cutlines for utilities

If a base cabinet must be fit over plumbing or electrical outlets, mark the cutouts on the back panel, using mini-story sticks for speed and accuracy (see the drawing above). The horizontal positions of the utilities should already have been brought up to the level reference line (see pp. 49-51). Hold the horizontal story stick to the reference line and transfer these positions to the stick. Also mark the predicted position of the cabinet case side, taking into account the overhang of the face frames.

To locate the vertical cutlines, extend level lines over to one side from the utilities. Now hold the vertical stick plumb, mark where it crosses the base-unit reference line, and then mark the position of the level lines on the side of the stick. Be sure

to keep the stick plumb and the reference line on the mark.

Now transfer the cutline positions to the back of the cabinet. For the horizontal positions, hold the stick along the top edge of the cabinet, aligning the case side mark to the actual case side (as shown in the top drawing on the facing page). Transfer the position marks along the top edge of the cabinet and then extend them down square to the top. For the vertical positions, transfer the vertical cutline marks to the side edge of the cabinet, aligning the mark indicating the base reference line with the cabinet's top edge (see the bottom drawing on the facing page). Again, bring the marks over with a square. The outlines of the cutouts are created where these lines intersect the lines brought down from the top edge.

TRANSFERRING LAYOUT TO BACK OF CABINET

Hold stick on cabinet to mark indicating side edge.

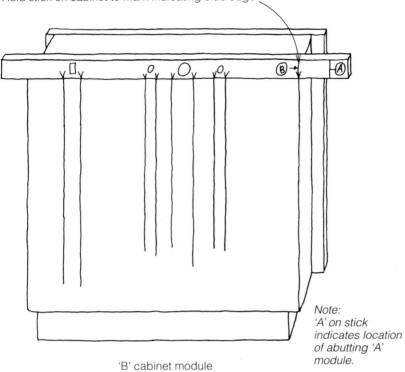

'B' cabinet module

*Note:
'A' on stick
indicates location
of abutting 'A'
module.*

Hold stick to side of cabinet at base-level mark.

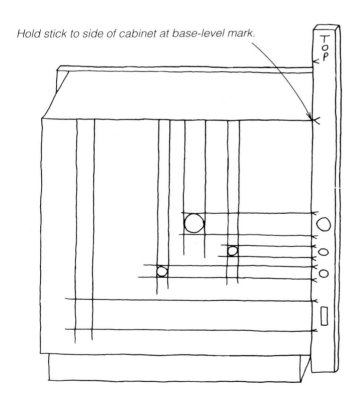

INSTALLING THE WALL UNITS

As you might have guessed, installing wall units is a bit trickier than laying down base units. Here, gravity works against you rather than with you. But with the help of a few car jacks (or a commercial cabinet lift if you prefer — see the Sources of Supply on pp. 194-196 for a source) and some clever prep work, it's not all that difficult.

Begin installation with a corner cabinet. If the face frame butts to a wall, remove the doors and temporarily set the cabinet in place (using the jacks to hold it in position). Scribe the ear as described on pp. 171-172. Take the cabinet back down, cut the scribe line and then, working on a flat section of floor, attach the next cabinet. Be careful to flush the ad-

joining face frames before running in the screws. Attach the other cabinets of this run while they sit level and flush-faced on the floor. (If the run is more than 6 ft., you may have to break it up into sub-runs to reduce the weight.)

Using story poles, lay out and then cut out any utility openings as described above. Also, find the stud locations and lay out and predrill shank holes through the nailer for the attachment screws. To simplify the process, I work on the outside of the cabinet, marking and producing the cutouts and pilot holes from the back of the cabinet.

Now set up a temporary counter surface — a scrap of ¾-in. plywood works well — on which to set the jacks at 4-ft. to 6-ft. intervals. (I prefer to use scissor-type jacks as they

With a pair of jacks set on a temporary plywood counter, crank up the cabinet until the bottom edge reaches the wall-cabinet reference line.

seem to fine-tune more readily than hydraulic jacks.) Crank up the jacks so you'll only need to raise the units up about another 2 in. I sit the jacks on some conveniently sized drawer boxes to help them gain the needed height. (I protect the boxes below with cardboard and above with a scrap of plywood.) With a helper, lift the assembled run of wall units onto the jacks. Work the jacks until the run sits level to the reference line (see the photo on the facing page). If the face of the wall unit goes out of plumb as you lay the cabinet back flat to the wall, insert shims where necessary to make the correction (see the photo below). Note that the end walls will be covered with applied panels, and the shims won't show here.

Fix the units to the wall by running in 2½-in. to 3-in. #10 screws through the predrilled shank holes in the nailer; be sure you are hitting the wall studs. Drill thread pilot holes in the studs to prevent stripping the heads. If you are working with a sub-run, don't screw the cabinet tight to the wall. Allow some play so you can align the face of the next cabinet run.

Installing peninsula or island overhead cabinets

Because a run of peninsula or island overhead cabinets has little, if any, wall to fasten to, installation is a bit more difficult. First, you must be sure there's sufficient blocking in the soffit or ceiling joists; you may have to install cross blocking if the joists run parallel to the length of the cabinets. Second, you may need to install blocking to the cabinets' top surface to hold the cabinets a predetermined distance away from the ceiling or soffit. And third, you must

If necessary, shim the face of the wall cabinet plumb.

INSTALLING ISLAND/PENINSULA UPPER-CABINET UNITS

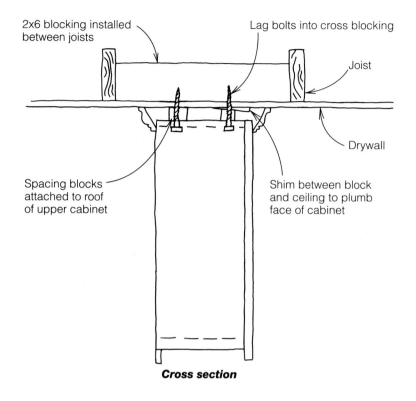

2x6 blocking installed between joists

Lag bolts into cross blocking

Joist

Drywall

Spacing blocks attached to roof of upper cabinet

Shim between block and ceiling to plumb face of cabinet

Cross section

predrill shank holes for the lag bolts or through bolts that will hold the cabinets in place.

To do the installation, set up the jacking stations and lift the cabinet(s) into place. While your helpers stabilize the unit, raise the jacks until the blocking comes snug to the ceiling. If all goes well, the cabinet will sit level lengthwise and crosswise. If not, back off the appropriate jack and insert shims between the block and ceiling. Resnug the jacks, check the levels and then drill pilot holes and run in the bolts.

INSTALLING END PANELS

The use of applied end panels or boards is one of the features of this style of cabinet construction that I really appreciate. After the cabinets

are installed, it's a simple matter to cover any gaps or shims showing between the back of a cabinet and the wall. The exposed edge of the cabinet's back panel and any case fasteners are covered as well.

To install an applied panel, follow this sequence of steps: Using either a tape measure or a story stick, measure the distance along the top edge of the cabinet between the front of the cabinet and the wall. (Distance A in the drawing on the facing page.) Transfer this measurement to the top edge of the applied panel (the panel should have been cut at least ½ in. over width). In a similar fashion, transfer the bottom spacing (Distance B in the drawing) to the bottom edge of the panel.

Set a scribing compass to about 2 in. and then hold the panel against the side of the cabinet. Keep the panel's top and bottom edges even with the cabinet edges as you slide the panel until the compass's pencil point touches the A mark; the leg of the scribe must be level with the pencil and touching the wall. Check the compass at the B mark; the pencil should touch the mark with the leg against the wall. If not, double-check your A and B marks for accuracy.

When you're satisfied with the alignment, run the compass along the wall, allowing the pencil to mimic the shape of the wall on the panel. (Note: If the panel is dark wood, apply a strip of masking tape on which to draw the line.) Be careful to keep the compass legs level with each other as you draw the line; otherwise the line will not be true.

Using a jigsaw, cut ¹⁄₁₆ in. away from the line and test the fit. Plane and file the cutline until you attain a perfect fit (you needn't fuss with it if you intend to cover the joint with a piece

SCRIBING AN APPLIED PANEL

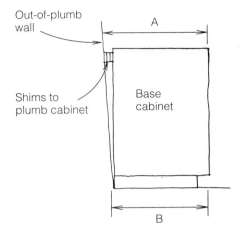

Out-of-plumb wall

Shims to plumb cabinet

Base cabinet

A

B

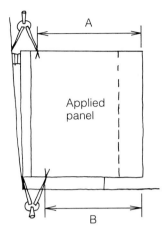

Applied panel

A

B

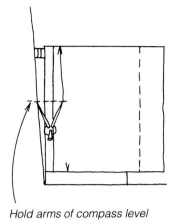

Hold arms of compass level

1. Measure distance A and distance B.

2. Mark A and B distances along top and bottom edges of applied panel. Open compass to arbitrary setting of approx. 2 in. Lock and hold panel so pencil touches A and B marks.

3. Draw scribe line mimicking wall from point A to point B.

Use a compass to scribe the cutline along the back edge of an end panel.

of molding). Then remove the panel, apply beads of panel adhesive to the side of the cabinet, and press the panel in place. Use clamps or finish nails to hold the panel in position.

To install tongue-and-groove boards, follow this sequence: Install the first board either flush to the face frame or tucked behind an overhanging frame; plane the edge if necessary to tune the fit. Use panel adhesive and brads to hold it in place. Continue to install boards, applying panel adhesive and tacking through the tongues so the nail holes won't show. To cut the closing board to fit between the last installed board and the wall, fol-

low the same procedure described above for scribing a panel to fit. Because the board must be "rolled" into place, you will need to undercut the scribed fitting line.

INSTALLING RUNNING MOLDINGS

Depending on the style of your cabinetry, you may have to run one or more of the following cabinet-bridging moldings: cornice moldings to tie the wall cabinets to the ceiling; corner moldings to cover the junctures of end panels and face frames with the wall; pilaster moldings to cover the joints between face frames or between face frames and end panels; a valance to hide under-cabinet lighting; a kickboard and a shoe molding to tie the kick to the floor; and perhaps an undercounter cove molding. You may also need to install a valance between two cabinets to surround a window, lighting or ventilation fixture.

Outside corners

Join the outside corners of profiled moldings with miter joints. Unless the corner isn't square, the cuts will both be 45°. To join an out-of-square corner, find the bisecting angle as shown in the drawing at left. Mark the location of the cut by holding a length of molding stock in place and marking an edge where it runs by the corner (see the photo on the facing page). Lightly mark the direction of the angle cut on the waste side of the cut to remind you which direction to set the miter saw. Before cutting and installing this piece, first mark the adjoining piece where it runs by the corner. Use a sharp block plane to fine-tune the fit of the joint.

Inside corners

You should not attempt to join inside corners with a miter joint, since any

FINDING A BISECTING ANGLE

1. Hold Stick I against face and mark intersection with corner.

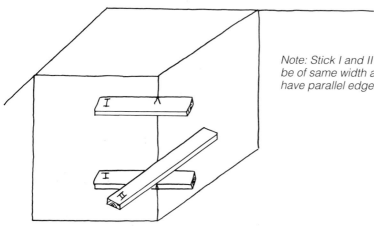

Note: Stick I and II must be of same width and have parallel edges.

2. Hold Stick II against other face and over Stick I. Mark where outside edges of sticks intersect.

3. Connect marks to find bisecting angle (setting of miter angle on chopsaw/miter box)

shrinkage or shifting of the cabinets may result in an unsightly, open joint. Instead, make a coped joint by following the sequence of steps shown in the drawing below. Install the first piece of molding into the corner, simply butting the end into the meeting wall. Back-cut the end of the adjoining molding at 45° to create the cutline for the coped joint – the line where the cut emerges on the face of the stock. Using a coping saw, cut the molding to this line, undercutting to create a sharp edge. Test the fit against the installed molding and fine-tune with a file or chisel.

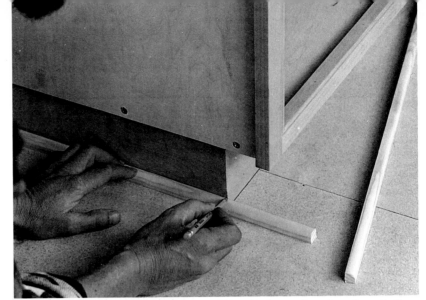

Hold the molding in place (shoe molding is shown here) and mark the location of the corner miter cut.

CUTTING A COPED JOINT

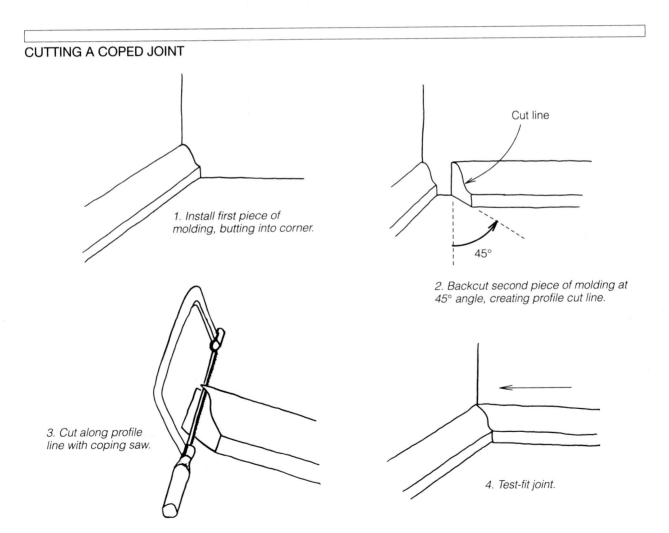

1. Install first piece of molding, butting into corner.

Cut line

45°

2. Backcut second piece of molding at 45° angle, creating profile cut line.

3. Cut along profile line with coping saw.

4. Test-fit joint.

Joining cornice moldings

Because cornice moldings sit at an angle between the face of the cabinets and the ceiling (called the "spring angle"), the corner joints must be cut at a compound angle. If you cut the moldings sitting at this same angle in the chopsaw or miter box, however, you do not have to deal with the bevel angle. Instead, you need only set the saw at the miter angle: 45° for square outside corners (or at the bisecting angle for non-square corners) and again at 45° to back-cut for coping. I build a simple jig with a stop to hold the cornice molding at the correct spring angle (see the drawing below). I set the molding on the jig upside-down for cutting — the back of the jig represents the wall surface, while the base represents the ceiling.

Installing kickboards and shoe molding

If you are using adjustable leg levelers, make the kickboards from ¾-in. hardwood plywood. Run a saw kerf about ¼ in. deep along the length of the back to accept the press-in clips that serve to attach the board to the leg shafts. To retain the advantage of removable kickboards, don't join the corners permanently. Instead, simply butt the boards together. I miter-return the exposed ends of the kickboards to eliminate the unsightly plywood edge. After locating and pressing in the clips, install the boards and slide them tight to one another at the butt joints and down to the floor. A wavy floor surface may require you to scribe the bottom edge to fit.

To create a good-looking toe kick with the 2x4 base-frame system, I

JIG FOR CUTTING CORNICE MOLDING

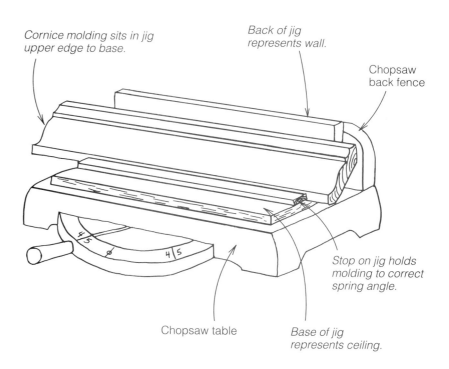

Cornice molding sits in jig upper edge to base.

Back of jig represents wall.

Chopsaw back fence

Stop on jig holds molding to correct spring angle.

Chopsaw table

Base of jig represents ceiling.

To install the kickboards, press the clips over the adjustable leg levelers. Note the spline biscuit, which helps keep the corner in alignment.

apply a shoe molding where it joins the floor (see the photo on p. 181). In general, I use a ³⁄₄-in. quarter-round molding. To keep water from seeping under the shoe and causing rot, I set the molding into a bedding of caulking adhesive. If you intend to lay a new floor surface in the kitchen, wait until you've done so before installing the shoe.

INSTALLING FIXTURES AND MAKING FINAL ADJUSTMENTS

At this point, the installation of your kitchen cabinetry is almost complete. All that remains is to reinstall any fixtures that were removed for shipping, set in the adjustable shelf clips and shelving, and reinstall the pull or knob hardware. Also install bumpers at the inner corners of the doors and drawers if you have not already done so.

Check to see how the doors and drawers sit in their closed positions. They should hang plumb and level. Where door pairs meet, they should show a uniform gap of about ⅛ in. or less. If the drawer faces and doors inset with a rabbet, there should be no binding against the face frame. Both the doors and drawers should open and close with no binding, and self-closing hardware should work smoothly and positively. Refer to Chapter 11 for details on how to make any necessary corrections.

13

BUILDING AND INSTALLING LAMINATE COUNTERS

While there are admittedly more traditional options from which to make kitchen counters (solid wood or stone in particular), I generally use plastic laminate for the majority of my countertops. If I'm careful in choosing the colors and textures, I find that this material can blend well into almost any period setting. And you just can't beat the price and relative ease of installation compared to working with the traditional materials.

In this final chapter, then, I show you how I make and install laminate counters with a solid-wood backsplash and facing edge. You can, of course, buy prelaminated counters with a molded backsplash and edge: They offer high performance (there

are no seams that might open up) and are relatively easy to install (assuming the supplier cuts the joints for you). I don't use prelaminated counters very often, however, since they rarely work well aesthetically with many of the traditionally styled kitchens that I build.

The process that I use to prepare and apply laminate to the substrate takes much of the anxiety out of using this notoriously unforgiving material. Instead of attempting to fit and install the laminate to a pre-installed counter, I first cut the substrate to size, joining runs where necessary and installing stretchers and cleats. Then I fit and attach the wood edging. I can then apply the laminate by overlapping it over the edges and ends of the substrate. The only criti-

cal fitting occurs where I have to butt the sheets of laminate to one another. Finally, I trim the laminate with a router and install the counter in one piece, covering the joint at the wall(s) with a wood backsplash.

PREPARATION

Setting the countertops can be a risky business for the cabinets. All it takes is a careless movement with a tool (or your tool belt) to ding a drawer or door face. If you have cardboard sheeting available, tape it over the front of the cabinets. Don't use masking tape since it can lift the finish if you leave it on for more than an hour or so. Instead, use clear packing tape. As another option, remove the doors and drawers that may be in harm's way.

Next, check the cabinet installation for adequate counter support. Where a corner cabinet doesn't extend all the way to the meeting wall, or across open spans in the dishwasher or trash-compactor areas, install ¾-in. by 2½-in. cleats to the wall. Align the supports to the base-unit reference line.

Choosing materials

Once you've decided on a laminate countertop, the hard part is choosing the color — the selection is almost limitless. Then you must choose from a wide variety of textures (and patterns if you are not satisfied with a solid color). If you'll need to make a number of butt joints, consider matte textures and rectilinear patterns, which tend to hide joints better than glossy, solid colors.

You also have a choice of substrate material. I use either ¾-in. A-C fir plywood or ¾-in. high-density ("industrial grade") particleboard. While the latter offers a smoother and denser surface than that of plywood, it is much heavier — a large counter of this stuff can be a struggle to install. Particleboard also has the potential to absorb moisture and expand. When I use particleboard, I always seal untrimmed edges (especially around the sink cutout) with glue or a caulking compound.

To determine how much substrate and laminate you'll need, first plan where you'll join the sheets of laminate along the counter. Of course, it's best if you can avoid butt joints entirely. The availability of sheets up to 5 ft. by 12 ft. makes it possible to cover large areas without having to join sheets, though their use might prove very wasteful unless you can use the offcut somewhere else.

I usually let joints fall in logical places. In the case of our sample L-

A laminate counter surface with a solid-wood backsplash and facing edge makes an appropriate countertop for most styles of kitchen.

shaped kitchen, this would be at the juncture of the two perpendicular counters. Although a miter joint would work here, it is a more difficult joint to make and it tends to open up more than a butt joint if any shrinkage or expansion of the laminate should take place (which is, unfortunately, a possibility). Sometimes I'll make the joint at the location of the sink or cooktop — with the sink or appliance installed there is very little of the joint left showing. A drawback, however, is the potential for water or grease to get into the joint. Their intrusion is not only unsightly but may also eventually cause delamination. Whatever their location, I plan the laminate joints to fall at least 6 in. or more from the substrate joints.

In the drawing below, I have laid out both the substrate and the laminate for a typical L-shaped kitchen. The cutlist shows the rough sizes of the pieces (note that I've listed the laminate at least ½ in. oversize all around to allow for trimming). A graphic cutting chart shows how I will lay out the cuts on the material. The substrate panels are either 49 in. by 97 in. (for particleboard) or 48 in. by 96 in.

(for plywood). The laminate is available in 26-in., 30-in., 48-in. and 60-in. wide sheets up to 12 ft. long.

Use contact cement to affix the laminate to the substrate. I've had good results recently with 3M's waterborne "Fastbond." It's non-explosive and outgasses much lower amounts of toxic organic volatile than solvent-based glues (to be safe, however, you should still wear a carbon-filtered respirator and provide adequate ventilation). The trick with this stuff

LAYOUT OF LAMINATE AND SUBSTRATE

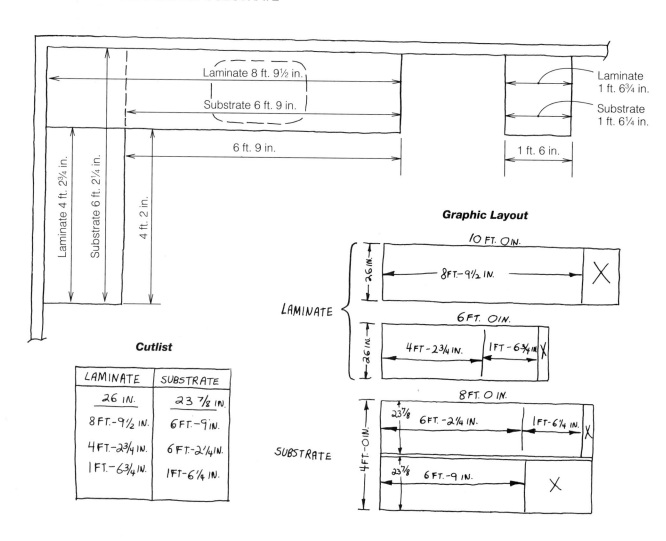

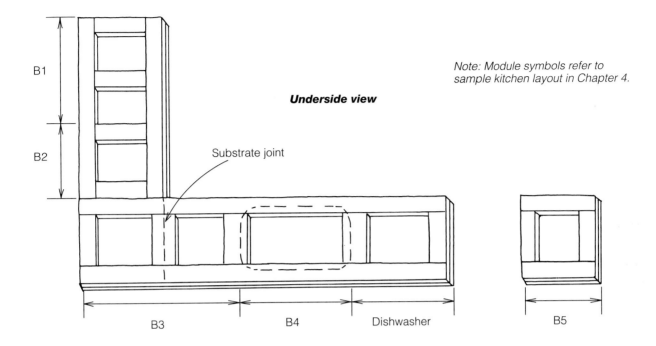

Note: Module symbols refer to sample kitchen layout in Chapter 4.

Underside view

Substrate joint

B1

B2

B3

B4

Dishwasher

B5

is to be sure your stock is fresh (the shelf life is a maximum of six months), never frozen, and to allow the adhesive to dry completely before you join the two surfaces.

If you should choose a solvent-based glue, opt for the non-explosive solvent formula. Be sure the filters are new in your respirator and give yourself plenty of ventilation. With any contact cement, plan to use at least two coats on both surfaces; 1 gal. is about the right amount to purchase for our sample L-shaped kitchen.

CUTTING AND JOINING THE SUBSTRATE

Begin by ripping out full-length runs from the sheet stock. Then, using either a crosscut box on the table saw or a saw guide clamped square across the panel (see pp. 60-61), cut the runs to length. In general, the substrate should overhang cabinet ends by $\frac{1}{4}$ in. and be flush with the face-frame stiles where they abut appliances. Because the edge meeting the wall will be covered by a $\frac{3}{4}$-in. thick wood splashboard, it's rarely necessary to allow extra width or length in the substrate for scribing.

Set the runs of substrate on the counters to make sure they fit (trim if necessary). Remove the runs and arrange them upside-down in a mirror image of the counter on a flat work surface. Mark the rough outlines of the sink, cooktop and any other cutouts. Now install 4-in. wide stretcher strips of $\frac{3}{4}$-in. plywood, as shown in the drawing above. Note that the short crosspieces should occur about every 2 ft., as well as across the substrate joint and the perimeter of the cutouts. Attach the plywood strips with glue and $1\frac{1}{4}$-in. self-tapping drywall screws.

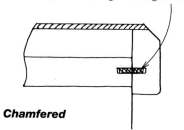

Optional spline biscuit
(for fastening and alignment)

Chamfered

1¼ in.

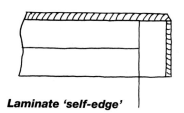

Cove with bed molding

Bed
molding

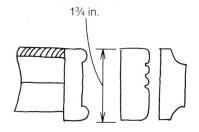

Laminate 'self-edge'

1¾ in.

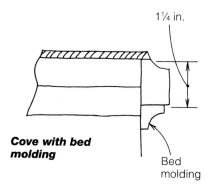

*These moldings are applied
after counter is laminated.*

Cutting out the sink and cooktop holes

Although cutting the hole for the sink or cooktop prior to installation makes the counter a bit more delicate to handle, I find that it's much easier to make the cut now with the counter off the cabinets. The tools are easier to manipulate, and there is no chance of damaging the underlying cabinets. Make the cut by turning the counter substrate right side up and then carefully measuring and laying out the cutout lines for the appliance (some units may include a cutting template). Drill a starting hole in one corner and then follow the cutline with a jigsaw. Make sure to remove any screws from the plywood strips that might come in contact with the saw.

Attaching the edge facing

The drawing at left shows a variety of options for trimming out the facing edge of the counter. The top three edging strips are applied before the laminate and then profiled with a router after the laminate is in place. The bottom three are preprofiled and then applied to the edge of the laminated substrate.

To ensure a tight fit where the edging strips meet a wall, temporarily install the counter in position. Run a few screws up through the stretchers to keep it from shifting. Now cut the edgings to fit. Cut outside and inside miter joints (cope joints are optional in this application) and attach the moldings by running a bead of wood glue or panel adhesive along the edge of the substrate and front stretcher and then nailing the strip in place. If you wish to avoid nail holes, use screws and fill the countersunk holes with plugs cut from a scrap of the edge stripping. As an aid to maintaining alignment, I sometimes add spline biscuits.

CUTTING AND APPLYING THE LAMINATE

Cut the laminate to rough length and at least ½ in. oversize in width. For a fast, clean cut, I use a router fitted with a top-bearing pattern bit (CMT 811-159B) and run it along a straight-edge clamped across the sheet of laminate, as shown in the photo on the facing page. I make two passes to remove any burrs or slight wavers in the cutline. When using this method, set the sheet down across a number of ¾-in. strips to give clearance for the router bit.

Where two runs of laminate butt together, you must make the adjoining cuts absolutely uniform. To do this with a minimum of fuss, overlap the ends of the runs to be joined about 1 in., clamping them together under a guide edge (see the drawing on the facing page). Then rout the cut with the top-bearing bit. Even if the guide edge is not perfectly straight or the bit wanders slightly, the joint will not be thrown off. This method ensures that the cut edges closely mimic each other.

Test the fit by pushing the two sheets together on a flat surface. A light pass with a sharp block plane or file is usually enough to attain a perfect fit. Be careful not to under-bevel the cut, creating a sharp top edge that may chip when you force the sheets together.

Applying the glue

To preparing for gluing, first undo the screws that are temporarily holding the substrate to the cabinets and move the counter back from the walls 3 in. to 4 in. (If you wish — and help is handy — remove the counter entirely and set it across some sawhorses.) Now thoroughly sweep away any grit or sawdust and spread

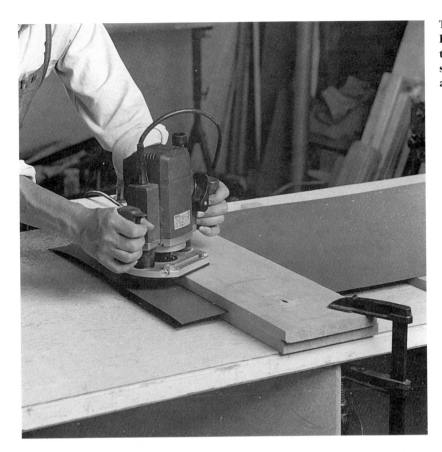

To cut the laminate to rough length, run a router fitted with a top-bearing pattern bit against a straight-edged guide clamped across the sheet.

CUTTING A LAMINATE BUTT JOINT

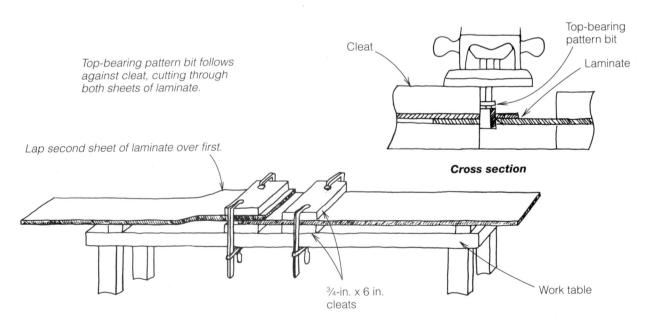

Top-bearing pattern bit follows against cleat, cutting through both sheets of laminate.

Cleat

Top-bearing pattern bit

Laminate

Cross section

Lap second sheet of laminate over first.

¾-in. x 6 in. cleats

Work table

the contact adhesive onto both surfaces — the underside of the laminate and the top of the substrate. Either use a good-quality short-nap paint roller (the cheap ones tend to fall apart with solvent-based glues) or pour the glue on the surface and spread it out with a grooved trowel.

Aim for an even film, being sure to wipe away quickly the high buildups at overlaps. When the first coat has dried to the point where a piece of brown paper bag ("kraft" paper) doesn't stick, apply a second coat. The goal is an even, slightly glossy film. Apply more where the glue dries to a dull finish. Keep the shop temperature above 65°F and the humidity below 80% to encourage drying. When the last coat passes the kraft-paper test, you're ready to lay down the laminate.

Laying down the laminate

You get only one shot to get the laminate right, because contact cement adheres instantly and powerfully the moment the two surfaces touch. To allow you to shift the laminate into position, lay ⅜-in. or ½-in. dowels (slats from old venetian blinds also work well) every 6 in. to 8 in. across the counter, then lay the laminate across them. Spread the sheets over the sink and cooktop cutouts. When you are satisfied that the sheet is overhanging all around, begin removing the dowels. Start with the middle dowel, sliding it out and then pressing the laminate to the substrate (see the photo at left below). Now work your way out, first to one side and then the other. Smooth the sheet down toward the ends to avoid trapping air pockets.

Position the laminate across a series of dowels, then remove the middle dowel and press the laminate down in the center area.

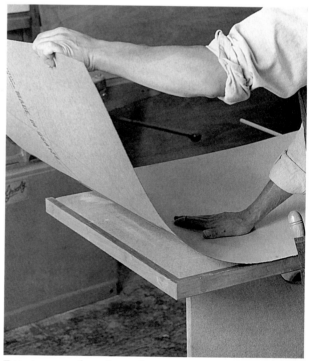

Remove one dowel at a time as you smooth the laminate down to either side of the center area.

To join two sheets of laminate, work your way out from the butt joint as you press the laminate into the glue. Use a smaller-diameter dowel next to the joint so you can see more clearly where to locate the laminate before pressing it down.

Butting one sheet to another requires a somewhat different procedure. Lay down one sheet as usual, then prepare the abutting sheet for installation. When spreading the glue, be careful to keep it off the edges of the sheet at the joint because its presence could hold the joint apart and create a gap. Set the sheet on dowels, using a smaller-diameter dowel ($^{3}/_{16}$ in. or $^{1}/_{4}$ in.) next to the joint, which makes it easier to see when the sheet is properly

aligned. Begin to lay down the laminate by pressing the end of the sheet down and against the butt joint. Now work away from the butt joint, sliding out the dowels as you press the sheet to the substrate.

Once you've removed the last dowel, exert pressure over the entire surface of the sheet to ensure that the adhesive reaches full strength. For best results, use a 3-in. rubber roller (and a "pinch roller" along the edges)

Once the laminate is down, use a small, rubber roller to exert pressure over the entire sheet.

designed for this purpose. You can often rent these tools at a building yard or tool-rental outlet. Avoid using larger rollers, such as a baker's rolling pin, whose large surface area reduces the amount of pressure you'll be able to exert. If these tools are unavailable, you can get by with hitting the surface with a mallet and a 3-in. square hardwood block (after first chamfering the edges with a plane). Remove any glue showing along the edges of the counter by rolling it off with your fingers while the adhesive is still rubbery.

Should you end up with an air bubble under the laminate, all is not lost. Heat up a fabric iron to the "silk" (low) setting and then warm the swollen area of laminate. Place a sheet of kraft paper under the iron to prevent scorching (reduce the heat if the paper discolors). As the laminate warms, you should be able to press out the bubble. Keep exerting

pressure until the laminate is cool to the touch. If you discover any gaps between adjoining sheets, you can fill them with a hard-drying seam fill compound supplied by the laminate manufacturer to match the color of your counter.

Trim the laminate to the edge of the counter using a lower-bearing flush-trim bit (CMT 806-096). (Avoid non-roller-bearing trim bits, which can scorch the wood edging.) Continually spray the cutting flutes and bearing with a lubricant such as WD-40 to help keep the bit from gumming up with adhesive and laminate dust. To cut the laminate to the sink or cooktop cutout, fit a "hole and flush-cut trimmer" bit (Bosch 85287 or CMT 816-064) to the router. This type of bit makes its own starting hole while also providing a flush-cutting pilot bearing; it's not a roller bearing, but any scorching here will not be seen.

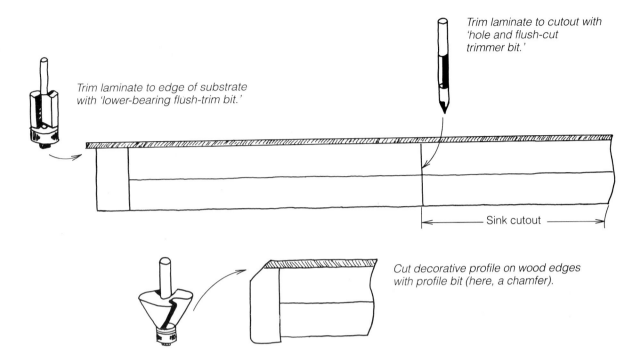

Trim laminate to edge of substrate with 'lower-bearing flush-trim bit.'

Trim laminate to cutout with 'hole and flush-cut trimmer bit.'

Sink cutout

Cut decorative profile on wood edges with profile bit (here, a chamfer).

Now choose the appropriate carbide router bit and cut the profile along the top edge of the wood facing strip. As the last step, slide the counter back into place and double-check its position. Clamp the counter down and screw it permanently in place by running up screws through the base-cabinet stretchers.

CUTTING AND INSTALLING THE BACKSPLASH

I usually use ¾-in. thick stock cut 3½ in. wide for the solid-wood backsplash. You can deviate from this height if necessary either to run under or around counter outlets. If I want a profile along the top edge of the backsplash, I rarely shape it into the board itself. Instead, to make the corner joinery easier, to account for any waviness in the wall, and to give a more traditional look, I'll add a bed molding (a cove, scotia or quarter round) as shown in the photo on p. 185. I lay out the backsplash so that the molding can run down the ends, dying into the counter surface.

Prefinish the backsplash (front and back) and run a bead of silicone caulking along the bottom edge before you install it. Fix it to the wall by driving finish nails or countersunk screws (which you will subsequently cover with wood plugs) into the wall studs. Shape the caulk squeeze-out into a smooth cove-shaped bead with your finger. Now, with the board in place, cut and install the bed molding to the top and side edges.

To complete the installation, set the appliances in place and hook them up. Now bring in the foodstuffs, install the cook, break open a bottle of champagne and prepare a meal — your kitchen cabinets are done!

SOURCES OF SUPPLY

LITERATURE

The following books have additional ideas on kitchen layout and design:

American Woodmark. *The Inch-By-Inch Guide to Kitchen Planning.* Winchester, Va., 1989.

Cary, Jere. *Building Your Own Kitchen Cabinets.* Newtown, Conn.: The Taunton Press, 1983.

Conran, Terence. *The Kitchen Book.* New York: Crown Publishers, 1984.

Cornell University Resource Center. *In Support of Mobility: Kitchen Design for Independent Older Adults.* Ithaca, N.Y., 1992.

Hylton, William. *Build Your Harvest Kitchen.* Emmaus, Pa.: Rodale Press, 1980.

Jankowski, Wanda. *Kitchens and Baths: Designs for Living.* Glen Cove, N.Y.: PBC International, 1993.

Levine, Paul. *Making Kitchen Cabinets.* Newtown, Conn.: The Taunton Press, 1988.

Thomas, Steve. *This Old House Kitchens.* Boston: Little, Brown and Co., 1992.

Wylde, Margaret, Adrian Baron-Robbins and Sam Clark. *Building for a Lifetime: The Design and Construction of Fully Accessible Homes.* Newtown, Conn.: The Taunton Press, 1994.

HARDWARE AND FIXTURES

Nearly every major metropolitan area has distributors that carry the major brands of cabinetmaking hardware and storage fixtures. You can locate them through the Yellow Pages or through the advice of a local cabinetshop. You may also be able to find much of what you need (albeit at a considerable markup) at your local building-supply store. The companies listed below are some of the mail-order sources that sell to the general public (the first four are those I most commonly deal with). Their prices generally fall somewhere between those of the retail stores and the regional trade distributors. Companies that sell only to the trade are listed on p. 195.

Woodworker's Hardware
P.O. Box 784
St. Cloud, MN 56302
(800) 383-0130
This is the most complete mail-order source I have discovered to date. Hard-to-find items such as the Confirmat RTA fasteners and drilling jig, the Blum drawer-slide installation jig, the Blum drawer-face fasteners, and adjustable leg levelers are all available here.

The Woodworkers' Store
21801 Industrial Blvd.
Rogers, MN 55374
(800) 279-4441

Woodworker's Supply
5604 Alameda Place, NE
Albuquerque, NM 87113
(800) 645-9292

Trend-Lines
375 Beacham St.
Chelsea, MA 02150
(800) 767-9999

Ball and Ball
463 W. Lincoln Hwy.
Exton, PA 19341
(215) 363-7330
Reproduction hardware.

Häfele America Co.
3901 Cheyenne Dr.
P.O. Box 4000
Archdale, NC 27263
(910) 889-2322
Full range of cabinet hardware and storage fixtures.

Horton Brasses
Nooks Hill Rd.
Cromwell, CT 06416
(203) 635-4400
Reproduction Colonial-era brass hardware.

Smith Woodworks and Design
101 Farmersville Rd.
Califon, NJ 07830
(908) 832-2723
Shaker knobs and pegs.

Van Dyke's Restorers
Fourth Ave. and Sixth St.
Woonsocket, SD 57385
(800) 843-3320
Wide selection of Victorian and other period hardware.

The following companies do not sell directly to the public, but they can provide product information and direct you to a local distributor:

Accuride
12311 Shoemaker Ave.
Santa Fe Springs, CA 90670
(310) 903-0200
Drawer and cutting-board slides.

Acorn Manufacturing Co.
457 School St.
Mansfield, MA 02048
(508) 339-4500
Reproduction Colonial-era wrought-iron, brass and copper hardware.

Feeny Manufacturing Co.
P.O. Box 191
Muncie, IN 47308
(317) 288-8730
Cabinet-storage systems, including revolving recycling bins.

Julius Blum, Inc.
Hwy. 16-Lowesville
Stanley, NC 28164
(800) 438-6788
Drawer slides and installation jig, face-adjuster fittings and centering pins, cup hinges and installation jigs, bumpers.

Knape and Vogt Manufacturing Co.
2700 Oak Industrial Drive, NE
Grand Rapids, MI 49505
(616) 459-3311
Side-mounted cabinet slides.

Rev-A-Shelf, Inc.
P.O. Box 99585
Jeffersontown, KY 40269
(800) 626-1126
Cabinet-storage systems, including tilt-out sink tray.

HAND WOODWORKING TOOLS

In addition to your local building store and the mail-order sources listed above for hardware sources, you may also order hand tools from:

Garrett Wade Co.
161 Avenue of the Americas
New York, NY 10013
(800) 221-2942

Highland Hardware
1045 N. Highland Ave., NE
Atlanta, GA 30306
(800) 241-6748

Lee Valley Tools
P.O. Box 6295, Station J
Ottawa, Ontario
Canada K2A 1T4
(800) 267-8767

Woodcraft
210 Wood County Industrial Park
P.O. Box 1686
Parkersburg, WV 26102-1686
(800) 225-1153

POWER TOOLS

You can find power hand tools at your local building-supply or hardware store. Lower prices can often be found at mail-order sources listed prominently in all the major woodworking magazines. (Be aware, however, that it is usually your burden to pay for the initial shipping and handling of the item as well as return charges should it prove defective.) Stationary machines can also be obtained through many of these mail-order sources — or through suppliers located in larger cities.

SPECIALIZED TOOLS AND MATERIALS

Here are the sources of the specialized cabinetmaking tools, jigs and materials mentioned in this book:

Layout Tools

Bridge City Tool Works
1104 NE 28th Ave.
Portland, OR 97232
(800) 253-3332
Finely made squares, gauges and rules.

L.S. Starrett Co.
121 Crescent St.
Athol, MA 01331
(508) 249-3551
Combination squares, compass scribes, rulers (trade only — call for local distributor).

Price Brothers' Tools
P.O.Box 1133
Novato, CA 94948
(800) 334-8270
Reservoir-type water level.

Drilling and Installation Jigs

J&R Enterprises
12629 N. Tatum #431
Phoenix, AZ 85032
(602) 953-0178
Adjustable double-bar drilling template for shelf-clip holes.

Kreg Tool Co.
P.O. Box 367
Huxley, IA 50124
(800) 447-8638
Hole-cutting jig for pocket screws, face-frame bit, Vise-grip clamp.

Trend-Lines
(address and phone on p. 194)
Cutting templates for curved door panels.

Veritas Tools
12 E. River St.
Ogdensburg, NY 13669
(315) 393-1967
Drill jig for cup hinges, shelf-hole boring jig, other measuring and layout devices.

Woodworker's Hardware
(address and phone on p. 194)
Blum drawer-slide installation jig, Confirmat RTA fastener drilling jig.

Woodworker's Supply
(address and phone on p. 194)
Glue bottles for spline-biscuit joinery, self-centering doweling jig.

Cutting Guides

American Design and Engineering
900 Third St.
St. Paul Park, MN 55071
(800) 441-1388
Extension tables and indexed sliding stop for chopsaws and compound-miter saws.

Excalibur Machine and Tool Co.
210 Eighth St. South
Lewiston, NY 14092
(800) 387-9789
Crosscut sliding-table fixture for table saws.

Matrix Enterprises
5926 Sedgwick Rd.
Columbus, OH 43235
(614) 846-0030
Crosscutting guide for circular saws (trade only).

Pat Warner Router Accessories
1427 Kenora St.
Escondido, CA 92027
(619) 747-2623
Extension base and knobs for routers.

Woodhaven
5323 W. Kimberly Rd.
Davenport, IA 52806
(800) 344-6657
Router equipment — tables, fences, guides.

Other Tools

CMT Tools
5425 Beaumont Center Blvd.
Suite 900
Tampa, FL 33634
(800) 531-5559
Manufacturer of a wide range of router bits, including the lock rabbet, shank-bearing pattern and cope-and-stick bits mentioned in text.

GIL-LIFT
1605 North River
Independence, MO 64050
(816) 833-0611
Cabinet lift and dolly.

Other Materials

The Bartley Collection
29060 Airpark Drive
Easton, MD 21601
(800) 227-8539
Wipe-on gel varnish.

Eco Design
1365 Rufina Circle
Santa Fe, NM 87501
(505) 438-3448
Non-toxic citrus-based finishing oils and varnishes.

Johnson Paint Co.
355 Newbury St.
Boston, MA 02115
(617) 536-4838
Raw materials — calcium carbonate, casein, alkali-proof earth pigments — to make your own milk paint.

Klingspor's Sanding Catalog
P.O. Box 3737
Hickory, NC 28603-3737
(800) 228-0000
Sandpaper, oil-free steel wool, shaped sanding blocks.

Old Fashioned Milk Paint Co.
P.O. Box 222
Groton, MA 01450-0222
(508) 448-6336
Premixed milk-paint powder.

WARP (Woodworker's Alliance for Rainforest Protection)
1 Cottage St.
Easthampton, MA 01027
(413) 586-8156
Information about where to locate wood products and lumber made or taken from sustained yield forests.

Wood-Kote Productions
8000 NE 14th Place
Portland, OR 97211
(503) 285-8371
Wipe-on gel stains, waterborne polyurethanes.

INDEX

EDITOR   Peter Chapman

DESIGNER/LAYOUT ARTIST   Henry Roth

ILLUSTRATOR   Jim Tolpin

PHOTOGRAPHER   Patrick Cudahy (except where noted)